The Art of
Management and
the Aesthetic Manager

The Art of Management and the Aesthetic Manager

The Coming Way of Business

JOHN DOBSON

Q

QUORUM BOOKS
Westport, Connecticut • London

Library of Congress Cataloging-in-Publication Data

Dobson, John, 1957–
    The art of management and the aesthetic manager : the coming way
of business / John Dobson.
        p. cm.
    Includes bibliographical references and index.
    ISBN 1–56720–232–2 (alk. paper)
    1. Social sciences and management.   2. Corporate culture.
    3. Postmodernism—Social aspects.   I. Title.
    HD30.19.D63   1999
    658—dc21   98–30541

British Library Cataloguing in Publication Data is available.

Library of Congress Catalog Card Number: 98–30541
ISBN: 1–56720–232–2

First published in 1999

Quorum Books, 88 Post Road West, Westport, CT 06881
An imprint of Greenwood Publishing Group, Inc.

Printed in the United States of America

The paper used in this book complies with the
Permanent Paper Standard issued by the National
Information Standards Organization (Z39.48–1984).

10 9 8 7 6 5 4 3 2 1

The life of money-making is one undertaken under compulsion, and wealth is evidently not the good we are seeking: for it is merely useful and for the sake of something else.

—Aristotle, *The Nicomachean Ethics*

And what is good, Phaedrus,
And what is not good—
Need we ask anyone to tell us these things?

—Plato, *Republic*

Contents

Preface

These days we frequently hear the term "corporate culture." This implies that business has some form of cultural force. But the history of business activity indicates that the relationship between culture and business is one of reflection rather than creation: business does not create or shape the surrounding culture, but rather reflects whatever culture prevails. From the street vendors of ancient Babylon to today's multinational corporation, the aspirations and attitudes of those engaged in business reflect the aspirations and attitudes of the prevailing culture. The businesses that flourish at any given time and in any given place are those that best reflect the prevailing characteristics of the existing culture. Specifically, it is the managers within these flourishing businesses who reflect these characteristics.

For example, Robert Cozine noted recently that "Royal Dutch–Shell, one of the world's largest oil companies, plans to shake up its tradition-bound corporate culture by increasing the number of women and range of nationalities in its top management tier" (1998, p. 17); currently, only about 4 percent of Shell's 400 senior managers are women. The main reason for this shakeup, according to Cozine, is that the

narrowness of Shell's senior management base has been cited by critics as one reason why it has struggled with rapid change in its business. Critics point to the controversy over the scrapping of the Brent Spar oil rig and Shell's problems with human rights in Nigeria. They say a broader management base might have helped Shell to respond more effectively to those issues. (Cozine, 1998, p. 17)

So culture changes, but Shell's culture in recent years has not: its male Anglo management structure reflects the cultural values of 30 years ago but not the values of today. Thirty years ago such a decision would not have been seen as making sense either ethically or financially; now it is seen as essential on both these fronts. The broad challenge of business management, therefore, is to develop an ability to read and interpret these often subtle cultural shifts and to understand how these shifts impact the role of business in society.

The central premise of this book is that business reflects culture. Building from this premise, I address two basic questions. First, what is the prevailing culture of the twenty-first century? Second, how is this culture going to be reflected in the attitudes and aspirations of business management? In answering the first question, I identify the dominant culture of the twenty-first century as that embraced by the general label of "aestheticism." Hence, in answering the second question, I label the manager of the twenty-first century the "aesthetic manager." The primary characteristic of the aesthetic manager, which distinguishes this individual from the modern manager, is the former's view of business as primarily an indeterminate aesthetic activity, rather than the characteristically modern view of business as a deterministic technical enterprise.

As with any cultural shift, this change or transition from the modern to the aesthetic is far from clean and unambiguous; indeed, vestiges of the characteristics that I identify here with the aesthetic manager have always been present to some extent. These characteristics are present in the modern manager, although they are dominated and suppressed by the characteristics of modernity. In a sense, therefore, the aesthetic manager can be viewed as one who is left when the veneers of modernism are peeled back.

My notion of the aesthetic manager clearly has links to the broad intellectual movement loosely known as postmodernism. For example, John Kay, director of Oxford University's business school, echoes the sentiment of this book when he concludes that "it is time to develop a theory of postmodern management" (1998). He reaches this conclusion after reflecting on the failures of modernist management. But what is the nature of this failure? To describe this, Kay uses the analogy of modernist architecture as pioneered by the likes of van der Rohe, Gropius, and Le Corbusier: he notes the latter describing houses as "machines for living in." Kay comments:

The point is, of course, that houses are not just machines for living in. They are homes and parts of communities. To serve these needs demands respect for conventional—even banal—aesthetics and for the social relationships that make homes and communities. (Kay, 1998, p. 12)

Houses are more than "machines for living in," and businesses are more than "machines for making money," as described by prominent financial economist Merton Miller; this is the essence of Kay's editorial, and this is the essence of my book. In what follows, I answer Kay's plea for a theory of postmodern management; however, I eschew the word "postmodern" in favor of the word "aesthetic" because the latter captures more succinctly the essence of my management theory. (Note, in the above quote, how Kay links the aesthetic with the postmodern.) Also, "aesthetic" does not carry the nihilistic baggage often attached to "postmodern." Postmodernism is often seen as merely an absence, an "absent modernity," but my manager as aesthete is very much a presence, a real moral character. The postmodern critique—the deconstruction of modernist management and modernist ethics—creates the metaphysical space for the aesthetic manager. This manager is the phoenix who rises from the ashes of modernism's smoldering pyre. Unlike many invocations of postmodernism, therefore, I conjure aestheticism in business as a real cultural force.

Although this is by no means the first book to invoke the notion of management as some form of aesthetic activity, it is, I believe, the first book to begin this invocation from within the realm of financial-economic theory. By trade, I am a financial economist, and this seems to me the most appropriate origin for a critique of the modern manager. The behavioral assumptions and general worldview embedded within finance theory's "Theory of the Firm" really provide the conceptual bedrock for the modernist view of business.

My critique of financial-economic theory in Part I of this book is similar to that found in my earlier work *Finance Ethics: The Rationality of Virtue*. (Dobson, 1997b). Those of you familiar with that earlier book will thus find Part I of this book somewhat familiar territory, albeit with a new aesthetic-focused twist. Also in that earlier book I introduced virtue ethics in a narrow, specifically finance context, but I did not recognize the potential for a broader contribution of virtue ethics to a business aesthetic. Although there are some connections between these two books, therefore, I view this current book as conceptually freestanding. Thus, the earlier book should in no way be viewed as a prerequisite for a full understanding of what follows.

Introduction

The ideas of the herd should rule in the herd—but not reach out beyond it: the leaders of the herd require a fundamentally different valuation for their own actions.

—Friedrich Nietzsche, *The Will to Power*

Imagine yourself as an anthropologist. You have been living with some isolated culture that has had no prior contact with the rest of the world; you have become conversant in their language and wish to describe to these people the substantive qualities of, say, plastic. The problem you face is that these people have never seen plastic, and consequently their language has no words relating specifically to plastic. Of course, if you happened to have brought some plastic object with you, then you could just show this to them, but what if you have no such object? To describe plastic to these people you would have to use whatever words they do have that relate to things similar to plastic. You would have to weave an elaborate web of analogy, comparison, simile, and metaphor, to circuitously get at the essential qualities of plastic.

Contemporary writers about aestheticism in business are in the same position as this anthropologist. Actually, they are in a worse position: modern English is, to a great extent, a product of modernism; thus, aestheticists find themselves having to define or deconstruct almost every substantive word or phrase they use in order to reveal the modernist context embedded implicitly in contemporary usage of the word. For example, note how, in the quote from John Kay in the preface, he resorts to analogy in his attempt to describe the aesthetic of postmodern management. Discussing the specific subject of *business* in an aesthetic context is even tougher because modern business English is absolutely a product of modernity. The aestheticist writers themselves, unless they come from some isolated tribe, are also the product of modernity. It's interesting to note that several of the most prominent postmodern or aesthetic writers are French or French/Algerian (e.g., Balandier, Baudrillard, Camus, Derrida, Foucalt, Lachau, Lascault, Lyotard, Mouffe, Sartre) and are thus the inheritors of an intellectual tradition that is in large part divorced from modern Anglo-Saxon culture; as such they are detached from the full force of Anglo modernism. These writers must at every turn conduct meticulous self-examination to reveal their own personal, innate, modernist bias; so words like "deconstruct," "difference," and "context," which crop up regularly in such writing, are characteristic of an attempt to reveal what is already there but is in some way not readily apparent to the modern intellectual gaze. These words tend to connote an activity concerned with an absence rather than a presence, with a peeling back, an exposition and removal, rather than an addition.

Much of what I supply in this book, therefore, is definitional. Rather than introducing something substantively new, like a new plastic, I try to define what is already extant, albeit latent. In this regard, my story above about the anthropologist is perhaps misleading. Unlike the concept of plastic to this isolated tribe, the aesthetic manager is already among us, within each manager. It is just that this aspect of management is swamped by modernism. The central challenge is thus to use the language of modern business to reveal what modern business has smothered and is consequently now largely blind to.

I discuss this question of etymology or semantics here because I want to make clear why it is necessary to describe modern business so carefully in a book that is ostensibly about aesthetic business. Once again, it goes back to the problem of describing an absence. The first step in clothing the naked emperor is to reveal the exact nature of his nakedness.

As a means of distinguishing the modern manager from the aesthetic manager, imagine three parallel business universes. These metaphysical universes are identical except for the moral orientation of the managers therein. In one universe managers adhere precisely to the epistemology of financial economics: they pursue personal material wealth in a logical, consistent, and unremitting fashion: they are *Homo economicus*. I term this universe the *Technical Universe*.

In the second universe, managers are also instrumentally rational in the sense that they apply logic and reason in the pursuit of some goal. However, their goal is not strictly and simply personal material wealth. They are what modern moral philosophy would call "enlightened" and thus may temper their personal material aspirations in deference to some moral principle. They may, for example, substitute some notion of societal welfare for personal wealth maximization, or they may restrict their actions to those that will most benefit the materially least advantaged, or they may act only on the basis of universalizable moral principles such as some conception of fairness or justice. These managers are still rational in the sense that they apply logic and reason, and indeed they may on occasion act in a way that is indistinguishable from the managers in the Technical Universe. These moral managers, however, because of their belief in some overriding moral principle, cannot be relied upon to act in ways that are predictable in financial-economic theory. This is not to say that the behavior of these managers would not be predictable—once their moral principles were made clear. Indeed, the fact that these managers still act in ways governed by logic and reason will make their behavior as predictable as those managers who comprise the Technical Universe. The essential difference, therefore, between the technical managers and the moral managers will be that the latter pursue goals and are subject to constraints that may be more nuanced and ethereal than the straightforward wealth maximization goals of the technicians. Just as invocations of the technician can be found in financial-economic theory, invocations of this moral manager can be found in the dictates of business ethics theory. I term this second universe the *Moral Universe*.

The third and final universe that I wish to conjure is the most opaque. It is a universe that we in modernity are least familiar with because the actions of managers therein are not governed by notions of scientific logic or instrumental rationality. Managers in this universe recognize the need for material profit, and they are cognizant of the conventional rules and logic of the Moral Universe; however, they do not view these reason-based enterprises as ultimate objectives. These aesthetic managers pursue a goal that is hard to define in modernist terms—indeed, to even call it a goal may be misleading. Sherwin Klein describes a similar individual in his analysis of Cervantes's *Don Quixote*:

The ideal of craftsmanship is to create that which has quality or excellence; personal satisfaction, pride in accomplishment, and a sense of dignity derived from the consequent self-development are the motivations. In an "excellent" company it is this ideal that permeates the firm, and management should provide the moral example of such an ideal; a business management craftsman attempts to create a quality organization, and quality products and services are the result of such an organization. (Klein, 1998, p. 55)

Klein's managers are involved in a quintessentially aesthetic pursuit. They recognize their business universe as essentially one of chaotic disorder and unpredictability where rules of logic and rationality will never fit comfortably. These managers endeavor to achieve some sort of aesthetic balance and harmony in their chaotic environment. In this endeavor they are not quixotic but rather are guided and tempered by conceptions of quality, excellence, the Good, Aristotelian *eudaimonia*, and desirable character traits—

virtues—that may lead to these ideals. The acquisition of these character traits and the concomitant pursuit of these ideals is not achieved simply by the application of certain rules of logic or of rationality. Indeed, the whole pursuit is characterized by a marked absence of rules and set goals. It is, to all intents and purposes, an aesthetic pursuit. At one time a manager's actions may be governed by economic interest, but at other times, they may be governed by compassion or courage or a conception of the beautiful or harmonious. Thus, unlike the previous two universes, the managers in this universe exhibit more complex and multifarious behavior. Their goal is not easily defined, if indeed it can be viewed in terms of a singular goal, and the means by which they pursue this elusive goal are not easily categorized, either. In essence, their behavior lies outside modernist logic or rationality. They pursue a type of aesthetic truth or beauty. Or, to put it another way, they pursue a convergence of economic and moral truth with aesthetic beauty. I term this final universe the *Aesthetic Universe.*

My essential thesis in this book is that business management exists and has always existed in all three of these universes. Every business manager is and has always been to a greater or lesser degree a technician, a moralist, and an aesthete. What has varied over time and between place is the extent to which one or more of these universes dominates the others. The dominance of any one of these three universes is generally determined by the encompassing cultural milieu. Crises in business management generally develop when the universe in which management believes it resides conflicts with that of the surrounding society. To a large degree, therefore, successful management entails the ability to perceive and predict the prevailing cultural conception of business. In short, business reflects culture. As paleontologist Jean Staune (1996) observes: "The vision of the world and the vision of mankind which prevail in a society have a determining influence on social and economic organization" (p. 145).

As we enter the twenty-first century, a Western corporate culture is becoming ever more geographically omnipresent. At the same time, however, the epistemological bedrock of this culture is crumbling. From its inception in the Reformation and Renaissance, Western corporate culture has been the child of the age of reason. All the facets of modern business—economics, rule-based or consequence-based business ethics, science, technology—are products of this reason-based instrumental rationality. The foundation of modern business is reason. But Western corporate culture itself, as with any culture, evolves and changes. In attempting to respond to this evolution and change, managers are continually confronted with the limitations of any fixed notion of reason; rationality itself evolves and shifts definitional emphasis between the Technical, Moral, and Aesthetic Universes.

For example, senior management at Royal Dutch–Shell recently decided to establish a division within the company whose sole purpose is to monitor the environmental and human rights implications of Shell's activities. This decision is undoubtedly a reaction to recent public relations gaffs: most notably, Shell's decision—which was subsequently reversed—to dump an obsolete oil platform in the mid-Atlantic, and its perceived tacit support of the oppressive government of Nigeria.

Shell's decision clearly exists, to some degree, within the Technical Universe of financial rationality; indeed, to be welcomed by shareholders, which it was, it would presumably have to be financially justifiable. But Shell's decision also reflects a genuine concern among managers and other employees for the environment and for human rights. For example, its most recent oil-drilling activities in Peru are the very model of environmental and cultural sensitivity: rather than following the usual procedure of cutting a road through the rain forest to its oil installations, Shell is, at great expense, flying all supplies in and out.

Of course, the cynic will readily dismiss Shell's recent behavior as thinly disguised public relations. It, the cynic will argue, resides firmly and entirely within the Technical Universe. But careful observation and reflection on Shell's activities do not support the cynic. Rather, they support the view that Shell's management is recognizing that—as with all multinationals— this massive company can no longer be run as a purely economic enterprise; it must also be run as a moral and aesthetic enterprise. Thus, Shell's management is awakening to the Moral and Aesthetic Universes. Indeed, the much better public relations image of British Petroleum (BP) is a direct result of BP's early recognition of this broader sociocultural shift. BP's operations in Colombia are as potentially sensitive, in terms of human rights, as Shell's in Nigeria, but unlike Shell, BP's management has from the outset been careful to distance itself from the morally questionable Colombian national government.

Similar examples abound. In the soft-drinks industry, PepsiCo has recently suffered a public relations disaster that resulted in its severing all ties with Burma, a country currently controlled by a military junta. Pepsi's interests in Burma were no doubt financially justifiable initially, but Pepsi failed to realize that financial justifiability is not sufficient today. Nike, the athletic apparel manufacturer, is having similar experiences with its (a priori economically rational) policy of targeting certain developing countries as locations for shoe assembly. Nike is now following the lead of Levi-Strauss, the world's largest clothing manufacturer, in its provision of a model living environment for employees in developing countries. In essence, Pepsi, Shell, and Nike tried to remain predominantly economic institutions within a culture that increasingly finds acceptable only predominantly moral and aesthetic institutions vis-à-vis the Moral and Aesthetic Universes.

The recent experiences of these multinational corporations (MNCs) are not unusual. In fact, as any perusal of a business newspaper will reveal, they are typical. Of course, one reason why the market mechanism is now effectively disciplining firms is the greater availability and dissemination of information about corporate activities. This, in turn, has much to do with the growth of nongovernmental organizations (NGOs) such as Greenpeace, Worldwatch, Friends of the Earth, Amnesty International, and the Rainforest Coalition. But the very fact that these NGOs have garnered such widespread support and influence is itself evidence of a broad cultural shift.

The rigidity and incompatibility of the modernist Technical and Moral Universes have in the past led to conflict—the familiar modern business ethics conflict of "profits versus ethics." But one beauty of the Aesthetic Universe is that its nondeterministic and nonjudgmental nature facilitates a more positive symbiosis of different business roles. This difference can be seen in the evolving relation between MNCs and NGOs. Until recently, this relation has been one of conflict, of protests (often violent), of subterfuge, of negative publicity campaigns. The individuals within these organizations saw each other as occupying different and incompatible conceptual universes. But there is now evidence that this is changing. In its aforementioned operations in Peru, for example, Shell is working in close cooperation with various nongovernmental organizations. A Shell-Mobil joint venture to develop Peru's vast hydrocarbon reserves in the region of Camisea's virgin jungle has invited the cooperation of more than 30 NGOs and local groups who will monitor the performance of these companies on environmental and social issues. Another example, also in Peru, is that of Yanacocha Inc., a hugely profitable U.S.-Peruvian gold-mining joint venture based in northern Peru. As a result of cooperation with various NGOs, "Yanacocha has the best-developed community assistance programme in Peru, spending some $3 [million] a year on projects in 35 communities around the mine" (Bowen, 1998, p. 6).

Thus, this interplay between MNCs and NGOs is rapidly evolving from one of conflict to one of cooperation and synergistic benefit. As Sally Bowen observes, "The alliance [between NGOs and MNCs] works both ways. As well as being a source of project funding, mining and oil companies can allow NGOs access to remote areas they would not normally reach" (p. 6). This cooperation took further tangible form recently with a conference in London sponsored by the oil industry, to which delegates of Greenpeace and other NGOs were "officially" invited. Rather than protesting outside the conference hall with placards, therefore, members of Greenpeace found themselves actually sitting around the conference table with senior executives of the largest oil MNCs.

The broad trend is clear. The distinction between NGOs and MNCs, once so sharp, is becoming increasingly indistinct. As we enter the twenty-first century, the very distinction—so pronounced in modernism—between the economic and moral in business appears blurred.

This blurring is now recognized not only by practicing managers but also by academic philosophers. Thomas Dunfee (1998), the president of the U.S. Society for Business Ethics, suggested in a recent presidential address that a

"Marketplace of Morality" would "provide a unifying framework integrating moral preferences, reasoning, behaviors and organizational contexts with broader political and economic concepts" (p. 142). Dunfee quotes Judge Richard Posner, observing "moral philosophy as a weak field, a field in disarray, a field in which consensus is impossible to achieve in our society" (p. 138). So why not let the market mechanism price the ebbs and flows of postmodern pluralism? Whether it's environmentalism, multiculturalism, speciesism, feminism, or child labor, Dunfee proffers a marketplace of morality to translate these moral concerns into economic concerns. But Dunfee's suggestion implies that every value in business can be priced. In what follows, I suggest otherwise. In the Aesthetic Universe, certain values transcend the price mechanism of the market. But more on this later.

What the above examples of Shell and others indicate, and what the remainder of this book will I hope establish, is that Western corporate culture is in the midst of a shift in the metaphysical universe of business. It is experiencing what Alasdair MacIntyre (1984) terms an "epistemological crisis" or what Thomas Kuhn (1970) terms a "paradigm shift." This shift or crisis is in Western corporate culture's very conception of rationality and reason in business enterprise. More precisely, business in the West is becoming increasingly unsure of the exact nature of reason. Whose reason? What is the reason behind reason? These are questions that would have had little relevance to nineteenth-century industrialists: the Vanderbilts, Rothschilds, Carnegies, Rockefellers, and Morgans. Their monocultural, Protestant ethic, encyclopedic bedrock was solid. Twenty-first-century business culture, however, is characterized, not by Victorian self-confidence but by radical self-questioning. Indeed, in contrast to the recent epochs of the age of reason and of self-confidence, the West of the next millennium promises to be an age of self-doubt and self-questioning. Staune (1996) sums up this transition by noting that

one of the great events of the end of the twentieth century is that, in all the disciplines of science, a new vision is emerging. Behind the study of the foundations of matter, the origin of the universe, behind the experiments studying how man's consciousness works, behind the playing out of the evolution of life appears a certain depth to reality. One can scientifically show that "what is" cannot be reduced to an objective, material and measurable level. (p. 146)

This approach of the age of self-questioning and self-doubt is reflected also in the philosophy and sociology of poststructuralism and postmodernism. These movements challenge the bedrock of modernity by deconstructing many of the constructs upon which modernism is built—constructs such as truth, reason, and logic.

These late twentieth-century critiques of modernity gained much of their impetus from the writings of Friedrich Nietzsche in the nineteenth century.

Nietzsche challenged the assumed certainties of his era by arguing that there is no absolute truth or absolute moral good. Truth is a "mobile army of metaphors"—a weapon used by society and individuals in their continual will to power: "This world is the will to power—and nothing besides! And you yourselves are also this will to power—and nothing besides!" (Nietzsche, 1967b, pp. 449–450). For Nietzsche the only absolute was this will to power, although he was equivocal even about this. For example, in his analysis of Nietzschean morality, Brian Leiter (1997) concludes: "I doubt whether a good argument can even be made out that 'will to power' provides Nietzsche with his standard of value" (p. 267, fn. 40). Nietzsche's whole approach (if indeed it can be viewed as something as purposeful as an approach) was characterized by a distinct lack of standards, at least of fixed standards. Nietzsche criticized the universal application of everyday moral dictums on the grounds that such application stifled those few individuals capable of real creativity and excellence:

Whoever reflects upon the way in which the type [i.e., typical] man can be raised to his greatest splendor and power will grasp first of all that he must place himself outside morality; for morality has been essentially directed toward the opposite end: to obstruct, or destroy that splendid evolution wherever it has been going on. (Nietzsche, 1967b, p. 450)

Although his insightful (and inciteful) aphorisms have led to much debate and misinterpretation, Nietzsche's contribution to the aestheticist canon is indisputable. He looked beyond modernism to a view of life as essentially a type of nondeterministic artistic quest. To Nietzsche, we are all Wagnerian Parsifals, engaged in our lifelong quest for an Arthurian Holy Grail. Those contemporary writers who attempt to look beyond modernism invariably acknowledge a singular debt to Nietzsche. His critique of the assumed self-evident truths of modernism augured our current age of radical uncertainty; the title of Alasdair MacIntyre's 1988 book really says it all: *Whose Justice? Which Rationality?* Of my three conceptual universes, Nietzsche would have undoubtedly felt comfortable only in the Aesthetic. But he would not have viewed the uncertainties of this universe as nihilistic; on the contrary, he would have viewed them as a liberation from the stifling delusions of the Technical and Moral Universes of modernity.

In business this current age of self-questioning is reflected in the growing debate over the role of business in society. Indeed, this debate has, within the last couple of decades, spawned an entire academic discipline, namely, business ethics. The acceptance of business ethics as a bona fide intellectual pursuit is really a reflection of this age of self-doubt. It reflects the current multiplicity of business self-conceptions. It is no longer obvious to our culture exactly what the role of business and the business manager is in society. Should business simply try to make a profit and let the logic of the Smithian invisible hand do the rest? Or must modern business actually in some way nurture some utopian concept of society? Indeed, is there still any meaningful concept of society that is wholly divorced from business? Is our culture now merely in a literal sense "corporate" culture?

Returning to our three business universes: the first two, those of the Technical and Moral, were products of reason. They reflect modernity as defined by the Enlightenment economic and moral philosophers, most notably Adam Smith in his two masterworks, *The Theory of Moral Sentiments* (1759; see Smith 1937a), and, *An Enquiry into the Nature and Causes of the Wealth of Nations* (1776; see Smith, 1937b). These works presaged and explained the Industrial Revolution and the rise of capitalism as economic expressions of the modernist principles of prudent reason and instrumental rationality. Smith saw no inherent conflict between what I have termed here the Moral and Technical Universes. For him, both were complementary facets of the modernist metaphysic.

Business may have existed comfortably in these two universes in the last two centuries; business of the twenty-first century will, however, no longer reside in these universes. The age of self-doubt, augured by Nietzsche, will necessitate business's moving to a different universe, an Aesthetic Universe. Management will also have to make this shift. It will be a shift in management paradigm. The management universe of the twenty-first century will be neither a Technical Universe nor a Moral Universe; indeed, it will be no reason-based universe. The dominant business culture will be a rekindling of a culture of business that was all but entirely eclipsed in the Industrial Revolution. In the age beyond reason, in the epoch of self-doubt, the manager will become the aesthete. That is the central prediction of this book.

By this prediction I do not mean simply that the aesthetic manager will arise as an additional alternative to the manager as technician or to the moral manager. I do not mean merely that another item will be added to the menu, that the smorgasbord of management paradigms will be extended. I see the implications of aestheticism as far more pervasive than this. The management aesthetic of the twenty-first century will not just compete with the technician and moralist as some parallel and incommensurable conceptual paradigm; it will actually eclipse the previous two paradigms. The aesthetic manager will expose the technician and the moral manager as logically insupportable. Even in terms of their own logical constructs, that is, even in terms of conventional rationality and logic, aestheticism will reveal the vacuous essence of the Technical and Moral Universes. But why will—and why *must*—this be so?

In his book *The Structure of Scientific Revolutions*, Thomas Kuhn (1970) describes the evolution of knowledge as "a succession of tradition-bound periods punctuated by non-cumulative breaks" (p. 208); he labels these breaks as "paradigm shifts." Kuhn recognizes that the evolution of knowledge is not uniform over time; rather, it tends to go in fits and starts. There may be long periods in which nothing more is achieved than merely fine-tuning of extant conceptual rubrics. Then suddenly, out of the blue, as it were, a radical new idea appears that recasts and redirects the entire discipline, namely, a paradigm shift. To illustrate this process, Kuhn notes how the heliocentric astronomy of Copernicus discredited the Aristotelian and early medieval theories of the solar system. It was not just that Copernicus's theory arose as some parallel and incommensurable theory that could coexist with earlier earth-centered theories. Copernicus was actually able to use the logic and methodology of the earlier theories to demonstrate their invalidity. Thus, Copernican astronomy did not merely compete with Aristotelian astronomy, in the way that one religion might coexist and compete with another; rather, Copernican astronomy eclipsed Aristotelian astronomy by demonstrating that the latter was insupportable *even in terms of the latter's logic and methodology.* This, according to Kuhn, was the essence of a paradigm shift: a complete eclipse of one intellectual foundation by another.

Similarly, in a philosophical context, Alasdair MacIntyre (1990) argues that the theology of Thomas Aquinas synthesized and eclipsed the earlier philosophical traditions of Augustinianism and Aristotelianism. Once again, it was not merely that Aquinas's theories arose as some competing and incommensurable doctrine, but rather that Aquinas was able to develop a philosophy with sufficient sophistication to embrace these earlier philosophies and to demonstrate the weaknesses and epistemological inferiority of Augustinianism and Aristotelianism when seen in the light of Thomism.

Finally, in the context of financial economics, paradigm shift labels may be applied appropriately in two cases. First, most recently, the formal recognition of the importance of market imperfections in theoretical finance in the 1970s revolutionized the field; this recognition generally takes the form of agency theory, to be discussed at length in Chapter 2. The second case of a paradigm shift is that of the capital structure–irrelevance propositions of Franco Modigliani and Merton Miller in the late 1950s. As Stephen Ross (1988) recently commented: "If the view of the progress of science that interprets it as one of changing paradigms has merit, then surely the work of Miller and Modigliani provides a laboratory example of a violently shifted paradigm" (p. 127). Whether in astronomy, philosophy, or finance, therefore, the arrival of a new paradigm affords not only a new way of viewing reality but also a new way of viewing antecedent paradigms.

Thus, in the current context, the incommensurability of the aesthetic manager with the technician and moralist of modernity does not mean that comparison of these viewpoints is impossible. The aesthetic and the modern manager may not share the same concepts of truth and rationality, but if it is possible for the aesthetic manager to accurately conceptualize the truth and rationality claims of modernism, then comparison is possible. Furthermore, if the aestheticist is able to demonstrate inconsistencies and ambiguities in the modernist worldview—that is, if the aestheticist is able to discredit the modernist even in terms of the modernist's rationality and truth claims—then it is reasonable to reject a modernist view of business management in favor of an aesthetic one. I suggest that, in business theory and practice, not only is such a rejection possible, but just such a rejection is already actually taking place.

It is important to note here that my claim of three parallel business universes is not a claim of relativism. I am not claiming that all are equally valid, that there are equally valid claims to rationality and truth in business. Indeed, to make such a claim would imply that I am occupying another, all-embracing context from which these other contexts or universes could be judged. Indeed, the deconstruction of the concept of relativism reveals it as self-contradictory. Relativism claims that all philosophical perspectives are equally valid. This in turn assumes some overarching moral context from which all other moral perspectives can be judged. If such a context exists, then it clearly invalidates the relativist's claim. Thus, relativism is logically insupportable by the standards of its own logic.

Thus, just because the modern manager and the aesthetic manager are in many respects incommensurable in terms of rationality constructs and truth claims, and just because no other all-embracing concept exists from which to evaluate these two, does not mean that the two paradigms cannot be compared meaningfully. Nor does it mean that one concept cannot be demonstrated as superior to the other. Indeed, it is just such a claim of superiority that I make in this book.

This point of the comparability of incommensurable constructs is a crucial one. To the extent that my entire argument here rests on an ability of the aesthetic manager to eclipse the modern manager, then it would not be excessive to claim that the justification of Kuhn's and MacIntyre's paradigm shift–type argument provides the justification for my thesis here: specifically, the thesis that the reemergence to prominence of the aesthetic paradigm will render the modernist technical and moral paradigms insupportable even in terms of their own modernist foundations, once these foundations are revealed in the aesthetic light. With this in mind, I would like to quote MacIntyre here at some length. In the excerpt below, taken from "Incommensurability, Truth, and the Conversation between Confucians and Aristotelians about the Virtues," MacIntyre makes very clear the conditions that must be satisfied for some meaningful progression from—or eclipse of—one conceptual universe to another:

Any particular tradition of enquiry, any body of well-developed theory and practice, may come in the light of its own standards of rationality, theoretical and practical, to be recognized by its own adherents as rationally inferior to some other rival and incompatible tradition, embodying in its theory and practice some alternative and incommensurable standpoint, if two conditions are both satisfied. The first is that its own history, as narrated in the light of its own standards, the standards internal to it, should lead in the end to radical and, so far as it is possible to judge, irremediable failure, perhaps by reason of its sterility and resourcelessness in the face of some set of problems which its own goals require it to solve, perhaps because, in trying to frame adequate solutions to its problems and an adequately comprehensive account of the subject matter with which it deals, it lapses into irreparable incoherence. (1991, p. 117)

In this book, I undertake just such a rational debate and encounter between the modernist and aestheticist concepts of business. I use the intellectual tools of aestheticism to demonstrate what is already becoming apparent in modern business, namely—to use MacIntyre's phrase—the sterility and resourcelessness in the face of some set of problems that its own goals require it to solve; whether in the guise of the technician or the moralist, the manager of modernity is exhibiting just this sterility and resourcelessness. In the case of the technician, contained within the universe of financial-economic theory, this theory is demonstrating—even within its own narrow financial-economic terms—both the descriptive inaccuracy and the prescriptive undesirability of the manager as technician. In the case of the manager as moralist, contained within its universe of modernist business ethics theory, this theory is being forced to recognize its failure at self-justification; however metaphysically desirable the moral manager may be, post-Enlightenment moral philosophy, which provides the basis for business ethics theory, has failed to provide the resources necessary to justify the existence of such a manager. In short, the moral manager is unable to provide any rational answer to the question, Why "ought" I be moral?

Parts I and II of this book explain these failures in detail. These explanations pave the way for the aesthetic manager in Part III. This shift to the aesthetic manager is, in the true Kuhnian sense, a paradigm shift. What Copernicus did to astronomy, and what Aquinas did to moral philosophy, aestheticism will do to management. Indeed, the evidence of this business culture paradigm shift is already apparent as we enter the twenty-first century. In the case of the technical approach to business—what I term here the Technical Universe—the collapse or "deconstruction" has begun. This collapse will be described in detail in Chapters 1 and 2. As will be seen, the collapse is from the inside, in true Kuhnian fashion. The foundations of the managerial Technical Universe have been logical consistency, descriptive accuracy, and moral neutrality. All of these foundations are crumbling.

Similarly, in the case of the Moral Universe, the collapse is already apparent. Moral management finds its justification in modernist moral philosophy. But the deconstruction of aestheticism has shattered this justification *in its own terms*. In a secular universe, which is the universe of modernity, the moral manager is revealed as resting on an illusory foundation of pseudoreligious terminology that, removed as it is from its theological context, is nothing more than empty rhetoric. On a theoretical level this may explain the growing interest among business ethicists in classical, pre-Enlightenment, virtue-based ethical theory. On a practical level, this may help explain the empirical observation that business managers tend to be more religious than other professionals; they may realize, albeit unconsciously, that their belief in divinity is the only way of logically sustaining their stance as a moral manager. But the Moral Universe that I discredit in Part II claims secular justification: The growing field of business ethics claims justification through Enlightenment philosophy, not theology. It is this Enlightenment bubble that aestheticism bursts, and with it any secular modernist justification for the moral manager.

Thus, the transition in management away from the Technical and Moral Universes is a reflection of the broader cultural shift away from reliance on a science-based concept of reason. Staune (1996, p. 146) encapsulates this shift by noting three broad cultural realizations that characterized the end of the twentieth century:

- The hope of being able to explain reality by reality, to find a definitive explanation for what is real, has vanished.
- The cutting edge of the sciences studying matter reveals the presence of an intangibility, another level of reality whose existence can be perceived but not reached.
- The question of meaning (of our own existence, of the existence of the universe) is once again at the heart of contemporary science after having been excluded for centuries.

Staune goes on to conclude that, taken together, these factors create a cultural impact that "constitutes a real 'change of paradigm,' in other words a change in the way we see things . . . [S]uch a change of vision cannot fail to have an impact on our society given the role that science plays" (p. 147).

With the collapse of the Technical and Moral Universes, business management in the twenty-first century will become not just more of an art than a science but almost entirely an art. The managers' guide to truth will become an aesthetic beauty rather than a technical formula or a moral dictum. The most successful managers of the next millennium will be those who "manage" to make this self-conceptual shift. A term that has all but disappeared since the inception of modern business will return as the best description of this new manager. It is the manager as *art*isan.

The paradigm shift that I have in mind here is thus one that moves away from management as a reason-based science and toward management as an aesthetics-based art. To those of us steeped in modernity, this notion of the manager as artist might, at first, seem fanciful. Isn't business about making money, not creating beauty? But then to those of us with some familiarity with the preindustrial communities of antiquity, that is, those of us who can to some extent at least put ourselves in the metaphorical shoes of members of such communities, we can imagine how preposterous and alien the contemporary manager as technician would be to such communities of antiquity. Art may seem very alien to those who craft modern business, but remember that classical Greek and Old English made no distinction between the words "art" and "craft" (nor, apparently, do most ancient Asian dialects). The craft of business was the art of business. The separation of the two and the cultural alienation of the artist are recent, modern phenomenan. Indeed we do not have to use our imagination entirely to conjure the artisan communities of premodernity. Vestiges of these cultures still survive in isolated pockets of modernity; the Aesthetic Universe has never been entirely eclipsed. What we will see in the next millennium is the return of this universe to dominance.

In a broader context, as is often observed by observers of aesthetic philosophy, much of aestheticism is premodernism. Aestheticism, as a cultural phenomenon, cannot be any kind of progression from modernity. The character of aestheticism, as we shall see, rejects the idea of linear progress. Aestheticism is better thought of as merely the absence of modernism. Aestheticism is the removal of something rather than the addition of anything. But more on this later. Suffice it to say here that the thrust of this book, the "reason" for this book, is to reveal business once again as an art. Those who read this book as some sort of guide to "successful" management can read my message as follows: The successful manager of the twenty-first century will be one who views himself or herself as first and foremost an artisan. This is not to say that the manager as technician, or the manager as moralist, will not still exist. As I mentioned earlier, these three metaphysical managerial universes always exist within every manager. What will change, however, is which universe dominates. For the first time since modernity, that is, for the first time in some 300 years in the West, the manager as aesthete will dominate. So, for example, Pepsi's management realized finally that its decision to pull out of Burma in January 1997 could not be made successfully by applying financial theory or by applying some moral dictum; it could only be made aesthetically; in having to make a decision not based on either financial theory or moral theory, Pepsi's management was forced, albeit kicking and screaming, into the aesthetic world.

Of course, the notion that successful decisions must now be based on aesthetic criteria rather than technical or moral ones entails some redefinition or deconstruction of the idea of "success." It means that success itself will become defined in aesthetic terms. The successful aesthetic manager may not even be recognizable to the contemporary modern manager as successful. How can a decision be successful, in the conventional notion, if it is not apparently profit maximizing? Measuring success in aesthetic terms such as "beauty" or "harmony" is clearly very different to measuring success in terms of some technical yardstick or moral dictum. Thus, when I say this book as a management guide is a guide to successful management, it is also implicitly a guide to redefining just exactly what success is.

Above I defined aestheticism as an absence rather than a presence, as a subtraction rather than an addition. This implies that the aesthetic manager as a phenomenon must in some sense be a nonphenomenon, an absence rather than a presence. More precisely, in shifting from a modern manager to an aesthetic manager, the individual loses or sheds something rather than adds something. The manager, through this transition, gains by losing, just as the naked emperor of yore gained true self-knowledge by losing his imaginary robes. Thus to say that aestheticism is an absence is not in any way to deride or dismiss it. The idea that more is always better, the idea that additions are better than subtractions, and the idea that presences are better than absences constitute just one more delusion of modernity—just one more invisible robe. Remember that nirvana, a very unmodern concept, is absence—it is literally "breathing out"; in a sense, the aesthetic manager can be viewed as searching for a type of Nirvana, a type of peace or even equilibrium through aesthetic harmony and balance. The very idea of maximization, whether it be maximizing profits or stock price or growth or societal welfare, is anathema to the aesthetic firm. Similarly, the "successful" aesthetic manager is one who has breathed out the delusions of modernity. Like the enlightened emperor, the aesthetic manager accepts his or her nakedness.

To describe an absence, one must first describe a presence. For without a presence there can be no absence. This accounts for the structure of this book. A specific description of the aesthetic manager must wait until Part III because first the modern manager—the presence—must be identified. This presence exists in two universes, that of the technician and that of the moralist. Parts I and II of this book describe these two modern metaphysical universes. This sets the stage for the description of the aesthetic manager in Part III.

TEST CASE: PEPSI/BURMA

Throughout this book, at various places, I will refer to one particular recent business event. Of course, this is not the only business event I will be referring to, but it is an event that I have chosen to use as a parable of my central thesis. I will thus be referring to "Test Case: Pepsi/Burma" explicitly at the end of several chapters. In a sense, it will provide the reality check for the theory.

The event to which I refer is PepsiCo's recent (January 1997) decision to sever all business ties with the East Asian country of Burma (renamed "Myanmar" by its military leaders in 1989, but I will stick with the more familiar name of Burma). Pepsi's decision was at least in part the result of growing public protest, generally on U.S. college campuses, concerning human rights abuses by Burma's ruling military junta. The junta took power

in 1988, and although national elections were held in 1990, the junta ignored the unfavorable pro-democracy election outcome.

The junta's activities have been widely condemned in the West. In April
1996, for example, Harvard University voted to change the school's $1
million contract from Pepsi to Coke, stating explicitly that the reason for
the change was Pepsi's continued involvement in Burma. Similar action was
taken by Stanford University, and several Pizza Hut franchises were forced
to close their on-campus operations because of student pickets (at the time,
Pizza Hut was owned by Pepsi).

I chose this event not because it is particularly unique; indeed, it is in
many respects typical of many contemporary dilemmas faced by multinational companies. I chose it, rather because it is typical and because it illustrates well the impoverishment of the modern conceptions of business
management. What I will show below in future discussions of this case is
how the modernist manager, whether technician or moralist, failed Pepsi in
its attempts to make the decision of whether or not to sever ties with Burma.
Initially Pepsi's management attempted to use the business tools of modernity but as with many other contemporary business decisions, Pepsi
found the tools of modernity both impotent and self-destructive; the continuation versus abandonment mathematics of capital budgeting theory in
the Technical Universe failed Pepsi; the integrated social contracts theory
of modernist business ethics failed Pepsi. Eventually—and I will argue inevitably—Pepsi's decision to pull out of Burma was one primarily of aesthetics. Pepsi was forced to recognize the real-world business implications
of the aesthetic critique.

Similarly, Royal Dutch–Shell's aforementioned decision to sink its massive
obsolete "Brent Spar" oil platform in the mid-Atlantic was optimal financially, and it did not appear to contravene any conventional moral dictum,
but it was a decision that Shell was forced to change in the aesthetic world.
Nike's recent experience with the sudden public furor over its employment
practices in developing countries, particularly in Vietnam, is another story
very similar to that of Shell and Pepsi. Whether the decision was to pull out
of a country, to dispose of an oil platform, or to employ children, the tools
of the Technical and Moral Universes failed. The management of Pepsi,
Shell, and Nike have been forced to recognize the paradigm shift under way
in business. They have been forced to recognize the growing prominence
and predominance of the Aesthetic Universe.

CHAPTER OUTLINE

The structure of the remainder of this book falls naturally into three sections. Each section invokes one of the three management universes outlined
above. Part I addresses the Technical Universe in two chapters. In Chapter
1, I show how the rational agent of financial-economic theory provides the

foundation for the manager as technician; rationality is defined in narrow terms as the individualistic and opportunistic pursuit of material wealth. The very nature of the rationality concept chosen, however, thwarts the agent in its attempts to maximize wealth. This Technical Universe, therefore, is subtly self-defeating. In Chapter 2, I extend the study of the Technical Universe from the individual agent to the role of the firm. The firm, in this context, is viewed essentially as a type of wealth-creating machine. Once again, however, the rationality assumptions that govern the behavior of agents within this firm render the firm and the economy in aggregate incapable of attaining the efficiency goal for which they are designed.

The critiques of Chapters 1 and 2 thus expose the internal inconsistencies of the Technical Universe. This is a business metaphysic built around the concepts of economic efficiency, yet the very nature of the metaphysic prevents the attainment of economic efficiency. Regardless of any critique from outside its own context, therefore, a careful deconstruction of the manager as technician reveals that this construct fails even within and in terms of itself. In short, financial-economic rationality is premised on, and finds its justification in, the economically efficient pursuit of material wealth. Chapters 1 and 2 demonstrate, however, that financial-economic rationality fails in this pursuit. Thus, this rationality construct and its surrounding metaphysic—what I call here the Technical Universe—satisfy the first of MacIntyre's two conditions that he identifies as necessary for a Kuhnian-type paradigm shift.

This internal deconstruction is even apparent at the heart of financial-economic theory. The very bedrock of this theory, namely, the notion of a risk-return trade-off and a time value of money, is being currently exposed to radical self-questioning and self-doubt.

In addition to its internal inconsistencies, the Technical Universe is also being increasingly criticized by reference to standards that are external. These external standards are those derived from modern business ethics theory, and they conjure the second of the three management universes, namely, the Moral Universe of Part II. As with Part I, Part II is split into two chapters, the first dealing with the individual moral manager as rational agent (Chapter 3), and the second dealing with the firm and the business environment that this moral manager invokes (Chapter 4). Another similarity between Part I and Part II is that both sections involve a deconstruction of the underlying concept contained within that section. In the case of Part I, as just discussed, this deconstruction involves exposing the internal inconsistencies in the Technical Universe. In similar manner, Part II involves an exposition of the internal inconsistencies and incoherences in our second business metaphysic, namely, the Moral Universe.

In Chapter 3, the moral manager invoked by the Moral Universe is shown to derive his or her substance from modern business ethics theory. As with the technician of Part I, this moral manager still applies conventional rationality and logic in decision making. Unlike the pure technician, however, this rationality and logic are governed by adherence to some moral principle. This rational moral principle is supplied by Enlightenment moral philosophy, for example, Kantianism or utilitarianism.

But there is a central inconsistency in these "rational" moral principles of post-Enlightenment modernity. Indeed, as with the Technical Universe of Part I, a careful deconstruction of this Moral Universe renders it logically incoherent. This logical incoherence stems from what I term modernity's "deafening silence." The silence stems from modernity's failure to address the fundamental question, Why "ought" I act morally? I label this silence as deafening because modernity's failure to address it brings the entire Enlightenment project into question. We may be able to derive abstract moral principles such as Kantianism and utilitarianism, but if we are unable to provide any reason why agents should abide by them, then these abstract principles will remain as such: They will remain abstract and will have no empirical force as regards actual behavior.

In Chapters 3 and 4 I proffer the standard aesthetic critique of modernity. I argue that the Enlightenment philosophies of modernity, upon which business ethics theory is largely based, are incapable of answering the fundamental question, Why ought I, as a business manager or otherwise, act morally? Thus, the moral manager and the moral firm, invoked by business ethics theory, fall victim to their own internal incoherences and inconsistencies. In essence, like the technician, the moral manager in practice is a chimera.

To summarize, Parts I and II of this book, by describing and deconstructing the two modern business universes, reveal the fundamental epistemological failure of modern business theory. At its very core, this failure stems from the blindness of the modern worldview—a blindness both to the reality of human nature and to the reality of the human milieu. In the case of human nature, the concepts that underpin both the manager as technician, namely, material opportunism, and the moral manager, namely, adherence to some reason-based moral principle, fail to grasp the complexity of human thought and action. From the outset of the Industrial Revolution in Europe, these "rationality"-based concepts of human behavior have helped to sanction and justify the wrenching economic and cultural changes that industrialization and commercialization have wrought. Thus, the self-deceptions of modernity, whether of a technical or moral nature, are understandable in terms of the accumulation and stabilization of power relations in the modern world. But this does not alter the fact that they are, at root, deceptions.

Indeed, almost from their very inception and dissemination in the nineteenth century, the deceptive natures of the principles of modernity, both moral and economic, were recognized by some. Those observers of the Industrial Revolution who were able to remove themselves from the intellectual intoxication of modernity, most notably Nietzsche, saw the naked emperor. But it is not until the late twentieth century, in the guise of aestheticism, that the observations of Nietzsche and other critics of modernity have begun to come to the fore of Western culture.

This brings us to the final part of the book: Part III. In Chapters 5 and 6 of Part III the aesthetic manager is invoked. The central prediction of Part III, that the aesthetic manager as aesthete will eclipse the technical and moral manager, builds from the deconstructions of modernity in Part I and Part II. As mentioned above, the aesthetic manager is thus not really an addition to, or something beyond, the modern manager. Rather, the aesthetic manager is what is revealed once the ontological veils of modernity are removed. Removal of these pseudoscientific and moralistic veils reveals the aesthetic nature of business management. The manager as individual person is revealed as a holistic being who recognizes the complex, multifarious, and ephemeral nature of reality. Reality is recognized as essentially chaotic and unpredictable. The aesthetic manager thus recognizes the futility of acting on the premise of some doctrine that assumes underlying order and reason.

In this Aesthetic Universe of business, many of the erstwhile dualisms of modernism disappear. Indeed, perhaps the fundamental dualism of the modern manager is highlighted by the structure of this book. Many see Part I's materially opportunistic technician of financial-economic theory as what the manager "is" and Part II's ethically constrained moral manager of modernity as what the manager "ought" to be. The aesthetic manager does not recognize this is/ought dualism. In Chapter 5, what the manager is and what the manager ought to be are indistinguishable. The manager is some kind of beauty-seeking and balance-seeking aesthete, and given the nature of business reality, this is indistinguishable from what the manager ought to be. Indeed, in this Aesthetic Universe the concept of "ought" loses the pseudoreligious ambiguity of the moral ought of modernity. To capture the essence of the aesthetic manager in Chapter 5, I resurrect a word that most people connect with a preindustrial age, namely, the concept of a manager as an *artisan*. This word will, I hope, capture the essential nature of business in the aesthetic world as an art form. If I had to describe the aesthetic manager in two words, I would describe him or her as a "practical artist"— in one word, an artisan.

Unfortunately, 200 years of modernity have severely warped the cultural image of the artist or aesthete. In terms of social role, the artist or aesthete is invoked as antisocial: someone outside the "real" world of instrumental and scientific rationality. This trivialization and marginalization of art have meant that managers have both consciously and unconsciously distanced themselves as far as possible from any conceptualization or self-conceptualization of themselves as artists. The reality that managers, and particularly senior-level managers, do and have to operate largely on aesthetic principles is carefully concealed. Decisions, whatever their true origin, have to be couched in terms of financial-economic theory or reason-based morality in order to be palatable to the social milieu of modernity. Any acceptance or justification of the aesthetic nature of management has essentially become taboo. Metaphorically, this is the taboo of the naked emperor.

So, for example, in reference to our Pepsi/Burma test case, the fact that Pepsi's final decision to sever all ties with Burma in 1997 was not based on any financial analysis or moral principle was never admitted by Pepsi's management. To admit that this decision was aesthetically based—which I argue later it was and indeed had to be—would have been to break the great taboo of modern business. But more on this in Chapter 6.

Although the aesthetic critique is familiar territory to philosophers, it may not be familiar territory to many theorists and practitioners of business. In developing this notion of the manager as aesthete, however, I do not have to navigate entirely uncharted waters. If you will excuse the mixed metaphors, to some extent, a trail has already been blazed by one fairly new area of business ethics theory. This new "postconventional" area of business ethics tends to stand apart from the accepted canon of modern Enlightenment-based business ethics. Indeed, the controversy surrounding it undoubtedly stems from the fact that it threatens this very canon. What I am referring to here is the growing application of classical virtue-based moral philosophy to business. Virtue ethics predates modernity and is essentially an aesthetics-based approach, rather than a reason-based approach, to ethics; but it is not just an approach to ethics—it is a holistic approach to life that embraces ethics. In conjuring my aesthetic manager, therefore, I draw heavily on virtue ethics. Indeed, this literature, specifically the recent renaissance in virtue-based thinking spearheaded by Alasdair MacIntyre, provides the metaphysical backbone of Part III. Thus, although the aesthetic manager may reject the moral dictums of modernity, he or she in no way rejects morality as such.

My rejection of the business Technical and Moral universes of modernity should not be seen—and, given an accurate reading of this book, will not be seen—as a rejection of reason and morality. The manager as artisan still applies, for example, the tools of financial-economic theory, but the goals implicit in these tools are not viewed as ultimate objectives; rather, they are viewed as inputs into a holistic worldview. Indeed, the aesthetic manager encompasses both reason and morality; they are, however, a different reason and a different morality than those with which modernity has made us familiar. This different reason and different morality understandably lead to a different concept of business. In the final chapter of this book, Chapter 6, business in the aesthetic world becomes an aesthetic community. Within this community, morality, albeit in an aesthetic virtue-based form, is the very core and essence of the aesthetic manager.

Part I

The Modern Manager as Technician

We've asked before and we'll ask again—why should we restrain our baser instincts if we fear no god, contain no soul, exist merely for the convenience of a string of genes?
> —Joe Rogaly, "Knowledge, Freedom and a Poison Pill"

Chapter 1

The Rational Agent
of Modernity

The idea that Man is not just a stimulus-response machine, that his
thought process, his intuition and his creativity cannot be reduced solely
to the level of calculations (even very complex ones) undertaken by neu-
ral networks, is coming into its own on the basis of recent neurological
research.

—Jean Staune, "Science and Management"

With the possible exception of the latter third of the twentieth century,
when the moral manager has gained prominence, the dominant management paradigm of modernity has undoubtedly been the manager as technician. This manager as technician exists within the metaphysic of what I
term here the "Technical Universe." This Technical Universe finds its justification in the theory and empirics of financial-economic theory. Indeed,
this manager as technician is purely the practical manifestation of the theoretically rational agent of financial economics: the wealth maximizer, the
opportunist, the logician. But who exactly is this person? We must never
lose sight of the fact that the manager *is* a person. So what type of person
is the rational agent of financial-economic theory?

A priori, we might reasonably expect that if nothing else at least this agent
will be profoundly rational, where rationality would be defined in an instrumental—that is to say, modernist—sense. Instrumental rationality is what
designates the manager as technician; it is the essence of financial-economic
theory; so surely the rational pursuit of rational objectives will characterize
this person. But does it?

When we look closely at this manager as technician, when we deconstruct this construction of financial-economic theory, we find something that is unexpected. This rational agent, who has the rational objective of personal material advancement, never actually achieves this objective. Indeed, more significantly, it is the very nature of the rationality adopted that ensures that this rational agent can never rationally achieve his or her rational objective.

Thus, in short, financial-economic theory makes the odd assumption that rational agents rationally choose a rationality construct that ensures that they can never rationally achieve the rationally determined objective. Simply put, the goal of wealth maximization or some variant thereof, as conjured by financial-economic theory, and as adopted by our manager as technician, is subtly self-defeating. This pursuit of wealth maximization never achieves maximum wealth either for the individual agent or for the group of agents who comprise the Technical Universe. Elsewhere I have termed this phenomenon the "finance paradox," for it is indeed paradoxical that a rational individual or group of individuals would knowingly adopt a mode of reasoning and behavior—namely opportunism—that they rationally know will render them incapable of achieving their a priori stated objective: to maximize their material wealth or, if they are risk averse or effort averse, their utility of wealth.

Furthermore, financial-economic theory in the guise of the technician has always claimed that this opportunistic pursuit of wealth, together with the firm-wide implication of it, namely, shareholder wealth maximization, is value neutral. By "value" here is meant moral value: Financial economics has always had a self-conception as a moral-free zone, exempt from the vagaries of moral philosophy. The careful deconstruction undertaken below, however, will reveal that financial-economic theory is not value free. It possesses an implicit moral agenda.

In the case of individual opportunism, financial economics defends its theories as morally free by either just tacitly accepting opportunism as a simplifying assumption (real behavior is too complex to model) or just tacitly accepting such behavior as natural (a sort of tacit application of some variant of social Darwinism). In the case of the first justification, it is noteworthy that this acceptance of opportunism as a simplifying assumption is made purely on the basis of the latter's mathematical convenience. The mathematical modelability of behavior is taken as a primary criterion for building a model of the manager. In the context of human behavior, "mathematical" and "model building" are all characteristics peculiar to modernity.

In the case of the cockeyed application of social Darwinism's survival of the fittest, more on this later. Suffice it to note here that the common usage of this phrase is merely a tautology with, in actuality, no cognitive bite: "The fittest" are implicitly defined as those that survive; therefore, the phrase deconstructs to "survival of the survivors," which—as Robert M. Pirsig points out in *Zen and the Art of Motorcycle Maintenance* (1975)—really doesn't tell us very much.

I highlight these ambiguities and paradoxes up front to whet the appetite of the reader. Those unfamiliar with the subtler nuances of financial-economic theory might think that the manager as technician is going to be a pretty dry and predictable character. Or more naive yet, dangerously naive readers might think that the manager as technician leads naturally to a material utopia of predictability and uniform prosperity. What a careful deconstruction of financial-economic theory actually reveals, however, is that these types of reasonable prediction are manifestly false. A managerial universe of pure technicians, where a pure technician is an agent who adheres strictly to the tenets of financial-economic rationality, will be characterized by economic inefficiency and instability in the short run and likely self-destruction in the long run. More significantly, these are not merely the predictions of an aesthetic critique. These are the predictions of financial-economic theory itself!

It is the gradual recognition of these tendencies during the twentieth century that has, to some extent at least, augured the inception and growth of the Moral Universe of business ethics theory and other alternative theories, to be discussed in Part II. One might also be tempted to say that this recognition and deconstruction of the Technical Universe justifies the aesthetic manager. But of course justifying something on the grounds of effectiveness or efficiency, which presumably are the implicit grounds assumed here, is itself a phenomenon of modernity. Any justification of the aesthetic manager must await a deconstruction of the concept of justification. But first let us take a closer look at the Technical Universe of modernity. Who exactly is this manager as pure technician? And why is this individual's *raison d'être* subtly self-defeating?

RATIONALITY AS OPPORTUNISM

> I carved a massive cake of beeswax into bits and rolled them in my hands until they softened. . . . Going forward I carried wax along the line, and laid it thick on their ears. They tied me up, then, plumb amidships, back to the mast, lashed to the mast, and took themselves again to rowing. Soon, as we came smartly within hailing distance, the two Sirens, noting our fast ship off their point, made ready, and they sang. . . . The lovely voices in ardor appealing over the water made me crave to listen, and I tried to say "Untie me!" to the crew, jerking my brows; but they bent steady to the oars.
>
> —Homer, *The Odyssey*

A significant contributor to the canon of financial-economic theory is Stewart Myers. In "The Determinants of Corporate Borrowing" (1977), Myers employs the above excerpt from Homer's *Odyssey* to illustrate the paradoxical nature of rationality in financial economics. The Sirens' song in financial economics is the opportunistic pursuit of personal material gain. The term "opportunistic" implies that the agent will do whatever is necessary in the interests of this pursuit. The agent will lie, cheat, steal, and so forth, so long as this behavior is construed as wealth maximizing. The agent is assumed to adopt opportunism even though the agent knows that such behavior is ultimately self-defeating. It is as if financial economists assume that opportunism is irresistible—hence, the Sirens analogy.

Understandably, the mass media tends to be fed watered-down versions of this rational agent: Milton Friedman's infamous *New York Times Magazine* version, for example, entitled "The Social Responsibility of Business Is to Increase Its Profits" (1970; reprinted in Hoffman and Moore, 1990). I say "infamous" because even though he watered it down by the caveats "within the law" and "constrained by ethical custom" (Friedman never expands on the term "ethical custom"; does he mean *his* ethical custom?), his rendition of the rational manager as technician still caused quite a stir among those not initiated already into the worldview of financial economists. Friedman's views on this subject are actually quite nuanced and, although ambiguous, give a good intuitive idea of the practical implications of financial-economic theory. Thomas Carson (1993a) has recently summarized Friedman's writings on this subject into two basic propositions on the role of the firm:

The first formulation . . . says that the one and only obligation of business is to maximize its profits while engaging in "open and free competition without deception or fraud." The second formulation . . . says that business executives are obligated to follow the wishes of shareholders (which will generally be to make as much money as possible) while obeying the laws and the "ethical customs" of the society. (p. 3)

As noted above, Friedman's admission of ethical custom into one of these statements appears to imply that he supports some sort of role for deontological (i.e., rule-based) ethics within a fundamentally shareholder-based consequentialist (i.e., utilitarian) structure, although he never defines exactly what he means here by "ethical custom." As we will see in Part II, contemporary moral philosophy would have great difficulty in providing a uniform definition of "ethical custom."

MacIntyre (1988), for example, makes very clear in *Whose Justice? Which Rationality?* that there exists no single unified ethical custom even within Western philosophical tradition. For example, one might argue that a predisposition toward honesty is an unequivocal ethical custom, but then some business ethicists have argued that, in business dealings, dishonesty and deception are justified (Carson, 1993a). Friedman's second statement on the role of business is thus thwarted with ambiguity. For this reason, Carson concludes his review of Friedman's writings with his own theory, which is essentially a distillation of Friedman's equivocal statements:

The one and only social (moral) responsibility of corporate executives is to act in accordance with the wishes of the owners provided that they 1) obey the law, 2) engage in open and free competition, 3) refrain from fraud and deception, and 4) warn the public about all serious hazards or dangers created by the firms which they represent. (p. 20)

But Carson's theory perpetuates much of the ambiguity found in Friedman. For example, is deception always wrong—even in a competitive bidding environment? What are serious as opposed to nonserious hazards?

What is perhaps more shocking than the mere existence of opportunistic managers as a theoretical prerogative, and something that has not, to my knowledge, been disseminated by the mass media, is that financial-economic theory postulates that agents will pursue this goal even though they know that such a pursuit is self-defeating. It is true that financial economists consider agents who voluntarily enter into agreements that curb their opportunism for mutual self-interest: This is the "reputation effect" construct, to be discussed in further detail below. But, as we will see, such agreements are always very fragile. The rationality assumption precludes any agent from actually possessing any genuine regard for the welfare of the other agent or the welfare of the group. So the agreement only holds when it is in the self-interest of every agent individually to honor the agreement. Otherwise, someone reneges, and the agreement collapses. Indeed, using the phrase "honor the agreement" in this context is perhaps misleading because honor, in any meaningful sense, never enters into the rational equation for these agents. The concept of honor, as a behavioral attribute or characteristic possessing intrinsic worth, is entirely alien to financial-economic rationality.

The paradoxically self-defeating nature of our technician's rationality as opportunism is apparent in the aforementioned Myers's (1977) model of debt markets. In Myers's model, lenders (e.g., banks, financial institutions) have to decide upon the appropriate interest rate to charge borrowers. Given that this model is developed within the metaphysical universe of financial economics, lenders assume that borrowers are opportunists. Thus, lenders assume that borrowers will take only those actions that are directly and explicitly in the interests of borrowers. So, for example, if borrowers are faced with the choice of whether or not to undertake a project that, albeit profitable, does not generate sufficient profits to cover the interest cost of the money borrowed to undertake the project, then borrowers will simply not bother to undertake the project. Specifically, even though this is a profitable project, and even though these profits will go some way to paying the interest cost owed to lenders, borrowers will not undertake it. Borrowers will not "rationally" undertake it because the project will not materially benefit them personally. Simply put, borrowers are assumed to not give a fig about the welfare of lenders, or anyone else for that matter; all borrowers care about is borrowers. Indeed, the atomistic nature of the rationality assumption precludes any individual borrower from caring about any other borrower. Each rational opportunist is a metaphysical island unto himself or herself.

Cognizant of the opportunistic nature of borrowers' rationality, therefore, lenders charge a higher interest rate in the expectation that borrowers will act opportunistically and underinvest (i.e., will reject certain low-payoff profitable projects). This phenomenon is termed the "underinvestment problem" in the agency theory literature of financial economics. Thus, the actions of lenders in setting higher interest rates ensure that agents—in this case, borrowers—pay the price for opportunism even before they act; they are "lashed to the mast" of opportunism. The possibility that at least some agents may be honest or trustworthy—in the sense that they may feel some "obligation" to temper their opportunism and "honor" as far as possible their agreement with lenders—is never considered and can never be considered, given the prevailing rationality rubric. Indeed, the very nature of the resulting equilibrium, in which lenders charge a higher interest rate a priori, really discourages the cultivation of any sense of obligation; trust is never offered, agents are universally assumed to fall victim to the Sirens' Song of Opportunism, so why should agents feel any compunction to act differently? Opportunism, in essence, is "built into" financial economics in a most fundamental way. Eric Noreen (1988) defines this opportunistic notion of rationality as one in which individuals always pursue personal material gain with "necessary guile and deceit" (p. 359). Indeed, characteristics such as guile and deceit really characterize the broader nature of opportunism—hence, the moral censure traditionally attached to the "opportunistic" literary character. (For example, the deceptively and distastefully " 'umble" ambitious accounting clerk, Uriah Heep, in Charles Dickens's classic novel *David Copperfield*.) But moral censure has never worried financial economists very much. After all, in their Technical Universe, moral censure is irrational.

A BRIEF HISTORY OF OPPORTUNISM

From whence does this financial-economic notion of rationality spring? A historical perspective reveals that even within economic and financial-economic theory, economic agents have not always been invoked in such conceptually narrow terms. An investigation into the early origins of economic philosophy in the writings of, for example, Adam Smith and David Hume reveals

the incredible finesse with which Smith and his contemporaries analyzed the human psyche . . . [versus] . . . the pitiful impoverishment that befell us, sometime in the nineteenth century, when Marxism and liberal economics conspired to assert the supremacy of interest and thus to extinguish an older and subtler tradition of moral psychology. (Holmes, 1990, p. 268)

As the following quotes illustrate, these classic economic philosophers envisaged a far richer paradigm of human interaction in the business sphere. In the case of David Hume (1955; from an essay originally published in 1751):

The epithets sociable, good-natured, humane, merciful, grateful, friendly, generous, beneficent, or their equivalents, are known in all languages, and universally express the highest merit, which human nature is capable of attaining. (p. 557)

And in the case of Adam Smith (1937a):

All members of human society stand in need of each other's assistance, and are likewise exposed to mutual injuries. Where the necessary assistance is reciprocally afforded from love, from gratitude, from friendship, and esteem, the society flourishes and is happy. All the different members of it are bound together by the agreeable bonds of love and affection, and are, as it were, drawn to one common centre of mutual good offices. (p. 42)

In *Wealth of Nations* (1937b), Smith used the invisible hand metaphor to illustrate the socially beneficial effects of individual prudence or self-interest. The work of Charles Darwin in the nineteenth century, which popularized notions such as "natural selection" and "survival of the fittest," seemed to lend further credence to Smithian notions of prudent self-interest. In addition, the great scientific and technical advances of the nineteenth century, based, as they were, on the application of strict scientific logic, augured the modernist conception of reality. The eighteenth-century social epithets of Hume, and the moral sentiments of Smith, were increasingly marginalized, if not entirely eclipsed, by the nineteenth-century mantras of natural selection and internal combustion.

Thus, in evolving from the self-interest invoked by Smith and Hume to the self-interest of the Technical Universe of financial-economic theory, something has been lost. In essence we have regressed in the last 200 years from a morally inclusive concept of self-interest to one in which the notion of what Adam Smith called moral sentiment has absolutely no rational place.

In the late nineteenth century, for example, British physicist Lord Kelvin (1891) reflected the Victorians' complete faith in the explanatory powers of scientific rationality when he declared that "physics has given a harmonious and, at first glance, complete description of the world" (p. 42). But the second glance taken by twentieth-century physicists, revealing such phenomena as general relativity and quantum mechanics, rendered a far less harmonious and all-embracing view of science. This complete confidence in a scientific approach to rationality can also be found in the behavioral assumptions of late nineteenth-century economists. F. Y. Edgeworth (1881), for example, declared that "the first principle of Economics is that every agent is actuated only by self-interest" (p. 16).

Once embraced, economists—and particularly financial economists—have been reluctant to relinquish this Victorianly scientific, Darwinian notion of human rationality. Indeed, the rationality premise of contemporary financial economics is founded squarely on this notion, and consequently self-interest is defined strictly in material terms. Specifically, it is founded on the five axioms of cardinal utility as enumerated by von Neumann and Morgenstern (1947), plus one additional axiom. These five axioms define rationality in terms of an individual's ability to make consistent preference orderings over a broad spectrum of choices: "We wish to find the mathematically complete principles which define 'rational behavior' for the participants in a social economy, and derive from them the general characteristics of that behavior" (p. 31). Furthermore, "people are assumed to be able to make these rational choices among thousands of alternatives" (Copeland and Weston, 1988, p. 80).

The axioms are thus based on a very mathematical and instrumental notion of what it means to be rational: the five axioms are *completeness, consistency, independence, measurability*, and *ranking*; they are all concerned with defining instrumental rationality in terms of the consistent ranking of preferences. For example, if you are an investor choosing stocks in which to invest, and you prefer IBM to Microsoft, and you prefer Microsoft to Netscape, then to be rational, you must prefer IBM to Netscape. Also, your degree of preference for one investment over another must stay constant, no matter how many more stocks are added to your opportunity set. *Star Trek*'s Mr. Spock would be an excellent example of this type of rational agent, as would a computer—hence, the label I use here of "technician."

Note that this type of axiom makes no normative statement concerning whether the agent has any specific goal, or *telos*, or what the goal of the agent should be, the axiom simply requires that the agent act in a consistent manner in ordering preferences. The *sixth* axiom, however, which is promoted particularly vehemently by financial economists, has just such normative implications. As Thomas Copeland and Fred Weston's (1988) leading finance text puts it: "Having established the five axioms we add to them the assumption that individuals *always* prefer more wealth to less" (p. 80; my emphasis).

In relating the five axioms to this sixth axiom, a useful distinction can be made between *instrumental* rationality and *substantive* rationality. In *The Protestant Work Ethic and the Spirit of Capitalism* (1948), Max Weber made this distinction in labeling two types of rationality as *zweckrationalitat* (formal or instrumental rationality) and *wertrarationalitat* (values-based or substantive rationality). In essence, instrumental rationality concerns how the agent goes about achieving the desired objective, whereas substantive rationality concerns identifying the desired objective itself. For example, Jennifer Moore (1991) distinguishes between the two concepts as follows:

The primary feature of instrumental rationality is that it does not choose ends, but accepts them as given and looks for the best means to achieve them. In instrumental rationality, reason is subordinated to and placed at the service of ends outside itself. In . . . [substantive rationality], in contrast, reason is free ranging. It is not the servant of any end. Rather, it subjects every end to its *own* standards of evaluation and criticism. (p. 63)

Von Neumann and Morgenstern's five axioms clearly pertain to instrumental rationality. They do not stipulate an ultimate objective but merely require that agents pursue some given objective in a consistent and logical manner.

The substantive rationality premise of financial economics is provided by the sixth axiom: the opportunistic and atomistic pursuit of material gain ad infinitum. No justification is supplied in the finance literature in the form of empirical evidence to support this substantive rationality premise, nor is any normative argument supplied to defend the notion that this is how agents *should* behave. Far from the application of sound logic and philosophy, therefore, the sixth axiom is applied merely in the interests of methodological convenience. It is imposed by fiat. Let's take a closer look at the "agent" in this conventional finance paradigm.

THE MODERN RATIONAL AGENT

In reference to the notion of the rational agent in financial economics, Norman Bowie (1991) notes that "there is considerable confusion as to whether the profit maximization claim is a universal empirical claim, an approximate empirical claim, a heuristic assumption, or an ethical obligation" (p. 14). Despite its potential ambiguity, the term "profit maximization" or "wealth maximization" captures succinctly the primary characteristic common to all financial-economic objective functions, namely, that they are purely acquisitive in nature, entailing solely the accumulation or consumption, or both, of pecuniary goods. The broad acceptance of this sixth axiom of individual wealth maximization is reflected in the behavioral assumptions made by financial economists. Hayne Leland and David Pyle, (1977) for example, in their capital structure signaling model, state that "the entrepreneur is presumed to maximize his expected utility of wealth" (p. 373). Kose John and David Nachman (1985) directly transfer the traditional objective of the firm to managers when, in their agency model, they assume that management's "overall objective is to . . . invest in nonnegative NPV [net present value] projects" (p. 867). Douglas Diamond (1989), in his model of reputation acquisition in debt markets, defines management's objective as an endeavor to "maximize discounted expected consumption over T periods" (p. 833). Some models assume management is risk averse or effort averse, or both, and therefore maximizes some measure of *utility of wealth*. But this utility is always strictly a positive function of wealth, ad infinitum. Thus, the sixth axiom holds throughout.

These six axioms are also subsuming any competing notions of rationality. One reason often cited for this popularity is the similarity between economic rationality and the aforementioned Darwinian ideas of natural selection and Richard Dawkin's (1972) invocation of "the selfish gene." Recent evidence indicates, however, that genes may not be entirely selfish; some form of tacit cooperation, in other words, a morality, may exist even at the molecular level. The preeminence of a notion of narrow self-interest, however, clearly endures, particularly in the social sciences. This was made abundantly clear recently by Richard Thaler's book *The Winner's Curse: Paradoxes and Anomalies of Economic Life* (1992):

The same basic assumptions about behavior are used in all applications of economic analysis, be it the theory of the firm, financial markets, or consumer choice. The two key assumptions are rationality [the five axioms] and self-interest [the sixth axiom]. People are assumed to want to get as much for themselves as possible, and are assumed to be quite clever in figuring out how best to accomplish this aim. (p. 2)

Viewing this rationality within the Technical Universe—what I call elsewhere the "finance paradigm"—in terms of the aforementioned dichotomy between instrumental and substantive rationality reveals that this paradigm's rationality premise has only a partial foundation in logic. The logic of the instrumental part of what the finance paradigm regards as rational behavior finds a sound logical foundation in the five axioms enumerated by von Neumann and Morgenstern. The same cannot be said, however, for finance's substantive rationality premise. This premise is applied merely by arbitrarily assuming—for reasons of mathematical convenience—that agents are atomistic and opportunistic wealth maximizers.

These agents are atomistic in that they never adopt any communal notion of self-interest. To be sure, the agents may at times cooperate, but only when they perceive such cooperation to be in their own personal self-interest. Their decisions are not affected by the impact that these decisions might have on other agents, except to the extent that this impact might in turn impact their own personal wealth. In other words, there is no such thing as empathy or a sense of community. The agents are opportunists in that they are assumed to take whichever action maximizes their wealth, regardless of prior commitments or agreements. To date, the universal existence of this type of agent has been accepted by financial-economic theory as its sine qua non.

THE DESCRIPTIVE ACCURACY OF OPPORTUNISM

If individualistic and opportunistic wealth maximization were the only conceivable types of behavior, then there would be little realistic point in considering alternatives. Such illusiory consideration would then indeed be a "nirvana form of analysis," as Michael Jensen and William Meckling (1976), two leading financial economists, argue. But there is ample evidence that this is not the only conceivable form of behavior. For example, David Schmidtz (1994) notes that "[l]ike Homo economicus, we have preferences, but unlike Homo economicus, we have preferences directly relating to the welfare of others" (p. 250). Similarly, while commenting on the notion of economic rationality as premised on wealth maximization, Amartya Sen (1987) makes the following comment:

While this view of economics is quite widely held [i.e., the view of rationality as atomistic and opportunistic wealth maximization] . . . there is nevertheless something quite extraordinary in the fact that economics has evolved in this way, characterizing human motivation in such spectacularly narrow terms. One reason why this is extraordinary is that economics is supposed to be concerned with real people. It is hard to believe that real people could be completely unaffected by the reach of the self-examination induced by the Socratic question, "How should one live?" (pp. 1–2)

Similarly, C. R. Plott (1986) notes that "the weakest forms of the classical preference hypothesis [i.e., wealth maximization] are systematically at odds with the facts" (p. S309). H. A. Simon (1986) suggests that "we stop debating whether a theory of substantive rationality and the assumptions of utility maximization provide a sufficient base for explaining and predicting economic behavior. The evidence is overwhelming that they do not" (p. S223).

In the context of financial economics, Meir Statman and David Caldwell (1987) find evidence to suggest that aversion to regret or unwillingness to admit defeat dominates managerial decision making in the continuation versus abandonment decision of capital budgeting. David Kahneman, Jack Knetsch, and Richard Thaler (1986) observe that conceptions of fairness often eclipse wealth maximization criteria in sculpting managerial behavior. Richard Roll (1986) proposes a "hubris hypothesis" to explain the apparently excessive premiums paid for target firms in takeover battles. Similarly, "regret aversion" or an egoistic unwillingness to admit defeat seems to dominate many project abandonment decisions: Project abandonment is delayed beyond the point where the "technical" criteria, such as NPV provided by financial economics, dictate immediate abandonment (see Dobson and Dorsey, 1992).

Laboratory experiments indicate that strategies based on fair distribution or tit-for-tat tend to be more popular—and often more materially successful—than outright opportunism (Axelrod, 1984; DeJong, Forsythe, and Uecker, 1985;). Thaler (1992) has amassed a disquieting array of behavioral "anomalies" and concludes that "assumptions aside, the theory [of opportunism] is vulnerable just on the quality of the predictions" (p. 4). He notes:

We can start to see the development of a new, improved version of economic theory. The new theory will retain the idea that agents try to do the best they can, but these individuals will also have the human strengths of kindness and cooperation, together with the limited human abilities to store and process information. (p. 5)

In concluding his book *On Ethics and Economics* (1987) Sen makes a plea for this "new theory": "The wide use of the extremely narrow assumption of self-interested behavior has, I have tried to argue, seriously limited the scope of predictive economics, and made it difficult to pursue a number of important economic relationships that operate through behavioral versatility" (p. 79).

In short, reasonable or rational behavior is more complex and multifaceted than simple opportunism. Although by no means exhaustive, the above examples are perhaps sufficient to illustrate the weight of evidence available that suggests the need for some broader notion of behavior than that currently embraced by conventional financial-economic theory.

DISPELLING THE MYTH OF THE AMORAL MANAGER

Another aspect of the modern notion of rationality in business is its claim to moral neutrality. For example, in their recent article "Corporate Ethics and Shareholder Wealth Maximization" (1996), Donald Chambers and Nelson Lacey consider the ethical implications of the conceptual foundation of corporate finance theory, namely, shareholder wealth maximization. They suggest that shareholder wealth maximization is neither ethical nor unethical; rather, it is non ethical: "[S]hareholder wealth maximization serves as a conduit of ethics rather than a net determinant of ethical behavior" (p. 93); if investors or consumers, or indeed any stakeholder group, do not like the moral flavor of a particular firm, then they can generally discipline the firm in the market. By viewing morality as just one more economic variable in the technical business equation, the authors locate themselves squarely within our modernist Technical Universe: "Market values can price ethics just as they can price anything else" (p. 93). Managers concerned with shareholder wealth maximization, therefore, will not merely be the puppets of shareholders; they will also have to be concerned with the reputation of the firm among other stakeholders and within society at large. As many studies have shown, a firm's reputation has real economic worth. This reputation may be for product quality, timely debt repayment, or environmental consciousness. Any action that the firm takes, whether financial or not, can influence the profitability of the firm and hence stock price. Thus, as Chambers and Lacey point out, the shareholder wealth maximization rubric is not as narrow and as purely shareholder driven as many business ethicists imply.

But is the notion of shareholder wealth maximization, so central to financial economics and indeed central to the modernist conception of business, really morally neutral? Superficially, this idea of moral neutrality is very appealing to corporate finance theorists and practitioners; it enables both to circumvent the complexities of contemporary ethical pluralism. But what exactly does it mean to label shareholder wealth maximization as an ethical conduit rather than as a net determinant of ethical behavior? I take this to mean that a manager acting in accordance with shareholder wealth maximization is not exercising any particular ethical judgment. The manager as technician is part of the market mechanism that, through reputation effects, prices the actions of stakeholders whether those actions be economically or ethically motivated. The manager takes an ethically neutral and passive stance and tries merely to make decisions based on ethical signals received from stakeholders through the market mechanism.

For example, the manager of Starkist Seafood Company may realize that the publication of evidence linking tuna fishing to the death of dolphins is reducing canned-tuna sales. Thus, the manager is receiving a market signal based on some ethical value judgment of consumers. If the signal from consumers is sufficiently strong, then the shareholder wealth maximization–consistent decision for the manager may be to redesign the nets used to catch tuna. Note here that in saving the lives of dolphins, the manager has not exercised any personal ethical judgments. The manager has merely reacted to the ethical judgments of a large body of canned-tuna consumers. The manager has not had to react directly to the ethical judgments of consumers because consumers are able to convert these judgments into an economic mechanism. The manager just makes an economic decision (to modify the nets) on the basis of an economic observation (lower canned-tuna sales). The manager does not have to act as moral adjudicator between dolphin-loving consumers and possibly dolphin-indifferent shareholders. Because of the economic impact of dolphin-loving consumers on sales, it is in the financial interests of shareholders that the manager choose to modify the nets.

In short, the manager acts as a conduit for the ethical beliefs of stakeholders. The manager does not need to become an expert on—in this case—animal rights, nor does the manager need to conduct some sort of stakeholder referendum to determine the moral beliefs of all stakeholders in the firm. The economic mechanism enables the manager to circumvent all this. As Chambers and Lacey (1996) conclude: "[S]hareholder wealth maximization puts money in the hands of shareholders who can efficiently pursue their own ethical agendas" (pp. 95–96).

But consider more closely the actions of this manager. In pursuing share-holder wealth maximization, is this manager really acting merely as an ethical conduit rather than as a net determinant of ethical behavior? Prior to taking *any* action, the manager has made a decision. He or she has decided that the best way of tackling decisions in business is to pursue shareholder wealth maximization. Is this not an ethical decision? Does this decision not determine the ethical tenor of the firm? In making this decision, therefore, is the manager not acting as a net determinant of ethical behavior?

In particular, by adopting shareholder wealth maximization the manager has adopted a certain moral "context." As MacIntyre (1977) comments: "[A]ll nontrivial activity presupposes some philosophical point of view [i.e., a context] and that not to recognize this is to make oneself the ready victim of bad or at the very least inadequate philosophy" (p. 217). So what is the moral context of shareholder wealth maximization?

The acceptance and implementation of shareholder wealth maximization entails the acceptance and implementation of several layers of philosophical context. First, it entails the acceptance of a rather narrow interpretation of utilitarianism, in which moral decisions within the firm can be based solely on the consequences of those decisions for the firm's stock price. Thus, shareholder wealth maximization chooses a specific moral context within the broader context of utilitarian or consequentialist moral philosophy. Utilitarianism, in turn, is just one context or ethical determinant within the broader context of modernist philosophy. This modernist or Enlightenment moral context also includes Kantianism, Rawlsian social justice theory, social contracts theory, and various versions of utilitarianism, to name but a few. In essence, all modernist philosophy shares the ontological foundation of a rationality based on means-end reasoning. It also presumes some absolute "truth," against which these competing theories can be judged. Conventional financial-economic theory also lies within this modernist epistemology.

But modernist philosophy is just one ethical determinant within yet broader contexts. Indeed, it is only when one steps outside this modernist context that one realizes that such things as cost-benefit analysis, means-end reasoning, instrumental rationality, and individualism are all ethical determinants. They entail a certain nonunique and nonstable view of what reality is and of what reality should be. These broader contexts are the focus of postmodern or deconstructionist philosophy. Perhaps the best, and most readable, deconstruction of modern philosophy is still that found in Mac-Intyre's *After Virtue* (1984a). (Also, in a specifically business context, see the special issue of *Business Ethics Quarterly* [July 1993] devoted to post-modernism.)

So, returning to the Starkist example, in adopting shareholder wealth maximization, the manager adopts a narrow interpretation of utilitarianism. Not only is this an ethical determinant, but it is also a subset of a subset of a subset of all known ethical determinants. This manager "determines" or "adopts the moral context" that the right thing to do is to act in the interests of whoever has the greatest economic influence on stock price. If this is the dolphin lovers, then money will be spent to save dolphin lives. If this is the dolphin indifferents, then shareholder wealth maximization "determines" that no resources will go to save dolphins. In essence, therefore, shareholder wealth maximization is a variant on "might makes right"—where "might" is defined purely in economic terms.

My objective here is not to pass judgment on shareholder wealth maximization, at least not yet. Indeed, to do so would assume the existence of some all-embracing context, from within which all other contexts could be judged. My objective is merely to dispel the conception of shareholder wealth maximization as an ethical conduit rather than as a net determinant of ethical behavior. Nothing exists outside of a metaphysical context, and shareholder wealth maximization is no exception. Perhaps the reason why financial economists like Chambers and Lacey tend not to see this is because shareholder wealth maximization exists within a context that modern economic academicians rarely, if ever, step out of.

WHY THE MODERN AGENT AS TECHNICIAN IS A "HE"

A recent development in moral philosophy is the growing recognition of a possible link between differences in attitude toward ethical decisions and the decision maker's gender. The extent of, and indeed the very existence of, these gender-based differences is still hotly debated. But one implication of this debate is that the financial-economic concept of what constitutes rational behavior may exhibit a distinct male gender bias. Another limitation of the rationality construct of the technician, therefore, may be its tendency to reflect only the archetypically male behavioral attributes. As this gender bias becomes more apparent, it provides further justification for a rejection of this invocation of the manager as the modern agent as technician.

A seminal work in this area is Carol Gilligan's book *In a Different Voice* (1982), which claims to present evidence of significant gender differences in moral orientation. She identifies "two voices," one predominantly female and the other predominantly male, which represent two distinct moral selves. The autonomous self separated from others in a hierarchical world is predominant among men. Ethics for this self adopts a gamelike quality; the moves that are acceptable and unacceptable are clearly defined before the game, disputes are refereed impartially according to the abstract principle of fairness, and setting a precedent becomes worrisome.

The self that is predominant among women is the connected self, joined to others in a web of relationships. The ethical outlook derived from this connected self is more situational and contextual than that which a separate self produces. Instead of the male orientation to "rules of the game," the dynamics and expectations involved in relationships are central. Women tend to conceptualize moral questions as problems of care involving empathy and compassion, whereas men conceptualize them as problems of rights.

In one study, for example, a sample of men and women were asked five questions relating to unethical behavior. The study revealed that men were more than twice as likely to be willing to engage in actions regarded as less ethical. The study also revealed that men are more likely to work long hours and break rules because men view achievement as competitive (Betz et al. 1987). Another study asked over 1,000 business students to evaluate the ethical acceptability of each of ten different scenarios. In four of the ten responses, there was no significant difference between the male and female responses. The results of the other six questions, however, support the above findings of significant gender differences in ethical orientation. Once again, the male responses tended to be rule based and to view the problem as that of a game. The female responses tended to be more compassion based and more contextual (Ruegger and King, 1992).

But Gilligan's dichotomy between male and female moral orientation is far from generally accepted. (See, for example, the October 1994 issue of the *Monist*, which is devoted entirely to this debate over feminist episte-mologies.) Harriet Baber (1994), for example, has recently argued that

the thesis of gender differences in moral reasoning hypothesized by Carol Gilligan . . . was early shown to be false on empirical grounds. Nevertheless, like a number of other "scientific fictions," . . . the myth of women's way of knowing took on a life of its own within the literature. (p. 404)

It may well be that these purported gender differences are in fact differences due to some other factor. Carol Tavris (1992), for example, notes that "[n]ew studies find that the behavior that we link to gender depends more on what an individual is doing and needs to do than on his or her biological sex" (p. 63). Even acknowledging these caveats, however, Gilligan's central message is viewed by many as possessing a kernel of truth. Males and females do often view an ethical decision from different perspectives.

In light of these possible gender differences in ethical orientation, this chapter's account of what—according to the finance paradigm—constitutes reasonable business behavior clearly exhibits a male gender bias. This concept of business behavior has been noted as one in which "work is a game with rules and customs geared to reward traditional male behavior" (Collins, Gilbert, and Nycum, 1988, p. 4). Similarly, a recent article in *Newsweek* magazine summarizes the views of various observers that "traditional business-school teaching methods are male-oriented" (Kantrowitz et al., 1992, p. 98). Specifically, three central attributes of the financial-economic concept of rationality favor the male orientation:

1. The narrow focus on individual wealth maximization as the ultimate and sole end of all human endeavor.

2. The increasing use of a game theory methodology and conceptualization to model business environments. As Daniel Hausman and Michael McPherson (1993) note: "[Game theory] does not rule out altruism or sympathy . . . but it does rule out a collective perspective, a perspective that considers what *we* should do and what the consequences will be for *us*" (p. 718).

3. The fundamentally rigid mathematical axiom approach to developing a concept of rationality reflecting a rule, rather than contextual, orientation.

By focusing on the manager as technician, therefore, the very foundation of business education, namely, its rationality assumption, may actively deter female participation. Possible evidence for this comes from enrollment trends in MBA programs. A disquieting trend is apparent in America's business schools. Although the number of professional women in the workforce continues to grow, the percentage of women enrolled in MBA programs has fallen noticably in recent years (Fuchsberg, 1992).

At Northwestern University's Kellogg Graduate School of Management, for example, female enrollment has dropped 37 percent since 1986, and similar trends can be observed at other major universities. These trends are particularly alarming when one considers the dramatically *increasing* percentage of women on corporate boards of directors and in management positions at all levels:

One of the most significant socio-economic trends of the past two decades is the unprecedented increase in the number of women in the labor force, particularly that of women holding executive/management positions in business organizations. (Akaah, 1989, p. 375)

This would imply a *greater* incentive and need for women to enter business education, yet the opposite appears to be the case. In addition, these trends show no sign of abating: recently, both Indiana University and the University of California at Los Angeles experienced 17 percent drops in female enrollment in their respective MBA programs.

Several nonethical reasons have been proposed to account for this declining female enrollment. There is evidence that women have traditionally been excluded from senior management positions by a "glass ceiling"; therefore, they have less incentive to pursue a business career. But the aforementioned increase in the number of women in senior positions over the last few years tends to contradict this argument. The high cost of MBA programs has been proposed as another reason, although why cost should deter women more than men is not clear. Other suggested explanations include the tendency for MBA programs to favor candidates in their late twenties and early thirties, which, for women, are prime childbearing years. Statistically, there is some evidence that the increasing numbers of students from foreign countries, most of whom are men, tend to be skewing the enrollment trends.

Although all of these suggested reasons undoubtedly have some validity, they do not explain fully either the scale of the gender shift or the fact that the shift appears to be a fairly recent phenomenon. In light of Gilligan's work, it seems at least possible that women may be increasingly avoiding graduate business programs because they find the value system promulgated therein not merely morally impoverished but also inherently hostile. In other words, they recognize that the modern conception of the manager as a technician is a conception of management as a male pursuit.

If the extant financial-economic approach to developing a rationality concept were the only feasible one, then the above evidence of male bias would seem inevitable. Indeed, it would imply that, in reference to Gilligan's "two voices," men are more rational than women.

Is this masculine firm as invoked by the finance paradigm economically optimal or even desirable? Financial-economic theory implies that it is not. Most interestingly, the inefficiencies of the masculine firm stem from precisely those value characteristics that identify the firm as male.

As discussed earlier, the contemporary theory of the firm, as reflected in the financial contracting models of financial economics, invariably engenders equilibria that are *second best*. Specifically, these equilibria are optimal (i.e., wealth maximizing) neither for the agent concerned nor for the economy in aggregate. As will be discussed in the next chapter, the costs resulting from these conflicts of interest in financial contracting are generally called "agency costs." Note that agency costs stem from an inability on the part of agents to reliably enforce contractual agreements: even though it is self-defeating, opportunism holds sway. Indeed, any notion of a value system other than that of narrowly defined self-interest is summarily dismissed by financial economists as no more than a " 'Nirvana' form of analysis."

This invocation of economic *man* is an invocation of Gilligan's "separated self," reflecting the archetypically male values of competition, individualism, game, and rule orientation—an autonomous self separated from others in a hierarchical world. The idea that a different yet equally plausible type of agent—namely, a more feminine, relationship-oriented, "connected self" type of agent—would ameliorate these agency costs seems appealing. Indeed, Richard Thaler (1992) predicts just such a future shift in economists' concept of rationality when he predicts a new theory of economic behavior that will "retain the idea that agents try to do the best they can, but these individuals will also have the human strengths of kindness and cooperation" (p. 5). As we've just seen, these "human strengths of kindness and cooperation" have been linked explicitly to a feminine value system. Thus, no doubt inadvertently, Thaler is singing the praises of economic woman over economic man. The economic superiority of what might be called a more feminine firm, therefore, derives from its broadened concept of what constitutes rational behavior.

Unlike the masculine firm invoked in financial-economic theory, the feminine firm will exhibit a tendency to nurture cooperation and a recognition of communal—in addition to merely individual—objectives. This tendency will dissipate the agency problems that plague our Technical Universe. In essence, within the feminine firm, *trust* becomes a rational and feasible implicit contractual enforcement mechanism.

The ideal firm, therefore, from both a moral and an economic perspective, may be feminine: where a feminine firm is one in which individuals' moral orientation is that identified by Gilligan as the—predominantly feminine—"connected self," as opposed to the—predominantly masculine—"separated self."

The moral and economic superiority of the feminine firm is implied by Thomas White's provocative essay "Business, Ethics, and Carol Gilligan's 'Two Voices' " (1992). White applies Gilligan's work on gender differences in moral orientation to organizational behavior. He notes that these gender differences may explain why various empirical studies find women relatively more sensitive to ethical dilemmas in business:

On this matter it is crucial to note Kohlberg's claim that only one in four people advances to the highest stage of moral reasoning. The vast majority of men, then, probably employ "conventional" moral thinking—an outlook that puts a premium on laws, rules, norms or conventions. The apparent ethical superiority of the women in the studies may suggest that ethical dilemmas in business register more strongly with the average possessor of an ethic of care [the connected self] than they do with someone at the conventional stage of an ethic of justice [the separated self]. (p. 57)

Thus, at the conventional levels of ethical reasoning, the connected self is more adept at moral deliberation in business than is the separated self. But White's observations are not limited to the moral worth of the firm. In addition, he suggests that a feminine moral orientation may enhance a firm's *economic* worth. He suggests that the feminine ethic may be more attuned to the essential nature of the firm as a nexus of relationships. A feminine firm, therefore, is both morally *and economically* superior. Given this essential nature of the firm as a nexus of communal relations, the exclusion of the feminine firm levies both a moral and an economic cost on our corporate culture. By establishing a sound logical conceptualization and justification for the feminine firm within the business disciplines, a more balanced portrayal of the financial milieu could be achieved.

Robin Derry (1996) has recently drawn an interesting distinction between the "feminine" firm and the "feminist" firm. In essence, according to Derry, a feminist firm would be characterized less by the feminine traits of compassion and caring and would be focused more on ensuring that women in business—regardless of their moral orientation—are afforded a legal and moral status equal to that of men. Others appear to combine these notions of feminine and feminist into a single concept of the firm. Consider, for example, the following description of a feminist-cum-feminine firm:

> A corporation run by feminist principles would oppose the exploitation of employees and the environment. A value on community welfare—and the collective—would foster concern with making the corporation a more habitable, hospitable, and equitable work environment. . . . Feminist management would protect the physical environment through recycling, cleaning up, or detoxifying industrial wastes, complying with regulations and rules that protect workers and the ecosystem, and using biodegradable materials. It would promote the public interest and return profits to workers and the community (in addition to officials and shareholders). Feminist managers would resist closing factories as tax write-offs or moving them to third world countries, where cheaper labor is found. Feminist managers would cooperate with and improve, rather than dominate and degrade, the community and environment. (Anonymous, From Dobson and White, 1995, p. 476)

Such a feminist corporation may be morally desirable, but would it be economically efficient in a competitive market economy? Would a firm that spent more on pollution control than its competitors, and did not produce where labor costs were lowest, be uncompetitive? As Thomas Gilmore (1986) observes: "[T]o build a smokeless factory when no competitors are incurring the cost is individual firm suicide" (p. 31).

Of course, if stakeholders were willing to pay a premium for such a "green" firm, then it might compete, but then such actions would become economically optimal, and any distinction between a male and female firm would be unobservable. Indeed, firms today are keenly aware that environmental sensitivity can be a powerful marketing tool. For example, Robert Solomon (1994) observes that "being green is a good way to bring in the green" (p. 5). Similarly, "the strategic use of philanthropy has begun to give companies a powerful competitive edge" (Smith, 1994, p. 105).

In the context of education, business schools can be seen as sculpting the attitudes and values of individuals who inherit and perpetuate our corporate culture. The business school is, in essence, the crucible of corporate culture. It is currently where disparate and undeveloped ideologies and values are cast or recast in the mold of economic rationality.

By adopting this broadened concept of what constitutes rational behavior, business schools could rebalance the extant gender imbalance caused by an exclusive preoccupation with the financial-economic notion of rationality—yet another reason to move beyond the *man*ager as technician.

TEST CASE: PEPSI/BURMA

In the introduction to this book, I mentioned that I would use the case of PepsiCo's decision to pull out of Burma to illustrate my argument at various points. If Pepsi's management had donned the hat of the technician, if they had believed that they were operating within the Technical Universe of financial-economic theory, how would they have addressed the decision of whether or not to cease operations in Burma?

Pepsi's ongoing operations in Burma can be viewed as a capital project undertaken by the firm. Within financial economics, the decision of whether to cease these operations would come under the nomenclature of a "continuation versus abandonment" decision in capital budgeting. As technicians, Pepsi's management would have been able to draw on the capital budgeting theory supplied by financial economics, namely, the net present value (NPV) rule.

THE NPV RULE

The net present value rule of financial theory supposedly gives management a clear and decisive criterion for choosing between abandonment versus continuation of capital projects. The rule can be summarized as follows:

[S]unk costs should be ignored and . . . projects should be terminated when the expected present value of cash flows, given that the project is terminated today, is greater than the expected present value of cash flows given that the project is continued for at least one additional period. (Statman and Caldwell, 1987, p. 7)

Theoretically, the process seems quite simple and eminently logical. Pepsi's management merely needs to estimate two cash flow streams, one relating to Pepsi's operations, given it stays in Burma, and the other relating to Pepsi's operations, given it pulls out of Burma. These two cash flow streams then need to be discounted at some appropriate discount rate. Whichever choice yields the higher discounted present value of cash flows is the choice that Pepsi should adopt. Thus, through capital budgeting theory, the technician in theory would seem to possess a very precise methodology for making this type of decision. But how about in practice?

First, even if we ignore the complications of this particular capital budgeting decision faced by Pepsi, we face difficulties in basic application of the NPV rule. Indeed, financial economists themselves recognize these difficulties. For example, even one of the gurus of financial-economic theory, Stewart Myers (1976), accepts that standard capital budgeting theory, based as it is on the NPV rule and similar discounted cash flow procedures, has its shortcomings:

An intelligent application of discounted cash flow will encounter four chief problems:

• Estimating the discount rate,
• Estimating the project's future cash flows,

- Estimating the project's impact on the firm's other assets' cash flows—that is, through the cross-sectional links between projects, and
- Estimating the project's impact on the firm's future investment opportunities.

Thus, even in terms of a very narrow financial evaluation of a project's worth, the net present value methodology rests heavily on certain key assumptions. The evidence indicates that Pepsi did adopt standard NPV-type analysis in making its decision to initially invest in Burma and, later on, to stay in Burma. But in retrospect, given Pepsi's eventual decision to pull out, and given the negative publicity in the run up to this decision, it seems that conventional financial-economic theory failed Pepsi. The NPV rule did not provide Pepsi's management with the correct decision *even from a financial perspective!* Thus, as discussed earlier, in practice as well as in theory, the manager as technician—relying as "he" does on financial-economic theory— is subtly self-defeating.

So what this chapter suggests is that the epistemology of the manager as technician, based on financial-economic theory, is not merely externally deconstructible: It is not merely criticizable from the vantage point of external criteria such as moral impoverishment or gender bias. No, the critique of the manager as technician goes deeper than this; the Technical Universe can be deconstructed from within. As will be shown in Chapter 2, the logical inconsistencies of the Technical Universe render it insupportable even in terms of its own logic and rationality. It is this internal epistemological crisis that leads to the deconstruction that in turn provides the metaphysical vacuum to be filled by our aesthetic manager. In short, business reflects culture, and our current cultural universe is not that of the technician. Finance theory itself is increasingly reflecting the internal inconsistencies of its worldview, and as we exit the twentieth century, we see the deconstruction, both from without and within, of what I have termed here the "Technical Universe." To see this more clearly, the next chapter will focus on the specific view of business implied by the Technical Universe: the view of business as a game and the view of the firm as a type of wealth-creating machine.

Chapter 2

The Business Game

> [W]hen the corporation is guided only by this goal of maximizing some
> narrowly defined "stockholder profit," great harm can result.
> —Ralph Estes, *Tyranny of the Bottom Line*

I began Chapter 1 by mentioning the "finance paradox." The importance of this paradox for the main argument of this book cannot be understated because it illustrates categorically how the epistemological foundation of the Technical Universe, namely, financial-economic theory, deconstructs itself. Thus, even by its own standards of logic and rationality, the manager as technician is insupportable: even, as it were, on its home turf, the notion of agent as opportunistic wealth maximizer is subtly self-defeating.

What I have yet to show is the precise nature of this self-defeat. We may criticize the technician from the perspective of gender bias or descriptive accuracy or failure to live up to "his" claim of moral neutrality, but regardless of any external criticisms from the Moral Universe or elsewhere, why is the Technical Universe, and the manager as technician therein, unsustainable even in its own terms? To answer this question, we must conjure the business universe as financial-economic theory conjures it. We must invoke the "Theory of the Firm," which provides the bedrock of the Technical Universe.

The Theory of the Firm sees business as a competitive game. Not surprisingly, therefore, the dominant methodology, as first invoked by von Neumann and Morgernstern (1947), is game theory. For example, in the introduction to his book *Games and Information*, Rasmusen (1989) notes that "during the 1980s, game theory has become dramatically more important to mainstream economics. Indeed, it seems to be swallowing up microeconomics" (p. 13): there are individuals with their atomistic objective functions; they compete; they try to win by maximizing a payoff; they may even for a time cooperate if they perceive this as instrumental to them individually winning; the game extends over time; sometimes there are multiple iterations of a given game. Viewed through this game-theoretic lens, the business milieu in the Technical Universe is a reflection of the scientific values of modernity. There is an absolute Truth here, an ontology: the constraints of the game, the mathematical objective function, the application of instrumental rationality in ordering preferences on the basis of individual material advantage, the desire to win. This is the manifestation of the age of reason, of the view of business as science, of "management science." In the vernacular of aestheticism, to be discussed further in Part III, these characteristics constitute the "presence" of the Technical Universe's view of business.

If there is a presence, there must be an absence, an "other." What is absent from the Technical Universe's view of the firm?

What is absent is everything that fails to fit into this scientific concept of business. I will discuss these absences at length in Part III but, just as a primer, consider these absences: placing the interests of another before one's own, or indeed even considering the interests of another; desire or passion as opposed to objective reason-based motivation; the intrinsic valuation of intangibles like beauty or harmony or excellence. These are just a sample of the absences from the Techical Universe.

So the Technical Universe and business therein is dry and unemotional, but why is it self-defeating even in terms of its dry and unemotional universe? Let's return to financial economics' Theory of the Firm.

THEORY OF THE FIRM

Through the metaphysically narrow conceptual lens of the Technical Universe, the firm is viewed purely as a passive structure—a structure whose efficiency depends upon its ability to mitigate the pecuniary costs engendered by conflicts of interest between these guileful and deceitful "rational" opportunists. This arbitrary and rigid rationality premise, therefore, not only determines the behavior of individuals in financial markets but also sculpts the very structure and function of the firm itself.

Traditionally in financial economics the firm has been viewed as an atomistic unit, a single unified decision node or "black box." Theories of this nuclear firm have been conjured in the pristine environment of perfect and frictionless capital markets: there are numerous buyers and sellers, no information or transaction or transportation costs, no barriers to trade of any kind, and the future is known with certainty by all market participants—clearly a contrived environment, to say the least.

Not surprisingly, models developed in such an environment exhibit minimal explanatory power in many actual economic environments: "The firm, in that literature, is an abstraction stripped of such intangible assets as reputation and with no distinction made between the profit objective of investors and the utility maximization objective of agent managers" (Chung and Smith, 1987, p. 146). Perhaps the most famous model to come out of this "traditional" finance theory is the Capital Asset Pricing Model (affectionately known by aficionados as the "cap-M"). This model claimed to generate a classic economics-style equilibrium process for securities markets. In addition to the scientific-style rationality assumptions that we have already discussed, and of course the perfect and frictionless markets assumptions, the model was premised and thus predicted a risk-return trade-off as the characteristic of financial markets, where risk was measured precisely by a single number (labeled "beta"). Without getting into the technicalities, beta measured an individual security's volatility relative to the entire market. Until fairly recently the cap-M was viewed from within financial economics as one of that discipline's greatest achievements. Indeed, in some ways the conceptual rubric of this model defined financial theory.

Recent evidence, however, supplied by none other than some of the leading progenitors of the original concept, has brought cap-M into serious question. It seems that the type of risk-return trade-off that lies at the heart of cap-M, and at the heart of most conventional finance theory, may in fact be illusory.

The fate of cap-M is not unique among finance theories; indeed, the whole idea of progress within financial-economic theory seems questionable. Even the most fundamental questions of corporate finance remain unanswered, such as what determines the firm's choice between debt and equity financing, or why some firms pay regular dividends. Of course, one of the problems financial economists face in attempting to model financial reality is the speed with which financial reality changes: finance theory is trying to hit a moving target that is moving faster and faster. For example, in the case of the dividends question, while financial theorists are still trying to figure out why firms pay dividends, it seems that fewer and fewer firms are actually paying dividends. It may be, therefore, that dividends will disappear from the corporate scene before financial-economic theory ever gets a chance to explain their existence. Indeed financial economists in the 1980s thought they had a pretty good reason in the form of "signaling theory": dividends are a means by which corporate managers signal their predictions concerning the firm's future earning capacity to shareholders. As seems so often the case with finance theories, however, recent evidence tends to discredit this signaling theory (DeAngelo, DeAngelo, and Skinner, 1996).

Peter Bernstein (1995) has recently chronicled a similar history of financial-economic theory's attempts to define and quantify one of the most important concepts in business, namely, risk. Bernstein takes pains to emphasize the importance in business of conceptions of risk: "[P]erceptions of risk are the most powerful symptoms of what a society is all about" (1995, p. 11). Following its modernist self-conception, financial-economic theory has endeavored to develop rigorous mathematical measures of risk in business, such as beta in the cap-M. As the twentieth century draws to a close, however, financial economists such as Bernstein have been forced to accept the fact that these attempts to quantify and rationalize risk have largely failed:

But time has proven once again that the world does not come in neat and familiar packages. In a world that is changing faster than any of us can understand, risk seems less amenable to measurement than most investors had come to believe. The result is that tried-and-true methods of risk management are on the defensive. (p. 11)

Part of the epistemological crisis faced by financial economics at the end of the twentieth century is undoubtedly due to the demise of cap-M, risk measurement, and other theories and the inability of finance theory to explain financial-economic reality. It is another dimension of what I termed earlier the "age of self-doubt."

Of course, the "information revolution" of the present day may render the assumptions underlying traditional finance more realistic: financial markets may indeed become virtually frictionless. But what this revolution will not make more realistic are the concomitant rationality assumptions that form the core of my critique here.

I mentioned signaling theory as a possible explanation for dividend payment behavior. Signaling is interesting because its logic arises from recent attempts by financial economists to relax perfect-market assumptions and so reveal the firm in a more realistic light. In this light the firm emerges not as an atomistic unit but "as a nexus for a set of contracting relations among individuals" (Jensen and Meckling, 1976, p. 311):

Viewed in this way, it makes little or no sense to try to distinguish those things which are "inside" the firm from those things that are "outside" of it. There is in a very real sense only a multitude of complex relations (i.e. contracts) between the legal fiction (the firm) and the owners of labor, material and capital inputs and the consumers of output. . . . In this sense the "behavior" of the firm is like the behavior of the market; i.e., the outcome of a complex equilibrium process. (p. 311)

This "contractual nexus" thus includes the overlapping interests, claims, and objectives of several groups: suppliers and customers, employees and the community, management, shareholders, and bondholders. These groups could be further subdivided into voting versus nonvoting shareholders, inside versus outside shareholders, secured versus unsecured bondholders, unionized versus nonunionized employees, and so on. Not surprisingly, the claims and objectives of these various groups frequently conflict.

The broader philosophical implication of these developments concerns the notion of a "corporate objective." If, rather than being an atomistic unit, the firm is in fact an amalgamation of stakeholder groups, then clearly the idea of a corporate objective is something of a misnomer. Management may have one objective, shareholders another, and debtholders yet another, not to mention customers, employees, and suppliers.

One might argue that management represents the pivotal stakeholder group in that it controls the immediate corporate decision making and acts as agent for other stakeholder groups in the corporate milieu. Thus, the term "corporate objective" is often taken as being synonymous with "management's objective." The corporate contractual fabric is constructed in such a way that management is vested with the fiduciary responsibility of making economic decisions that affect all stakeholder groups. The challenge that all diversely held organizations face is to structure their contractual relations in such a way that one stakeholder is not able to exploit other stakeholders. Eugene Fama and Michael Jensen (1983) note the existence of boards of directors as the stakeholder group that adjudicates these conflicts of interest.

The board of directors is rarely an autonomous group; there is overlap. Some directors are also managers, and some are also shareholders, and some are all three. But some directors are neither managers nor shareholders. These are the "outside" directors. This eclectic board is, in theory at least, necessary in order to control conflicts with sufficient expertise. The inside directors provide expertise on the internal organization of the firm, whereas the outside directors, who ideally are aligned neither with management nor with shareholders, ensure fairness and objectivity. As Fama and Jensen note:

The outside board members act as arbiters in disagreements among internal managers and carry out tasks that involve serious agency problems between internal managers and residual claimants, for example, setting executive compensation or searching for replacements for top managers. (p. 315)

Evidence indicates, however, that the board of directors in practice is often different from—and less unbiased than—the board of directors in theory. For example, for the 500 corporations that comprise the *Fortune* 500, the chief executive officer (CEO) frequently also holds the position of chairman of the board. Thus, in many cases we have a situation of what T. Boone Pickens calls the "fox guarding the henhouse." The results of this corporate incest are readily predictable. Decisions tend to be made that serve the interests of incumbent managers, rather than all stakeholders. Indeed, in a recent *Harvard Business Review* (1989) article, Jensen predicts that these conflicts of interest or agency problems may lead to the "eclipse of the public corporation" in which the passivity of outside shareholders is replaced by a more highly leveraged corporate form in which the actions of management are closely monitored and constrained by bondholders. The leveraged buyout (LBO) craze of the 1980s—in which a large and diverse group of shareholders were replaced by a small and homogeneous group of bondholders—appeared to augur Jensen's "eclipse." In the 1990s, however, many of these erstwhile LBOs have returned to their pre-1980s structure by issuing public shares to replace debt.

Whether or not the traditional notion of the widely held public corporation is waxing or waning is clearly debatable. What seems certain, however, is that some form of corporation comprising an amalgamation of various interest groups—whatever form these interest groups may take—is going to be the dominant economic and socioeconomic force in world commerce for the foreseeable future. But is the view of these organizations, as supplied by the conceptual lens of financial-economic theory, the only view? If it is not the only view, then is it the most accurate or the most desirable?

In essence, this view is one in which the firm is a machine designed to derive the benefits of divisions of capital and labor while controlling the conflicts arising from irretrievably opportunistic agents. This financial-economic theory of the firm presents itself as a morally neutral descriptive construct that merely endeavors to define the firm and explain the actions of agents therein. But can a theory that bases itself on such a narrow and rigid concept of rationality be strictly morally neutral, or is it merely another facet of what Richard De George (1990) terms the "Myth of Amoral Business"? If this theory of the firm does have a normative dimension, then is it normatively justifiable? Will any attempt to make it normatively justifiable tend to compromise its descriptive accuracy?

Few would argue that, from the perspective of descriptive accuracy, the conceptual shift away from viewing the firm as a black box and toward the view of the firm as a contractual nexus has been a beneficial one—particularly when one considers the sheer size and complexity of the contemporary corporation (not to mention the virtual corporation). These firms clearly have more in common with the multiheaded Hydra of Greek mythology than with a unit or box.

Thus the question, What is the objective of the firm? has become as abstruse as the question, What is the objective of the market, or the city? Both are increasingly complex human organizations. It is the individuals within who possess the multifarious objectives that characterize these Hydras. Indeed, the analogy between firms and cities is an edifying one. Like the city, the firm is increasingly becoming a social, as well as an economic, phenomenon—hence, the increasing usage of the term "corporate culture."

CORPORATE CULTURE

Whatever ethnic, religious, or other cultural boundaries may have evolved through history, a global corporate culture is increasingly subsuming these traditional divisions, with transnational corporations bridging both geographic and cultural boundaries. Indeed, this corporate culture is not merely implicit; many firms now publish internal codes of acceptable behavior, as do several regulatory bodies, for example, the Organization for Economic Cooperation and Development's (OECD) "Guidelines for Multinational Enterprise." But despite the contemporary firm's size and complexity, its fundamental raison d'être remains the same. As Milton Friedman (1970) succinctly puts it: "The social responsibility of business is to increase its profits" (p. 153). This may be constrained by what Friedman calls "ethical custom," but, by definition, the firm would be misconstrued if it were not a Hydra concerned primarily with the creation of material wealth.

Thus, a culture, albeit a corporate one, premised solely on the accumulation of material wealth—however that might be constrained—inevitably raises questions of a moral nature. These questions are not explicitly or implicitly answered within such a culture—hence, the growing interest in the subject area of business ethics.

But as two heads of the Hydra, business ethics and financial economics clearly comprise—at best—an uncomfortable alliance. Indeed, if ethics is, as Friedman argues, merely some constraint within the wealth-maximizing rubric, then its role in business affairs would appear at best peripheral, and at worst vanishingly trivial. Under these circumstances, for ethics to exist at all within such a strictly material culture the colloquialism "good ethics is good (i.e., profitable) business" *would have to be* believed.

If it were not generally believed, then individuals would find ethics an entirely irrational and unintelligible concept, and they would consequently view the practice of ethical behavior as entirely unjustifiable. In the Technical Universe, business must justify morality, which is a far cry from Adam Smith's prioritization in *The Theory of Moral Sentiments* (1759; see Smith, 1937a) in which the pursuit of the moral *good* justified the pursuit of economic *goods*. In other words, the technician seeks economic justification for ethics (e.g., with statements like "Good ethics is good business"), whereas the early economists such as Smith and Hume tended to seek some moral justification for economics.

Rather than a leap into the future, therefore, conjuring the aesthetic manager may require a step into the past. What caused the morally rich behavioral paradigm, implicit in Smith's *The Theory of Moral Sentiments* and the *Wealth of Nations* (1937b), to become the morally impoverished paradigm reflected in the modern Theory of the Firm?

Interestingly, this historical route is also being taken by a new branch of economic philosophy labeled by some as "radical subjectivism": "The essential characteristic of the radical subjectivist position that marks its critical departure from a neoclassical framework is, at the same time, the feature that it shares with the new evolutionary synthesis . . . [its] conception of "a world in which time plays a vital role' " (MacIntyre, 1984, p. 208). Similarly, a central tenet of much aesthetic critique is the importance of viewing morality in the historical context of a genealogy or tradition of belief: "Narrative history of a certain kind turns out to be the basic and essential genre for the characterization of human actions" (p. 208).

As a manifestation of human action, the firm is thus a phenomenon inseparable from its past. Some focus on this narrative history may also explain why the behavioral assumptions of financial economics have, via the rise to prominence of the Technical Universe, inherited the role previously played by the behavioral prerogatives of religious dogma, namely, that of cultural progenitor. Another contribution of the aesthetic manager, therefore, will be an explicit recognition of the extent to which the notion of what constitutes rationality is historical and cultural.

Before turning to an explicitly moral evaluation of business in Part II, however, I'd like to take a closer look at the economic implications of financial rationality. This is important because the finance paradigm is often defended by some quasi-utilitarian/invisible hand–type argument, to the effect that opportunistic self-interest leads to economically optimal equilibria. What the remainder of this chapter will show is that this argument is false. A predominantly technical business universe, like the one currently in existence, *never* reaches economically optimal equilibria.

In short, extant financial rationality—in which everyone is an opportunist—is economically self-defeating. As Norman Bowie (1991) sagaciously observes in a broader context: "It only pays to lie or cheat when you can free ride off the honesty of others. . . . The conscious pursuit of self-interest by all members of society has the collective result of undermining the interests of all" (pp. 11–12). The central weakness of a corporate culture existing wholly within the Technical Universe, therefore, is its conceptual blindness to the intrinsic value of moral concepts such as trust and honesty. In fact, the deconstruction that I am about to undertake of the Technical Universe stems directly and solely from this blindness. A corporate culture devoid of trust and honesty, no matter how financially and technically sophisticated, is a corporate culture doomed to self-destruction. But why must this be so?

LOOKING INTERNATIONALLY

As finance becomes more global, the need for implicit contractual enforcement becomes more pressing. The lack of an effective global regulatory infrastructure renders explicit enforcement infeasible in many situations. In the case of implicit enforcement through reputation, given the impersonal and often infrequent nature of international transacting, reputation effects become even more fragile and ephemeral than in domestic markets.

One of the most significant financial developments of this century has been the globalization of business commerce. Traditional national, religious, and political boundaries are weakening in the wake of this internationalization of Western "corporate culture." With international securities markets and sophisticated transportation and communication systems linking all industrialized countries, the world is rapidly becoming a single financial market.

The extent of these international money flows is reflected in the phenomenal growth in currency trading: as we enter the twenty-first century the average volume of currency-trading activity (adjusted for double counting) is approaching a staggering $3 trillion per day! Perhaps the most dramatic illustration of the degree to which financial markets are now interconnected was the stock market crash of October 19, 1987 (alias "Black Monday"); on this day all major securities markets experienced a one-day decline in value of 20 percent or more almost simultaneously; in essence, the London, New York, Tokyo, and other major equity markets acted as one market.

The globalization of financial markets is being mirrored by a similar process in product markets. Robert Reich (1990) supplies a typical example:

Mazda's newest sportscar, the MX-5 Miata, was designed in California, financed from Tokyo and New York, its prototype was created in Worthing, England, and it was assembled in Michigan and Mexico using advanced electronics components invented in New Jersey and fabricated in Japan. (p. 79)

Today most large firms operate transnationally, that is, their operations extend across one or more national boundaries. Indeed, during the postwar expansion of Western economies, the transnational corporation (TNC) has risen to a role of dominance. Today the largest 100 corporations in the world are all TNCs. The annual earnings of any one of these companies exceeds the annual gross national product (GNP) of many developing nations, for whom international trade generally represents more than 50 percent of gross domestic product (GDP). TNCs control "80 percent of the world's land cultivated for export-oriented crops. . . . Eighty to ninety percent of the trade in tea, coffee, cocoa, cotton, forest products, tobacco, jute, copper, iron-ore, and bauxite is controlled in the case of each commodity by the three or six largest transnationals" (p. 79). In the case of U.S.-based TNCs, these companies increased overseas capital spending by 24 percent in 1988 and by a further 13 percent in 1989. American firms now employ 11 percent of the industrial workforce of Northern Ireland, manufacturing a broad range of products from cigarettes to software. Singapore's largest private employer is General Electric (GE), while AT&T, RCA, and Texas Instruments are three of Taiwan's largest exporters. Texas

Instruments is currently constructing a new $250 million semiconductor fabrication plant in Taiwan, and AT&T plans to build a similar facility in Spain. In their book *Managing across Borders*, Christopher Bartlett and Sumantra Ghoshal (1989) account for this dramatic growth in TNCs as follows: "[T]echnological, social, and economic developments over the last two decades have combined to create a unified world marketplace in which companies must capture global-scale economies to remain competitive" (p. 5).

But when a U.S. corporation expands its business beyond the domestic economy, it is no longer protected by a comprehensive and familiar regulatory environment. Indeed, few would argue that U.S. commerce is the beneficiary of the most sophisticated regulatory environment in the world. More important, this environment is designed generally to foster commercial activity rather than to inhibit or exploit it. As J. C. Francis (1986) notes, in the case of financial markets, "[N]o foreign markets are as efficient as the large, deep, and resilient securities markets in the United States" (p. 737).

The additional risks associated with international diversification are generally categorized into one of four types: political risk, foreign exchange risk, reduced liquidity or marketability risk, and inferior information risk. Clearly, these categories are not mutually exclusive, and all international transactions will likely be exposed, in varying degree, to all four types of risk. In general, therefore, a firm expanding outside the U.S. regulatory web is faced with the risks involved in enforcing transnational business contracts. Thus, the issue of contractual enforcement is particularly pertinent in contemporary global markets.

This chapter identified two fundamental mechanisms by which business contracts may be enforced: explicit enforcement via some legal mechanism or implicit enforcement via the firm's or agent's desire to maintain a reputation. Under scrutiny, both of these mechanisms appeared to have serious weaknesses—hence, the role for ethics as a contractual enforcement mechanism. In this chapter, a recognition of the increasing extent to which business relations extend across national borders reveals that the roles of law and reputation as *effective* contractual enforcement mechanisms become even more questionable. The weaknesses of these mechanisms, which were identified earlier in a domestic setting, are extenuated as business becomes more international. In a global marketplace, therefore, the need for some other enforcement mechanism in business interaction becomes even more pressing.

Outside the United States, the lack of a cohesive global regulatory body and the dramatic difference in economic power between nations combine to make the probability of explicit enforcement through law much lower than in domestic transactions. Consequently, in international dealings, corporations are forced to rely heavily on implicit contractual enforcement mechanisms.

Information availability was identified as critical to the effectiveness of reputation as an implicit contractual enforcement mechanism. But in an international context the complexities of implicit enforcement multiply: Business interaction becomes even more impersonal, and the degree of informational asymmetry—given minimal corporate disclosure laws in many countries—increases commensurably. These points are made clearly by Donaldson in his book on *The Ethics of International Business* (1989). Donaldson argues that, given the impersonality of most international transactions, the chances of any type of implicit cooperation along the lines of a reputation effect—or like that suggested by David Gauthier's *Morals by Agreement* (1988) in which enlightened self-interest leads to cooperation—become much lower:

[Gauthier's] attempt to generate international ethics from the concept of refined self-interest fails in the end. . . . [A] major problem for Gauthier's theory in application to international contexts is that an individual nation is not so impotent as an individual person. In international contexts the fruits of interaction are less certain. (Donaldson, 1989, p. 27)

In international business, therefore, the lack of information disclosure across borders tends to obfuscate the power of a "reputation effect" to act as an implicit contractual enforcement mechanism. Once again, reputation is not enough. The Technical Universe is not self-enforcing. The finance paradox holds sway.

TEST CASE: PEPSI/BURMA

As discussed at the end of Chapter 1, the decision faced by Pepsi's management of whether to pull out of Burma can be viewed as a continuation versus abandonment decision in capital budgeting. This type of decision-making construct is an archetypal Technical Universe–type decision: it entails the agent (project manager) choosing between two mutually exclusive and exhaustive alternatives, namely, whether to terminate an investment project immediately or to continue the project until the next evaluation. As discussed earlier, however, this theoretical precision proves illusory in practical application. Thus, even if he or she genuinely wishes to apply the NPV rule, the manager as technician would be unwise to base any practical decision solely on its prediction.

But, given our focus here in Chapter 2 on the business context as a contractual nexus, would our technically rational manager as agent even rationally *want* to apply the NPV rule of financial theory? Remember that this agent is a personal wealth–maximizing opportunist. Rationally, therefore, the agent will only strive to apply the NPV rule, in other words, will strive to maximize firm value, when it is within his or her personal self-interest to do so.

So although only two courses of action are observable—continuation or immediate abandonment—there may be many possible *motivations* under-lying this action. Financial-economic research in this area has supplied at least four possible motivations for the manager's choice between continua-tion versus abandonment. Business ethics theory supplies a fifth, and Part III of this book will supply a sixth. And, of course, in reality any individual manager may be motivated by some combination of these.

1. *No agency problem*. The manager may believe that his or her interests do dovetail with those of the firm. Specifically, the maximization of the manager's personal wealth or utility of wealth is seen by the manager as synonymous with the maximization of the firm's stock price—in which case, the manager as technician will rationally endeavor to apply the NPV rule. Of course, this endeavor will be thwarted with all the problems discussed in Chapter 1 concerning the practical application of this theoretically sound criterion.

2. *An agency problem*. Managers' concern for their personal reputations may induce them to delay project abandonment at the expense of firm value (Kanodia, Bushman, and Dickhaut, 1989). Managers might choose to con-tinue a negative-NPV project in an attempt to, at least temporarily, preserve their reputation for successfully completing capital investments. They would thus be acting in accordance with the tenets of narrowly defined economic self-interest (i.e., they would be acting within the finance paradigm), but they would not be acting in the interests of firm value maximization.

3. *Signaling*. Some researchers have argued that the NPV rule itself, out-lined in (1), is misspecified (Dobson and Dorsey, 1992). It fails to account for the real costs associated with tarnishing *the firm's* reputation: a reputation for successfully identifying and completing profitable projects. Assuming in-formational asymmetry, these costs are incurred by the announcement of a project abandonment. Such an announcement, at the time dictated by the NPV rule, represents a significantly negative signal. Thus, a project aban-donment may be more costly than the NPV rule implies.

Firm value may in fact be maximized, therefore, by continuing with a project that according to the NPV rule should be abandoned immediately. The length of the abandonment delay would be a function of the degree of informational asymmetry and the amount of reputational capital at stake as dictated by the perceived importance of the project. A *reputation-adjusted* NPV rule (RANPV) may therefore be the appropriate, firm-value-maximizing decision criterion.

4. *Psychology*. Individuals are generally reluctant to admit defeat, and thus managers' regret aversion may lead them to delay the termination of un-profitable projects (see Statman and Caldwell, 1987; similar arguments have been presented by Thaler [1988; psychic accounting], Laughhunn and

Payne [1991; framing], and Staw [1981]). For example, Staw and Ross (1986) note that a certain personal and social esteem accrues to those individuals who "stick to their guns" (p. 59) in the face of adversity. Managers pursue a *psychic* payoff rather than a personal or corporate *economic* payoff. An agent may therefore continue an unprofitable project in the hope, rather than any realistic expectation, that the project will become profitable in the future.

5. *The moral manager*: The manager may not operate within the rationality construct of the Technical Universe. The manager may instead operate within the Moral Universe, to be discussed in Part II—in which case, the manager will rationally reject the NPV criterion in favor of, or at least render the NPV criterion subservient to, some overriding moral criterion. But more on this in the next two chapters.

6. *The manager as aesthete*. The aesthetic manager, to be defined in Part III, will reject the criteria supplied by both the Technical and Moral Universes. In making this or any capital budgeting decision, the aesthetic manager would recognize the NPV rule of the technician and the ethical principle of the moralist as too conceptually limited, given their own internal inconsistencies and incoherences. A precise elucidation of exactly how the manager as aesthete *would* make this or any capital budgeting decision will have to wait until Part III.

In summary, even though the Technical Universe provides a cut-and-dry method for Pepsi's management to make its decision, namely, the NPV rule, it does not provide any compelling reason why any given individualistic and opportunistic manager should rationally abide by this method. Indeed, the opportunistic nature of the rationality assumption embedded in the Technical Universe suggests that management will not abide by it, unless there is some fortuitous congruence of the individual's objectives with those of the firm. My discussion so far in this section illustrates the variety of motives that may, in actuality, determine the manager as technician's behavior.

In actuality, the evidence indicates that Pepsi's management did initially occupy this Technical Universe in choosing whether or not to pull out of Burma. Pepsi's Burma operation was profitable. There was no law prohibiting Pepsi from operating within Burma. So, in true "Friedmanesque" fashion, Pepsi perceived its prerogative as maximizing profits within the law.

Indeed, all of Pepsi's decisions, even its eventual decision to pull out of Burma, can be seen as not inconsistent with the application of the NPV rule. Pepsi merely reevaluated the future cash flows and discount rate in light of the mounting economic costs from student boycotts and the like. At some point Pepsi calculated these costs to yield a higher NPV for abandonment versus continuation; so the managers as technicians at Pepsi pulled out.

But this type of reading of Pepsi's case history in no way vindicates even the economic efficacy of a practical application of financial-economic theory's NPV rule. An apologist for the latter might argue that the fault here lies not with financial-economic theory but rather with Pepsi's ability to apply it. Specifically, Pepsi failed initially to estimate the magnitude of the—moral outrage–induced—future economic costs associated with continuing operations in Burma. Thus, if Pepsi's management had been better financial economists, they would have made the right decision. But, I would argue, given the uncertainties at the time these cash flow estimates had to be made, how could Pepsi's managers, or indeed any managers, have estimated them accurately, not to mention estimating an appropriate risk-adjusted discount rate? In short, in application to many contemporary capital budgeting decisions, the problem of accurately estimating future cash flows and discount rates renders the NPV rule and similar methodologies supplied by financial-economic theory extremely inaccurate.

Consider, for example, the decision of Coke's managers. Coke decided never to get involved in Burma in the first place. If both the firms were applying the dictates of financial-economic theory, then how is it that they could both come up with such dramatically different decisions? Perhaps there were economic reasons relating to Coke's greater size and public exposure, perhaps not. But if we keep expanding the conceptual boundaries of cash flow estimation to cover all these estimates of intangibles, such as the probability of future moral outrage, then two things happen. In theory, the NPV Rule becomes little more than a tautology: the "right choice" (economically) is the one with the highest NPV, and this highest NPV will result from making the "right choice" (pseudomorally). In practice the criterion become impossible to apply because of the necessity of placing numerical values on such things as the probability of future "pseudo moral" outrage.

And of course, even if we are willing to accept all these internal problems with the NPV and similar rules, we still have to justify our existence solely within the Technical Universe itself. Should Pepsi or any company make this type of decision purely on the basis of maximizing the firm's economic value? As we enter the twenty-first century, is the notion of shareholder wealth maximization as the determining factor in decision making still justifiable? Clearly it provides the conceptual bedrock for the manager as technician within the Technical Universe. But is the Technical Universe, albeit still popular among financial economists, the *real* universe of contemporary business? If it is not, then what is? And, if it is not, then such criteria as the NPV rule lose any practical justification. As we will see in the next two chapters, a firm that believes it is operating within the Technical Universe, when the true surrounding culture is that of the Moral or Aesthetic Universe, is a firm that is in serious trouble, morally, aesthetically, and financially. In the context of their decisions regarding Burma, is this the real source of the different approaches of Pepsi and Coke? Were these firms' managers in different conceptual universes? And were Coke's managers in the correct, that is, "real," conceptual universe?

PART I SUMMARY

I began this book by identifying three business universes. Each of these universes conjures its own epistemology, or what MacIntyre might call its own "tradition of inquiry" into, in this case, the nature of business. In Part I, I have focused on that conceptual universe that has dominated much of twentieth-century business epistemology, namely, the Technical Universe.

What I have attempted to show is that—as a coherent tradition of inquiry or epistemology—the Technical Universe fails. It fails in terms of its own standards of logic and rationality; it conjures a business milieu of opportunistic individuals pursuing wealth maximization within a contractual nexus, yet it provides no mechanism within its construct for the adequate (that is, economically efficient) enforcement of these contracts. Without such enforcement, the rationally determined economic goal of material advancement is thwarted. In short, a dominant epistemology of individualistic wealth maximization ensures that individuals within that universe never maximize wealth; it is a classic "catch-22" scenario. As Aristotle and others have pointed out, to really achieve what is in one's self-interest, one cannot directly pursue what one perceives to be in one's self-interest; the Technical Universe lacks the philosophical sophistication to realize this.

Thus what I have endeavored to show in this section is that a deconstruction of the Technical Universe and its methodological foundation, namely, financial-economic theory, satisfies the first of MacIntyre's conditions for a Kuhnian-type paradigm shift:

This internal deconstruction of the Technical Universe has left a void in the business metaphysic. In Part III, I will argue that this void is increasingly, indeed inevitably, being filled by the aesthetic of the manager as artisan. But first the second of our three business universes requires attention, namely, the Moral Universe of modernity. Why does the modernist Moral Universe—epitomized by late twentieth-century business ethics theory—also fail in terms of its own incoherences and inconsistencies? This is the question I turn to now in Part II. This question must be answered to account fully for the metaphysical void left by the collapse of modernity—a void to be filled by the aesthetic manager of Part III.

Part II

The Moral Manager

The more one examines the motives—what Nietzsche would call the "genealogy"—of these theories of obligatory action [i.e., the theories of modern moral philosophy], the stranger they appear. Because it seems that they are motivated by the strongest of moral ideals, like freedom, altruism, universalism. These are among the central moral aspirations of modern culture, the overarching goods which are distinctive to it. And yet these ideals drive the theorists towards a denial of all such goods. They are caught in a strange pragmatic contradiction, whereby the very goods which move them push them to deny or de-nature all such goods. They are constitutionally incapable of coming clean about the deeper sources of their own thinking. Their thought is inescapably cramped.
—Charles Taylor, "A Most Peculiar Institution"

Chapter 3

The Enlightened Agent

The rosy blush of [Calvinism's] laughing heir, the Enlightenment, seems also to be irretrievably fading, and the idea of duty in one's calling prowls about in our lives like the ghost of dead religious beliefs.
— Max Weber, *The Protestant Work Ethic and the Spirit of Capitalism*

The Technical Universe, described in the previous section, has been the dominant business universe of modernity. But within the latter half of the twentieth century it has been increasingly embellished (some would argue tarnished) by another universe that is also particularly characteristic of modernity. This is the Moral Universe.

Of course the link between business and morality is an old one. Indeed, in *Nietzsche and the Origin of Virtue* (1991), Lester Hunt notes Nietzsche arguing that the very origin of morality—and specifically rules of morality—was in business dealings: "[T]he most fundamental moral concepts and sentiments originated in 'the oldest and most primitive personal relationship, that between buyer and seller, creditor and debtor,' and in the contracts that arise from this relationship" (p. 100). This merger or synthesis of the moral and the technical in business has gained recent academic and practitioner respectability in the form of the discipline of business ethics. Indeed, upon listening to the current controversy surrounding the role of ethics in business, managers may understandably feel somewhat bemused. On the one hand, they will remember their business school training, during which they were continually instructed that the primary objective of the firm is to maximize the wealth of shareholders. Or as Milton Friedman (1970) puts it in his oft-quoted *New York Times Magazine* article: "The social responsibility of business is to increase its profits" (p. 14). Sherwin (1983) sums up Friedman's argument as follows:

Friedman categorically disqualifies managers taking social action on two grounds: first, in complex situations, business managers will probably not know the correct action to take to achieve the desired result and, second, by taking social action, managers would be acting as unauthorized civil servants. (p. 183)

But these financial managers may also come across statements from leading business ethicists such as: "[The] primary obligation . . . [of business] is to provide meaningful work for . . . employees" (Bowie, 1991, p. 15) or, "[I]f in some instance it turns out that what is ethical leads to a company's demise . . . so be it" (DeGeorge, 1990, p. 421); not to mention such proclamations as, "Provision to meet need is the highest purpose of business; provision to satisfy unreasonable and socially harmful desire . . . perverts the purpose of business" (Byron, 1988, p. 528) and, "[I]t is usually profitable to be honorable, and virtue is more than its own reward" (Barach and Elstrott, 1988, p. 546).

How, if at all, can these views be reconciled? Is shareholder wealth maximization antithetical to honor and virtue? Are finance issues, such as management remuneration or management's delay in releasing negative financial information, also ethical problems? Assuming that it is relevant, is ethics too nebulous a concept for serious consideration within business? In practice, on what basis should decisions be made when an apparent conflict exists between profits and ethics? If corporations should temper their pecuniary aspirations with some ethic, then which of the various moral philosophies is most practical in a financial context? These are the types of questions faced by the moral manager to be discussed below.

Of course, the origins of business ethics in general and our moral manager in particular can be found much earlier than its recent renaissance. On the theoretical side, as discussed in Chapter 1, early business philosophers such as Adam Smith recognized the need for moral sentiment to temper narrow material self-interest. On the practical side, many early industrialists embraced some notion of morally enlightened business management. Perhaps the most famous of these was Robert Owen, who built a model community based on some modernist conceptions of a morally enlightened factory; he had regulated work hours and administered schools for the children, although these children still worked in the factory.

What is different about late twentieth-century business ethics is that it conceives of itself as a dominant paradigm. Business ethicists view the financial-economic idea of the firm—the idea of the firm as a machine and the individual as a wealth maximizer—as just one impoverished subset of the "true" business universe. This true business universe is a morally inclusive one in which the firm plays some broader social role. The firm is no longer viewed in merely a technical light, as a wealth-creating machine. This shift from the technical to the moral is reflected in the numerous explicit credos, enumerated by many companies; as we enter the twenty-first century, practically every company has developed an explicit corporate credo. These credos increasingly view the objectives of the firm in some broad social context. In its credo, for example, Johnson & Johnson states that its primary obligation is to the doctors, nurses, and others who use its products. I have never yet seen a corporate credo that listed shareholder wealth maximization as the firm's primary objective. These credos, therefore, whether actually adhered to by management or not, demonstrate some conceptual shift from the Technical Universe to the Moral Universe. But who exactly are these morally enlightened managers of modernity? What exactly motivates them, and how do they differ from the technicians of Part I?

THE ENLIGHTENED MANAGER

The contractual impasse of the Technical Universe, as described in Part I, implies that if agents acted ethically in the sense that contracts could be reliably enforced with trust, outcomes could be obtained in finance that are "first-best" (i.e., there would be no deadweight residual agency loss). As Noreen (1988) observes in the case of moral hazard: "The best solution, which is costless, is for the manager to truthfully report his effort and his consumption of perquisites" (p. 362). But what could motivate the manager to do this? Is this always the best solution? And, more fundamentally, what exactly is meant by the "best solution"? Is the best solution when the agent's wealth is maximized, or when society's wealth is maximized, or when everyone is honest and treated fairly, or what?

In attempting to answer this question, business ethics theory has tended to focus on what are commonly called the *Enlightenment* ethical theories, or what are often called "traditional" or "conventional" ethical theories. These theories have been labeled by Sherwin Klein (1988) as "action-based" because they focus on the actions of agents in a given contractual situation. The theories can be further categorized into two broad types: deontological and consequentialist.

DEONTOLOGICAL ETHICAL THEORIES

Deontological ethical theories focus on developing rules or guidelines that can be universally applied in contractual situations. A defining characteristic of this group of theories is that a decision of whether some action is morally right or wrong does not centrally depend on the consequences of the action: these theories are "nonconsequential."

Perhaps the most famous deontologist was Immanuel Kant, a German philosopher of the eighteenth century. Kant's broad philosophy can be distilled into two fundamental dictums: first, that people should be treated as ends rather than as means; this is generally referred to as Kant's "categorical imperative." In practical terms, this means that people should not be exploited for some ulterior end. An example of contravening this rule would be a firm that attempts to make money by attracting customers through deceptive advertising.

Second, Kant developed the "universalization" principle: People should choose to take only those actions that they would wish to become universal law. This principle is essentially the same as the "Golden Rule" principle adopted by most world religions, for example, "treat thy neighbor as thyself."

The application of these rule-based ethical theories to corporate activity has generally taken the form of developing corporate credos, or codes of conduct. As John Dienhart (1995) has recently pointed out, not all codes are rule-based; indeed, in the next chapter, we will look in some detail at non-rule-based corporate codes. But many codes are based on rules—on a set of do's and don'ts—and these types of code invariably find their philosophical foundation in deontological ethical theory. How successful have these rule-based codes been?

RULE-BASED CORPORATE CODES

Just how effective these codes are, and the motivations of the managers who introduce them, has been the source of much debate. Messod Baneish and Robert Chatov (1993) analyzed the content of 160 rule-based corporate codes of conduct in relation to the respective firm's business environment. The authors find that "managers choose code content so as to reduce the expected cost of adverse legal or regulatory action"(p. 15). They go on to conclude that "our findings are consistent with code adoptions and development as good *business* decisions" (p. 33). The results of this study indicate that the underlying objective behind this type of code is economic, not ethical. We are still firmly *within* the Technical Universe.

Implementing this type of code is notoriously difficult. For example, Michael R. Rion, CEO of Cummins Diesel—a company with an extensive corporate credo that will be discussed further in Chapter 6—notes that "Cummins does not meet its goals with perfect accuracy and the problems of sustaining and implementing ethical management arise regularly" (Rion, 1982, p. 420). Of course, actually measuring how successful these programs are is very difficult since what really needs to be evaluated are the underlying motives, whereas only the resulting action is observable. A single financial action could conceal a variety of possible motivations for that action. Thus, managers may be seen as complying with the *letter* of a corporate credo through their actions, whereas their latent motivations reveal that they are by no means complying with the *spirit* of the credo; their motivations may be strictly unethical and unobservable. This problem of identifying latent "motivation" from observable "action" will be illustrated clearly in the capital budgeting test case in Chapter 4.

In summary, the implementation of a corporate credo or code of conduct may have some benefit to the extent that it makes finance practitioners aware of the existence of ethics. But it could not be said to in any way *integrate* ethics with finance. A credo, in and of itself, does not rationalize ethics in finance.

This is no doubt why firms like Cummins and Johnson & Johnson, which take their credos seriously, must go to such lengths to get managers to respect and abide by the code. To a manager imbued with the conventional notion of financial rationality, the stipulations and language of such a code would seem fundamentally alien and would likely be viewed as merely some constraint to be circumvented in the pursuit of wealth maximization—hence, the frequent justification of these codes in terms of "Good ethics is good business."

Indeed, as the evidence presented earlier indicates, most firms probably adopt codes strictly for financial reasons: "[M]anagers choose code content so as to reduce the expected cost of adverse legal or regulatory action" (Fay, 1989, p. 44). And who can blame them, given the lack of any rational justification for such constraints in a financial world defined entirely in terms of the finance paradigm?

CONSEQUENTIALIST ETHICAL THEORIES

The other broad category of modernist ethical theories are those based on the consequences of an action. Utilitarianism is a prime example of a consequentialist ethical theory. A utilitarian endeavors to choose those actions that will create the greatest expected benefits for some entire economic or social group; the focus is thus entirely on consequences. A less extreme rendition is rule utilitarianism, in which the consequential objectives are tempered by some deontological-type ethic.

In the context of business ethics, examples of consequentialist theories would be "stakeholder theory" (Freeman, 1991) and "social-contracts theory" (Dunfee and Donaldson, 1995). Although these theories comprise deontological elements, in the form of certain corporate rights or obligations, the underlying premise is that a firm should be run to benefit all participants, or stakeholders, directly. This premise is in sharp contrast to the standard model in finance, in which the firm is organized around the idea of shareholder wealth maximization.

Of course, as we discussed earlier, apologists for the finance model such as Milton Friedman argue that a focus on benefiting shareholders will also indirectly benefit all other stakeholders. Thus, even Friedman's position can be viewed as a utilitarian-type argument, or more precisely rule utilitarian. Also, although desirable in principle, utilitarianism's focus on the broad consequences of an action presents certain real problems in business practice. At the time a decision has to be made, it is often very difficult for the manager to have any very clear idea of what the broad consequences of the action will be. For one thing, in many business situations, the consequences of an action depend in large part on how other agents or other firms react— hence, the popularity of game theory.

Also, a focus on the broad consequences of an action could well lead a manager to behave in ways that fail to comply with a strict rule-based corporate credo. Indeed, the most recent theories of business ethics tend to recognize the integrated nature of deontological and consequentialist ethics. Theories such as integrated social contracts theory are built around the notion that any meaningful modernist ethical precept must encompass a notion of both moral rules and a notion of the consequences of adhering to those rules. As I argue below, however, such theories still fall victim to the central logical inconsistencies and incoherences internal to modernist moral philosophy.

INTEGRATED SOCIAL CONTRACTS THEORY

To illustrate this failure, consider perhaps the most comprehensive and widely accepted business ethics theory yet developed, namely, integrated social contracts theory (ISCT). Donaldson and Dunfee (1994) desribe ISCT as a "realistic, comprehensive, and global normative theory of business ethics" (p. 32). This is clearly not a modest claim. The theory claims to establish certain hypernorms that provide a moral foundation for business throughout the world. Essentially these hypernorms all center around what we in the West call "human rights." In addition to the hypernorms, ISCT attempts to preempt any charge of western cultural imperialism by recognizing the existence of culturally distinct mininorms. These mininorms, however, according to ISCT, are always subject to justification in terms of the hypernorms.

Clearly, if it is to possess any normative bite, ISCT needs the hypernorms to be omnipotent. Otherwise, with a multiplicity of contradictory and culturally distinct mininorms, the theory would just descend into ethical relativism. But does ISCT live up to its claims? Does it provide a normative foundation for a global business ethic, without any Western bias?

Surely human rights, however desirable we in the West may feel them to be, are a peculiarly Western and more specifically a peculiarly "modernist" phenomenon. Human rights are an invention of Enlightenment moral philosophy. How can anyone claim these to be universal while simultaneously claiming no Western bias? To claim human rights such as personal freedom (whatever that is), informed consent (whatever that is), and ownership of property (whatever that is), as universal and unequivocal hypernorms is to claim that Enlightenment moral philosophy (whatever exactly that is) has some absolute justification, that it is the Truth, the absolute presence. MacIntyre (1984a), for example, observes that "there are no such [human] rights, and belief in them is one with belief in witches and in unicorns" (p. 69). He goes on to explain this position:

The best reason for asserting so bluntly that there are no such rights is indeed of precisely the same type as the best reason which we possess for asserting that there are no witches and the best reason which we possess for asserting that there are no unicorns: every attempt to give good reasons for believing that there are such rights has failed. The eighteenth-century philosophical defenders of natural rights sometimes suggest that the assertions which state that men possess them are self-evident truths; but we know that there are no self-evident truths. Twentieth-century moral philosophers have sometimes appealed to their and our intuitions; but one of the things that we ought to have learned from the history of moral philosophy is that the introduction of the word "intuition" by a moral philosopher is always a signal that something has gone badly wrong with an argument. (p. 69)

In his recent business ethics text, David Fritszche (1997) states that "there are certain practices (hypernorms) such as stealing, killing, and slavery which are not condoned by any community worldwide" (p. 55). Really? I am not familiar with every community worldwide, but I am familiar with my own Western community, and I could argue that—given reasonable definitions of "stealing," "killing," and "slavery"—all of these are condoned in my community. For example, ask a Native American whether the West condones stealing. Ask a Palestinian, or even perhaps a black American, whether the West condones killing. Ask the animal rights activists who have compiled a declaration of primate rights whether the West condones slavery.

In reality, as the central aesthetic critique of this book shows, ISCT, like business ethics theory in general, suffers from all the internal inconsistencies and incoherences characteristic of modernity. Simply put, there is no such thing as a hypernorm. Ethics is always contextual. As Paul Buller, John Kohls, and Kenneth Anderson note in their recent article "A Model for Addressing Cross-Cultural Ethical Conflicts, "[A] number of recent empirical studies provide evidence for different ethical perspectives across national cultures on a wide variety of specific issues" (p. 173). They go on to give numerous examples of such studies. They conclude:

[T]he preponderance of the research to date suggests strongly that different national cultures have different perspectives regarding ethical values and [hyper]norms . . . [N]ational culture plays a central role in shaping moral values and standards of ethical behavior. Strong cross-cultural differences make it difficult to develop universal moral values, reasoning, and behaviors that will be meaningful and adhered to across national boundaries. (pp. 173–174)

The notion of a hypernorm erroneously assumes that the Western modernist context is *the* context. In addition, the internal inconsistencies in the theory become apparent when attempts are made to apply it. For example, consider a recent attempt to apply it by Fritszche (1997). Fritszche considers the example of a Western firm doing business in China. Initially he notes that "nepotism might be a micro social contract norm in an Asian community. Equal opportunity may be a norm in a Western community" (p. 45). But then, of course, would not nepotism (or at least the Western definition of it) contradict our human rights–induced hypernorm? Later in his discussion of ISCT, Fritszche states: "Once the [Western] firm has landed a contract and begins hiring Chinese employees, it should observe equal opportunity norms (the norms of its local [Western] community that do not have an adverse effect on the Chinese) in its hiring practices" (p. 46). But wait a minute—did we not just decide that nepotism was a moral norm in China? So by adopting Western hiring practices, are we not guilty of precisely the moral imperialism that ISCT was supposed to avoid? We are in essence saying that our Western hiring practices are in some absolute moral sense superior to your Eastern hiring practices, which once again broaches the question, from where is this is absolute moral "ought" of Western modernity derived? For example, in the case of bribery, Manuel Velasquez and Neil Brady (1997) note that "moral views on bribery appear to be culturally conditioned, and in some cultures the absolutist view of the wrongness of bribery is perceived as a form of Western cultural imperialism that is deeply ethnocentric" (p. 100). Not surprisingly, given its existence entirely within the context of modernity, ISCT has no answer to this. Indeed, its conceptual contextlessness precludes it from even realizing this as a meaningful question. We are brought once again face-to-face with modernity's deafening silence.

DECONSTRUCTING THE ENLIGHTENED MANAGER

Although the widespread publication of modern business ethics texts now spans a period of nearly 40 years, these texts are all remarkably similar in their invocation of the moral manager; or perhaps this is not so remarkable since they all draw their inspiration from Enlightenment philosophers. At root, the moral manager is the same person as the technician of the previous section. Both are wholly products of modernity, and therefore both use conventional logic and reason to achieve some objective. Unlike the technician, however, the moral manager is peculiarly characterized by some sense of obligation. Either this obligation might be to other people, as with utilitarianism, or it might be to some sort of principle, as with deontology (e.g., Kantianism or the Golden Rule of "Do unto others as you would have them do unto you").

Thus, in the very structure of the subject area of business ethics we see something particularly characteristic of modernity, namely, a dualism. Either the manager is a utilitarian, or the manager is a Kantian. But, as recent aesthetic critique has made clear, a careful deconstruction of this apparent dualism reveals it as illusory. Both utilitarianism, or Kantianism, and the various hybrids thereof all really represent the same intellectual construct. This is the construct of obligation of "ought" or "owe." A utilitarian or Kantian is at root the same individual applying the same modern assumptions and principles of logic and rationality and fiat.

To see this, consider how a utilitarian manager would actually make a decision. Remember that a utilitarian strives to maximize some notion of overall welfare. Note already the modernist overlay of "obligation," "ordinal calculation," amd "maximization." And the invocation of the "other." There is the manager "the same" and the general welfare "the other," a dualism again, a subject and an object. As we will see in Part III, these are all characteristics of modernity. These are all robes/contexts that will be shed by our aesthetic emperor/manager.

But returning to our deconstruction of utilitarianism. How is our utilitarian moral manager going to make decisions? How is he going to act so as to maximize overall welfare? For example, Donaldson (1982) states that "[c]orporations . . . exist to enhance the welfare of society" (p. 54). But Donaldson fails to give a precise definition of this "welfare"; he goes on to say "through the satisfaction of consumer and worker interests" (p. 54), but what interests exactly, and might these interests not have been created by the corporation in the first place through advertising? Which brings us back to the question, How is our modern manager going to act so as to maximize overall welfare?

Well, before he can take any actions, he will have to make some decisions. To what extent is his firm, through advertising and perhaps through the enforcement of ISCT's hypernorms, responsible for society's conception of what its welfare actually is? In terms of overall welfare, how is he going to define "overall"? Is this the entire world population? Or is this all stakeholders? But then, if one stakeholder group is society at large—which is often the case in the business ethics stakeholder literature—then what is the difference between the entire world population and all stakeholders? Or maybe the manager will define "overall" as simply all stockholders in the firm. In which case, utilitarianism collapses into something like the shareholder wealth maximization dictum of financial economics' Theory of the Firm: How close these two would be depends upon how our manager chooses to define "welfare." If he defines welfare as financial wealth, then the two are identical; if the manager himself holds stock, then the moral manager once again becomes the technician, or something very close; but that surely is not what our utilitarian moral manager has in mind.

Going back to defining "overall." Should we even limit this "overall" to people? What about the physical environment? No doubt environmentalists would argue that this should be part of the utilitarian equation. Or what about animals? Animal rights activists would no doubt argue that all sentient life should be part of the utilitarian equation.

Also, however our manager decides to define "overall," he must also consider what time frame is relevant. Is this overall welfare today? Or for this year? Or the present discounted value (more financial-economics jargon) of all future overall welfare?

The utilitarian paradigm will not help our manager in his attempts to define "overall." If the manager says, "I will define 'overall' in whatever way leads to the maximization of overall welfare"—in other words if the manager does attempt to define "overall" by applying the utilitarian paradigm—then he finds himself caught in a logical circularity: using the word "overall" to define the word "overall."

Before even making a single utilitarian decision, therefore, the manager must apply some moral concept not derived from utilitarianism in order to define just exactly what the utilitarian principle will be. This is why I said earlier that a deconstruction of utilitarianism will render the distinction between it and deontology illusory. To meaningfully define the application of utilitarianism, some deontological moral principle must be applied. And of course we haven't even started to worry about how we are going to define "welfare" yet. As any honest utilitarian knows, "welfare" is a real Pandora's box. Is welfare wealth? Or is it happiness? Or is it pleasure over pain, as Jeremy Bentham (1789) argued in his original formulation of utilitarianism? (We're going to be referencing almost exclusively white European males in our discussion of the moral manager, but then of course these are the minds from which modernity sprang.) But then, what is wealth? What is happiness? What is pleasure? How are these to be measured, because, as with all good modernist paradigms, they must be measurable: there must be some ordinal "order." John Stuart Mill, arguably the father of utilitarianism (if we assume that Jeremy Bentham was the grandfather), thought there was pleasure . . . but then there was pleasure, that is, there are lower pleasures and higher pleasures: "[B]etter Socrates dissatisfied than a pig satisfied," as Mill famously puts it. There are higher pleasures and there are lower pleasures, and this is a moral absolute. So Mill blatantly and explicitly places a deontologically derived moral absolute at the heart of utilitarianism.

So, in short, somewhere along the line, before he takes any action, our utilitarian manager is just going to have to apply some absolute ought. But from whence is the justification for this "ought" going to come?

In *Against the Self-Images of the Age* (1984b), Alasdair MacIntyre notes that in classical Greek, Latin, and Anglo-Saxon and Middle English, the words "ought" and "owe" are indistinguishable. The "ought" of the Moral Universe is a type of taboo, or what MacIntyre calls a survival:

We make a social practice intelligible by placing it in some context where the point and purpose of doing things in one way rather than another is exhibited by showing the connection between that social practice and some wider institutional arrangements of which it is a part. So the passing of a verdict has to be understood in the context of a legal system, and the concept of a home run has to be understood in the context of baseball. When we cannot make a practice intelligible by providing such a context, there are two possibilities. The first is that we have not been adequately perceptive or understanding in our investigation of that particular social order; the other is that the practice just is, as it stands, unintelligible. One hypothesis which we may advance as a result of coming to the latter conclusion, a hypothesis which has the additional merit, if it is independently supported, of supporting the latter conclusion, is that the practice in question is a survival. That is to say, we explain the practice in its present form by supposing that it is the historical product of an earlier practice which existed in a social context that has now been removed and of the consequences of the removal of that context. What do I mean by a context? A set of beliefs expressed in institutionalized social practice. Hence what I want to maintain is that the use of the . . . moral "ought" can perhaps only be made intelligible as a social practice by supposing it to be a survival from a lost context of beliefs, just as the eighteenth-century Polynesian use of "taboo" can perhaps only be made intelligible by supposing it to be a survival from a lost context of beliefs. (p. 167)

So the moral "ought" of modernity is, according to MacIntyre, a taboo word in the sense that it has become divorced from its original religious context. Consider the fundamental question, Why "ought" I be trustworthy?

The classical philosopher could meaningfully answer this question as follows: "You 'ought' to be trustworthy because you 'owe' it to yourself to be trustworthy. That is to say, that acting in a trustworthy manner is consistent with your own pursuit of excellence and the good life. In essence, exercising the virtue of trustworthiness is in your own self-interest."

Similarly, the pre-Enlightenment Augustinian or Thomistic philosopher cum theologian would have no problem answering this question: "You 'ought' to be trustworthy because you 'owe' it to God. That is to say, that you are subject to the will of God, and it is the will of God as revealed in the Scriptures that you are trustworthy."

But how does post-Enlightenment modernity answer this question? When the moral "ought" is wrenched from the context of the classical virtues, and from the context of religious dogma, then from whence does it derive its substantive meaning? This is what I referred to in the introduction to this book as the deafening silence of modernity, because as Nietzsche, MacIntyre, and other critics of modernity have pointed out, post-Enlightenment moral philosophy has no answer to the fundamental question, Why ought I be moral? I call modernity's silence on this question deafening because failure to answer it defeats the entire Enlightenment project. Modernity has failed to find a secular, reason-based justification for morality. The moral "ought" of modernity is indeed a taboo word: a survival from a pre-Enlightenment, God-based, rather than reason-based, age.

The Enlightenment philosophers of the eighteenth and nineteenth centuries were so imbued with the God-based certainties of their age, reflected (as MacIntyre notes in *Three Rival Versions of Moral Enquiry* [1990]) in the unified Victorian worldview of the ninth edition of the *Encyclopeadia Britannica*, that they were largely blind to the implicit biases in their philosophies. The utilitarian utopia of Mill is, on close inspection, a peculiarly Victorian concoction. The deontological principles of Kant must at some point, as Kant himself admitted, rest on Divine authority. Indeed even within the nineteenth century itself, this central fallibility of the Enlightenment "ought" was recognized, most notably by Nietzsche.

To illustrate this point in a contemporary business context, consider the following example. A skillful financial accountant may be able to enhance her company's reported results of operations by crafting a sale-leaseback arrangement whereby some of the company's assets are sold, a gain is recorded, all the appropriate accounting pronouncements are adhered to, and the company still has use of its assets. The intent of the transaction was never to rid the company of unwanted assets, but rather to record a gain and thus possibly avoid breaching debt-covenant agreements or circumvent regulatory requirements. A recent example of a major corporation adopting this practice is IBM during its financial crisis of the early 1990s. IBM attempted to artificially bolster its financial statements by undertaking major sale and leaseback arrangements. It rapidly dropped the practice in the face of critical public scrutiny.

To examine whether or not this example of creative accounting is unethical, traditional approaches would have the individual step out of her accounting role and don the hat of a Kantian (e.g., "Does this action violate the rights of users of the financial statements to fairly presented financial information?") or of a utilitarian (e.g., "Does this action maximize the welfare of all stakeholders?").

In this traditional approach, therefore, a professional—whether accountant or otherwise—adopts a type of moral schizophrenia in which being a good professional in the sense of being an economically effective accountant becomes separable from being a good professional in the sense of being an ethical accountant. Thus, given this action-based approach, an accountant could be a "good" accountant, in the sense of being very efficient and effective, yet at the same time not be a "good" accountant, in the sense of being ethical.

Similarly, statements such as "You 'ought' to be an ethical accountant!" become problematic. Clearly, given the aforementioned separation of ethics and efficiency, such a command of "ought" cannot be premised on the idea that being an ethical accountant will in some way engender greater efficiency. If one were to challenge this command with the question, Why "ought" I be an ethical accountant?, the modernist approach to ethics would have trouble providing a simple answer beyond, "You ought to be an ethical accountant because being ethical is what accountants ought to be," which clearly does not really answer the original question. Given this dual concept of the "good" professional, therefore, it is not surprising that many practitioners feel confused. They may find themselves being simultaneously tugged in two opposing directions: in the direction of economic efficiency or profit maximization, and in the direction of adherence to some abstract professional code of conduct.

The implicit implication for managers in the Technical Universe is essentially utilitarian: Maximum aggregate wealth is the best solution, which in the models of finance is generally taken to be no broader than maximizing the value of a single firm. Financial economics does not invoke utilitarian individuals directly because such motivation is deemed unrealistic—what O. D. Hart (1983) terms "bounded rationality: individuals simply cannot conceive of all the eventualities that may occur" (p. 23). But what if this utilitarian best solution is attained by means of dishonesty? Should the utilitarian objective be constrained by a stipulation that all agents are honest—that is, some form of rule utilitarianism? Is honesty always the best solution, regardless of the economic cost? If honesty is actually to be inserted as a nonabsolute constraint in an objective function, then it must be financially measurable. But is honesty or trustworthiness quantifiable? Even if honesty could be quantified, there is no universal agreement on the ultimate desirability of honesty in all situations. Even deontological ethical theories, which do not concern themselves with consequences and therefore need not necessarily quantify moral attributes, fail to supply universally applicable rules of conduct (MacIntyre, 1984a).

Clearly, the ultimate desirability of any of these ethical theories depends fundamentally upon the desired ultimate objective. If a single ultimate objective were universally accepted and logically proven, then the corresponding ethical theory could merely be inserted into the business rubric. Business would thus fulfill its normative obligation. The central problem is that Enlightenment moral philosophy has failed to distill a clear ultimate objective. Any agent attempting to apply these types of ethical theory is thus set adrift in an unnavigable sea of ambiguity between the two pedagogical extremes of Kantianism and utilitarianism:

The existence of these divisions makes one wonder why [Enlightenment] theory is viewed as helpful in any way. On the surface, it would seem that the opposite would be true: that a familiarity with theoretical debates would only complicate students' approaches to concrete cases. . . . It would seem that the presence of fundamental disagreement at the theoretical level would tend to reinforce the impression . . . that ethics is ultimately "subjective." (Derry and Green, 1989, p. 4)

An additional complication in finance is that some individuals are invariably constrained by a fiduciary responsibility to other individuals. To the extent that a fiduciary duty can be construed as an ethical obligation, a manager may be ethically justified in deceiving bondholders if such behavior increases the wealth of stockholders.

Given the Enlightenment view of ethics, therefore, the morality of agency problems is unclear. Given managers' special fiduciary "duty" to shareholders, agency problems concerning the interaction of debtholders and management could be viewed in a different moral light to agency problems between management and shareholders. Two examples of the former type of agency problem discussed earlier are *underinvestment* (Myers, 1977) and *risk shifting* (Jensen and Meckling, 1976). In both cases, managers undertake deceptive behavior that is designed to expropriate wealth from unwitting debtholders. But surely, from a Kantian or a utilitarian perspective, one could argue that managers are morally obligated to attempt such behavior in order to honor their fiduciary duty to shareholders. Far from being unethical, therefore, the existence of these agency problems can be construed as evidence of managers fulfilling their moral obligations.

The same defense cannot be made for agency problems between management and shareholders. When managers act deceptively by consuming excessive amounts of perquisites, to the detriment of firm value, they are also breaching their fiduciary duty to shareholders. Any moral defense of such behavior, therefore, would be extremely tenuous. But to the extent that such behavior is expected and is priced by shareholders, a utilitarian-type defense is no doubt possible. Indeed, the fact that such a defense could conceivably be made further illustrates the ambiguity of Enlightenment moral philosophy. This school provides no clear direction for the accommodation of ethics in finance.

Futile is not too strong a word, therefore, with which to label any attempt to imbue the mathematical objective functions of business vis-à-vis the modernist Technical Universe with some ethic derived from Enlightenment approaches. In short, the conceptual logic from which the six axioms of the finance paradigm are drawn is simply irreconcilable with these conventional ethics. On closer inspection, therefore, despite its fiery rhetoric in corporate codes and business ethics textbooks, the attempt to build a moral manager on the foundations of Enlightenment philosophy in fact collapses into incommensurability and incoherence. The deafening silence prevails.

THE PRESCRIPTIVE DESIRABILITY OF OPPORTUNISM

But is there not perhaps another approach, perhaps a more feasible approach to invoking a modernist moral manager? Rather than attempting to replace the opportunistic technician of Part I by a moral manager, might it not be more feasible to use modern moral philosophy to defend the moral worth of the technician? That is to say, might it not be possible to construct a moral defense of the rational technician of Part I? Regardless of the descriptive accuracy of opportunism, could we as modernists not perhaps defend this as how agents *should* behave? This question can be interpreted from either an economic or a moral perspective. Are these agents economically efficient? Are these agents morally desirable?

In the case of economic efficiency, Chapter 2 made clear that opportunistic agents inevitably engender equilibria that are inefficient in that wealth is not maximized either for the agents involved or for the economy in aggregate. The equilibria are "second best." But, regardless of their economic efficiency, are opportunists morally desirable?

Even the most cursory review of ethical theory reveals that opportunism is not a favorable behavioral attribute. About the best moral defense that one could make is that it is harmless: it is merely a behavioral assumption that expedites finance theory and has no impact on actual behavior. But, as we've already seen, even within their theoretical constructs, these agents are not harmless in that they levy a cost on the financial system. More important from a moral perspective, several recent empirical studies find evidence that these behavioral assumptions have influence beyond the boundaries of financial modeling. These studies find that the assumptions of financial theory influence financial practice: "Is" does indeed imply "ought." For example, from his experience as a business professor, Bowie (1991) supplies anecdotal evidence that exposure to this narrow rationality paradigm and related rubrics modifies behavior: "They [business school students] believe that they will have to be unethical to keep their jobs. They believe that everyone else will put their [own] interests first" (p. 9). But he goes on to note that "the evidence here is not merely anecdotal. . . . [E]conomics graduate students are more inclined to behave in a self-interested fashion" (p. 9).

For example, in one recent study involving 267 prisoners' dilemma–type scenarios, economics students defected (i.e., failed to cooperate) 60 percent of the time, whereas noneconomists defected only 30 percent of the time. Also, when compared to students in different disciplines, economics students were found to be less honest in hypothetical situations, and both economics students *and professors* were found to be less likely to donate to charity (Frank, Gilovich, and Regan, 1993). Bowie (1991) observes that "people change their behavior when confronted with assumptions about how other people behave" (p. 9). In "Challenging the Egoistic Paradigm," he concludes that "[l]ooking out for oneself is a natural, powerful motive that needs little, if any, social reinforcement. . . . Altruistic motives, even if they too are natural, are not as powerful: they need to be socially reinforced and nurtured" (p. 19). Such nurturing is not to be found in the behavioral assumptions of finance.

In a broader context, the susceptibility and suggestibility of human behavior were made very clear in the famous laboratory experiments conducted by Stanley Milgram (1974). In these experiments volunteers were asked to administer progressively larger electric shocks to some individual. Even though these volunteers could see the "victim" in considerable distress from the shocks, the volunteers were generally willing to administer ever higher voltages, given the encouragement of an "authority figure." Milgram concluded:

Ordinary people, simply doing their jobs, and without any particular hostility on their part, can become agents in a terrible destructive process. . . . [E]ven when the destructive effects of their work become patently clear, and they are asked to carry out actions incompatible with fundamental standards of morality, relatively few people have the resources needed to resist authority. (p. 6)

Similarly, Gregory Dees (1992) argues that the value systems of business theory influence those of business practice. He observes that "how concepts are introduced in an academic setting can have a significant influence on their use later on" (p. 38). While commenting on the value system underlying business theory, Ronald Duska notes that "as it gets accepted as a legitimating reason for certain behavior in our form of life, it becomes subtly self-fulfilling" (p. 149). Thus, the finance paradigm presents itself as morally neutral but fails to recognize that its narrow and rigid invocation of self-interest has *moral* implications. MacIntyre (1984a) makes a similar point:

Managers themselves and most writers about management conceive of themselves as morally neutral characters whose skills enable them to devise the most efficient means of achieving whatever end is proposed. Whether a given manager is effective or not is in the dominant view a quite different question from that of the morality of the ends which his effectiveness serves or fails to serve. Nonetheless there are strong grounds for rejecting the claim that effectiveness is a morally neutral value. (p. 74)

Models developed within the finance paradigm, therefore, do not merely endeavor to explain observed phenomena. To a significant degree they create those phenomena. When, in their seminal article, Jensen and Meckling (1976) propose that managers' thirst for perquisites at the expense of firm value is as inevitable as "a world in which iron ore is a scarce commodity" (p. 328), they make a value judgment: They promote increased perquisite consumption by managers who no longer bear the full cost of that consumption as the right mode of behavior. They make a value judgment concerning the behavioral prerogatives of management. They do not attempt merely to describe reality but to—however inadvertently—shape it. So by assuming that the only reasonable motivation for human behavior is personal wealth maximization, the financial paradigm has sanctioned and promoted such behavior among the financial community. Although many practitioners and theorists realize the need for ethics in finance, the financial paradigm's conceptual rigidity has led them to view ethics only within this light. This has resulted in a fatal dilution of ethical precepts. Ethics is forced into the subservient and ambiguous role of merely supporting some fundamental materialistic objective.

By assuming away other motivations and thus elevating wealth maximization to the status of a necessary law of nature, finance may be sanctioning behavior that society at large regards as at best morally questionable and at worst downright criminal. In the corporate milieu, by assuming unbridled self-interest, finance promotes unbridled self-interest. Furthermore, even if empirical evidence were to overwhelmingly support wealth maximization as the dominant motivation among contemporary economic agents (which, as we've just seen, it does not), finance's normative dimension would still obligate it to consider alternatives.

BUT WHY CAN'T EXISTING FINANCE THEORY ACCOMMODATE ETHICS?

Consider our die-hard financial economist again. He (as we saw in Chapter 1, he probably would be a "he") might well remain unmoved by our argument so far. He might retort that through the aforementioned reputation effect rational agents in finance do exhibit ethical-type behavior such as cooperation and honoring contracts. He might argue that the apparent schism between ethics and finance that I have conjured here is, at root, illusory. I have, he might argue, in effect constructed a "straw man."

The argument has indeed been made that financial markets do in fact have some implicit control mechanism that sanctions unethical behavior. An excellent example of this argument is Clifford Smith's (1992) analysis of the investment banking firm of Salomon Brothers in the wake of its Treasury bond bid-rigging scandal. Treasury bonds are initially issued through an auction market. Smith summarizes the process as follows:

When auctioning Treasury bonds, the U.S. Treasury awards them first to the highest bidder at its quoted price, then moves to the next highest bidder. This process continues until the issue is exhausted. If the Treasury receives more than one bid at the price that exhausts the issue, it allocates the remaining bonds in proportion to the size of the bid. Treasury auction rules limit the amount of an issue sold to a single bidder to 35% of the issue. (p. 3)

In an endeavor to circumvent this 35 percent rule and to, in effect, corner the market for a given bond issue, Salomon's bond-trading desk submitted bids under the names of some of its customers without the customers' prior authorization thereby making one large bid under the auspices of several smaller bids. When these clandestine activities became known to the public, Salomon found itself embroiled in a classic Wall Street scandal.

Smith tallies the economic costs incurred by Salomon as a result of the Treasury bond bidding scandal. Smith attributes these costs to Salomon's tarnished *reputation for trustworthiness* among the financial community. He notes that a reputation for trustworthiness in investment banking has economic value. This value stems from the reduced uncertainty involved in dealing with an agent who has demonstrated a consistent mode of behavior in the past. Salomon's unscrupulous T-bond bidding activities represented a breach of trust between it and its stakeholders. This breach of trust increased the market's perception of the risk involved in doing business with Salomon. This, in turn, lowered the market's valuation of Salomon's reputability, as reflected in a lowered stock price and reduced underwriting revenues. Thus, the recent history of Salomon can be summarized in three stages:

1. Over the years, by demonstrating a consistent mode of dependable behavior, Salomon had built a reputation for trustworthiness and expertise in its investment banking activities. This reputation had real economic value as reflected in a higher stock price and underwriting revenues.

2. Some employees of Salomon chose to free-ride on this reputation. They in essence exploited lax enforcement of rules governing Treasury bond auctions.

3. The subsequent revelation of these individuals' activities caused outsiders to revalue Salomon's reputation for trustworthiness. This revaluation was reflected in Salomon's lowered stock price and underwriting revenues.

Note that the scenario described here is strictly economic. But in the title of his article, in addition to the word "economics," Smith uses the word "ethics." He goes on to imply that financial markets *punished* Salomon for its *unethical* behavior and that this punishment took the form of the economic costs incurred by Salomon as a result of the scandal. Smith implies, therefore, that financial markets are not merely an economic mechanism but also a moral one.

But is this the most plausible explanation for the market's reaction? Is it not far more plausible to explain all these events in strictly economic terms, as above, without recourse to moral censure? "Reputation" as a morality-based concept implies more than merely a dollar value placed on behavioral consistency. Clearly, financial markets and the individuals that comprise them *value* reputation in an economic sense—hence, Salomon's postscandal stock price decline. But Smith fails to realize that this says nothing about whether or not these individuals value reputation in a *moral* sense. In order to address this question, we must look beyond the actions of individuals. We must, instead, focus on the underlying *motivation* for the observed action.

In the wake of the scandal, when individual market participants sold Salomon's stock or chose not to avail themselves of Salomon's investment banking services, was their *motivation* economic? If the answer to this question is yes, then these actions have nothing to do with ethics. We may observe financial markets valuing a reputation for trustworthiness, just as they value dividend consistency and timely debt repayment, but what they are valuing is the reduced uncertainty engendered by the observed action. Indeed, even if they did want to value ethics, investors would be very naive to do this on the basis of an agent's observed action. Clearly, an agent who acts in a trustworthy manner could be doing so for economic, not ethical, reasons.

ENTER WARREN BUFFETT

Interestingly, this ambiguity concerning the ethical versus economic concept of reputation was highlighted in the wake of the above scandal by Warren Buffett in a statement made shortly after his appointment as the interim chairman of Salomon Brothers. While testifying before the House Telecommunications and Finance Subcommittee, he gave the following warning, to paraphrase: "If I hear of an employee losing the company money, I'll be understanding. However, If I hear of any employee losing Salomon one shred of reputation, I'll be ruthless!"

This powerful and concise message garnered kudos from the financial community. The popularity of Mr. Buffett's declaration presumably stems from a belief, both on and off Wall Street, that abuse of financial regulations—either in letter or in spirit—has become far too prevalent in recent years. By elevating reputation above profits, therefore, Mr. Buffett is seen as resurrecting the heretofore downtrodden banner of honesty and integrity among financial practitioners. But how exactly is Mr. Buffett defining "reputation" here? Is this economic reputation vis-à-vis the finance paradigm or some deeper reputation concept?

The various motivations for acquiring a reputation provide a good example of the financial paradigm's conceptual rigidity. Mr. Buffett's statement can be used to demonstrate why this paradigm affords no place for ethics. Consider the statement's meaning within the finance paradigm. The concept of "reputation" was clearly defined in Chapter 2:

A reputation is a behavioral trait. A firm builds a reputation by demonstrating a consistent mode of behavior through a series of contractual situations. Once built, a reputation increases the value of implicit claims sold by the firm to stakeholders. Thus, a firm's desire to earn future profits by maintaining its reputation may act as an implicit contractual enforcement mechanism.

Thus, firms build and maintain reputations in order to garner future profits. Reputation is defined in purely materialistic terms. Finance's underlying precept remains intact, namely, that the objective of all activity within the firm should be directed at maximizing firm value. Reputation building is solely another means to this end.

Applying this precise definition of "reputation" to Mr. Buffett's statement renders its logic circular: Tarnishing the firm's reputation and losing the firm money become synonymous. One way to possibly salvage some meaning from the statement is to assume that tarnishing Salomon Inc.'s reputation would lose the firm a very large amount of money, perhaps through the loss of significant future profits and a dramatic stock price decline. Given this interpretation, Mr. Buffett is merely stating that if employees lose a modest amount of money, he will be understanding, whereas if they lose a large amount of money, by tarnishing the firm's reputation, he will be ruthless.

This interpretation, however, is clearly a distortion of the statement's original intent. It is certainly not how the statement was interpreted by the financial community. The distortion stems from finance's narrow definition of "reputation." But the underlying behavioral assumptions of finance force it to define "reputation" in this way.

The Technical Universe of financial economics is premised on the assumption that the underlying objective of all economic agents is the accumulation of personal wealth. Thus, although agents may act in an apparently ethical manner (they may be trustworthy, for example), they may not be motivated fundamentally to act in a trustworthy manner; the only reason for trustworthiness is that it may increase personal wealth; the motivation is always personal material gain. One possible reason, therefore, for an apparent lack of ethical conduct among financial practitioners is engendered by financial theorists: The finance paradigm's assumption that motivations other than personal wealth maximization are irrational may send a dangerous message to the financial community.

Clearly, Mr. Buffett was attempting to send a different message. He was looking beyond the narrow economic definition of "reputation." His intent was to invoke some moral standard that goes above and beyond the profit motive. In order to clarify this intent, his statement could be usefully rephrased as follows: "If I hear of an employee tarnishing Salomon's reputation through ineptitude or bad luck, I'll be understanding. However, if I hear of any employee losing Salomon one shred of its reputation through unethical behavior, I'll be ruthless!"

For example, Mr. Buffett would be only moderately upset with an employee who, through lack of experience and expertise, misprices an initial public offering (IPO): Salomon has a reputation for accurately pricing IPOs, and this agent's error will undoubtedly tarnish Salomon's reputation in this regard; but the problem here stems from the agent's ability, not her motivation; the agent is inept, but assuming that she was attempting to price the issue accurately, she is not unethical.

Contrarily, Mr. Buffett would be *very* upset with an employee who knowingly overpriced an IPO in order to enrich Salomon at the expense of outside (less-well-informed) investors. The problem with this employee is clearly not that he is inept, nor does the problem lie in the employee's allegiance to the company (i.e., an agency problem): if the employee believed that such action would significantly increase underwriting revenues and that any reputation costs—should the activity be discovered—were likely to be outweighed by these increased revenues, then his actions and motivation are consistent with shareholder wealth maximization. The problem with this individual is purely and simply that he is unethical in a modernist deontological sense: The fact that he is willing to deceive in pursuit of profit betrays a predisposition to circumvent generally accepted ethical standards. More fundamentally, this employee may be characterized as one whose primary motivation is material gain rather than some "higher" form of excellence. But what is meant here by "excellence"? Surely a certain amount of deception is just an inevitable and accepted facet of doing business? Anyway, is this morally inclusive "excellence" a reasonable objective to have in a business environment?

Before addressing these questions by defining "excellence," some clarification of the argument so far may be useful. One might reasonably ask, from a practical standpoint, Why does the agent's motivation matter? The above analysis may be of interest to moral philosophers, but surely—from a practical perspective—all that really matters is whether or not the employee acts in a trustworthy manner. As long as the employee upholds the firm's reputation for trustworthiness, then this question of whether her motivation is primarily economic or moral is purely *academic* (i.e., irrelevant).

I would counter this argument as follows. From a practical perspective, the agent's underlying motivation matters because an agent who is not motivated to act ethically will sooner or later act unethically. An agent whose primary motivation is material gain will only act in a trustworthy manner for as long as she believes that such action is in her material best interests. She will readily sacrifice her reputation and the firm's reputation when she believes that such action is economically optimal. Game theorists label this point the endgame, at which time the agent adopts a ripoff strategy (i.e., cashing in one's reputation for an immediate payoff). Thus, a reputation for trustworthiness built for economic reasons can be a very fragile edifice.

But, returning to Mr. Buffett's statement, our analysis presents an interesting paradox. His statement essentially places ethics above profits: he does not mind about employees losing the firm some money so much as he minds if they are unethical. But even the most casual reflection indicates that there are situations in which unethical behavior is economically optimal (in game theory, for example, ripoff strategies and the like are often the optimal strategies in competitive games).

Mr. Buffett's declaration, therefore, is not necessarily in the interests of shareholder wealth maximization. As agent to shareholders, Buffett is presuming that shareholders en masse also wish to place ethics above profits—a noble presumption but clearly contrary to the assumptions of financial-economic theory. This brings our discussion full circle by addressing the original question of whether Salomon's stock price decline in the wake of the T-bond bidding scandal was the result of moral outrage or economic adjustment. What was the primary motivation of shareholders in selling Salomon's stock?

Most market practitioners would undoubtedly agree that the primary motivation behind this or any stock price adjustment is economic rather than ethical; but this fact does not make market participants unethical. Financial markets are economic mechanisms. It would be highly disruptive and ineffectually arbitrary for shareholders en masse to act as some moral police force. Ethics is too complex to identify and too personal to be punished and rewarded in a marketplace, particularly in light of the fact that the majority of today's shareholders—certainly the majority of Salomon's shareholders—are themselves institutions with economic obligations to their respective stakeholders. Enticing agents to act ethically through economic rewards and punishments will only encourage superficially ethical acts, not ethical motivations.

Ethics, like charity, begins at home. Specifically, it begins with a process of educating individuals about ethics and the moral ideal. But what form exactly should this education take? How, for example, can the logical and sophisticated minds of senior executives in an investment bank—handling billions of dollars on a daily basis—be convinced of the absolute superiority and desirability of ethical motivations over and above all others?

THE "CONFIDENCE SCHOOL": A FALSE JUSTIFICATION FOR ETHICS

Many listeners understood Mr. Buffett's intent in using the concept of reputation. "Reputation" was not meant to be defined in a manner consistent with finance theory, but rather in broader terms. Reputability was envisaged as possessing some intrinsic quality, beyond mundane materialism. But in a world where material gain is the measure of all things, what role can reputation possibly play except that of a vehicle for material gain?

The Confidence School represents an attempt to answer this question within the confines of finance. It attempts to justify and promote ethics as a necessary constraint on the ultimate objective of wealth maximization. But, albeit popular in current discourse, it is a corruption of the ethical ideal.

As the name implies, the Confidence School argues that scandals within the financial community—like that recently perpetrated by some employees of Salomon—erode confidence in financial markets. Over time, a loss of confidence could result in fewer market participants, which would lower the efficiency of financial markets as a vehicle for allocating risk and generating wealth. Thus, ethical behavior is desirable because it maintains confidence.

This confidence justification for ethics, therefore, views ethical behavior as a type of lubricant in the financial machine: actions are unethical if they inhibit economic efficiency. A simple dialectic can illustrate this argument's logical ambiguity. Assume that the questioner is an employee of Salomon Inc. and the respondent is a business ethicist of the Confidence School:

Q. As an employee of Salomon Inc, my job is to maximize the value of the company. Given that I believe that I can make more money for the company in a given situation by acting in a manner that is generally regarded as unethical (being dishonest, for example), why should I act ethically? Specifically, I am cognizant of the fact that the firm's reputation has economic value and that unethical behavior may tarnish this reputation. However, I believe that the economic benefits of my behavior will outweigh the possible economic costs to the firm. Thus, my unethical action is entirely consistent with financial theory.

R. It is entirely possible that your unethical actions may increase firm value, even net of reputation costs. However, the likely revelation of your unethical conduct, at some future time, will lead to a loss of confidence in financial markets.

Q. Given my fiduciary responsibility to Salomon Inc.'s shareholders, why should I put the objective of maintaining financial market confidence above that of maximizing firm value?

R. Salomon Inc. is part of the financial marketplace—a very significant part. If you damage financial markets, you will therefore be damaging Salomon Inc.'s future earning potential.

Q. But you already conceded that my actions may increase firm value. You are merely implying that I must add another variable to my decision—namely, the possibility that my unethical action will lower firm value through some loss of confidence in the financial system as a whole. What if I believe that my action, albeit dishonest, will maximize firm value, net of reputation costs to Salomon and "loss-of-confidence" costs to the system as a whole?

R. Then, by my definition of ethics, your action is ethical.

Q. So dishonesty or deception, if it does not lead to a significant loss of confidence in the financial system, is ethical?

R. Correct.

This simple example illustrates the tenuous nature of ethics in the Confidence School. If ethics is merely a constraint in the wealth maximization rubric, then an individual may easily rationalize unethical behavior given some low-probability estimate of information disclosure or public concern. As Sherwin Klein (1988) observes, this Confidence School justification for ethics has led to a moral schizophrenia among the financial community: "Corporate people, then, function according to a double standard—amorally as an official of an organization and morally as a private person" (p. 63).

Given this logic, therefore, in governing business behavior, "ethics"—together with legal and economic factors—becomes just one of many constraints.

THE ROOT OF THE PROBLEM

Any failure to find an adequate justification for ethics has certainly not been through lack of trying. If the growth industry of business ethics consulting is any guide, the idea that corporate behavior should be ethically motivated, as well as financially motivated, is becoming increasingly popular and increasingly voiced. For example, the Harvard Business School recently received a $30 million grant to fund a new program in Ethics and Leadership, whereas many other business schools are implementing similar programs.

This increasing popularity is probably due in part to the recent scandals on Wall Street and in the trading pits of Chicago and also due to a general conception that over the past few decades individuals have become increasingly motivated to maximize personal wealth without regard to religious or other moral strictures. Recent financial scandals include the Bank of Credit and Commerce International's (BCCI) money laundering and financing of organized crime, the excessive lending practices of U.S. savings and loans, fueled by unrestricted federal deposit insurance, insider trading and unauthorized trading scandals involving prominent individuals (Nigel Leeson, Ivan Boesky, Dennis Levine, and Micheal Milken) and institutions (Drexel Burnham Lambert); and Salomon Inc.'s manipulation of the Treasury note auction market. There are many others. In the context of securities trading, for example, the Securities and Exchange Commission (SEC) estimates that it successfully identifies only a small fraction of all insider trading activity.

In addition, recent financial scandals are by no means limited to the United States Japan, for example, which in the 1980s temporarily overtook the United States as the largest financial market in the world in terms of the total value of securities traded, has had its fair share. Sumitomo Bank, one of Japan's largest, has recently been connected with financing organized crime and nepotism among its senior executives. Industrial Bank of Japan (IBJ), Fuji Bank, and Tokai Bank all appear to have been involved in excessive real estate speculation and the related forgery of deposit verification documents. The major scandal currently rocking the Japanese securities industry involves the paying of compensation to large investors who have lost money in the recent equity market downturn. These compensation payments were made by brokerage houses in order to retain large customers. For example, the big four brokerages, Daiwa, Nikko, Nomura and Yamaichi, paid 128.3 billion yen in compensation to large clients in 231 incidents. "Even after the Ministry of Finance specifically directed the firms not to compensate their clients, from April 1990 to March 1991, another 43.5

billion yen was paid out in 78 separate incidents" (Okai, 1991, p. 4). Another recent scandal in Japan's securities markets concerns Nomura and Nikko, the two largest brokerage houses. Both have been identified as having links to organized crime. Specifically, "in October 1989 Nomura . . . 'loaned' Mr. Susumu Ishii, the don of Tokyo's most powerful criminal organization—the Inagawa-Kai—16 billion yen, and Nikko 'loaned' him 20 billion yen" (p. 4).

The recent apparent resurgence of interest in business ethics both in the United States and abroad, precipitated no doubt in part by this litany of scandals, has two interesting implications. First, it implies that some form of ethical code is important in business dealings. Second, it implies a general perception that whatever ethical code may have existed in the past is no longer being adhered to. Is our business environment indeed becoming less ethical?

Financial scandals in the United States are often blamed on cultural or regulatory factors. In the case of the former, a tradition in the United States of individualism and wealth as the ultimate measure of success is often cited as the cause of financial scandals. Also, U.S. insider trading laws—the most stringent in the world—are blamed for driving insider trading activity underground unnecessarily. Japan, for example, has minimal insider-trading regulations.

If financial scandals were limited to the United States, then these cultural and regulatory arguments might be vindicated. But as the Japanese examples clearly illustrate, the "scandalization" of financial markets has not been limited to the United States. Japan and other Eastern markets have experienced similar phenomena. It appears, therefore, that one needs to look beneath the surface of Western individualism and materialism when attempting to account for these egregious activities. Consider the following three factors:

1. *Dehumanization of financial markets.* As discussed earlier, the existence of imperfect markets is a necessary condition for reputations to have value. But if substantial asymmetries of information exist between stakeholder groups, the relative value of building a reputation will be diminished because opportunistic behavior will not be exposed. As a necessary condition for reputation effects, the efficient flow of information is even more critical in contemporary corporate culture where individual stakeholders rarely, if ever, meet repeatedly on a face-to-face basis. It is essential, therefore, that the information gleaned from the experiences of one stakeholder be made generally available. Alas, informational asymmetries are so pervasive in our financial markets that the necessary track record of individuals and institutions is often not generally available.

Specifically, computerization of stakeholder interactions has dramatically reduced the frequency with which individual stakeholders deal with each other on a face-to-face basis. In addition, the increasing size of our corporate culture means that any individual is less likely to deal more than once with any other individual. Thus, the impersonalization of corporate culture has increased the incentives for individual stakeholders to breach any generally accepted moral code. This dehumanizing trend supplies the central weakness in Frank's *Passions within Reason* (1988) argument, to be discussed in detail shortly, and it is also the source of reputation's impotence as a sufficient contractual enforcement mechanism in contemporary markets.

2. *A short-term consciousness.* Building a reputation generally entails immediate sacrifice in the expectation of future compensatory gains. It is clearly inconsistent, therefore, with behavior designed solely to attain short-term goals. U.S. corporate culture, however, appears to be increasingly motivated toward such myopia.

For example, the continual threat of takeover is forcing corporate managements to adopt short-term defensive strategies such as leveraged buyouts. These strategies encumber firms with burdensome debt loads that require immediate and continual cash flows to service. Similarly, the rapid growth of financial futures and options has given contemporary securities markets a casino atmosphere where short-term program-trading strategies, such as index arbitrage, create volatility and uncertainty in markets originally designed as a means by which corporations could raise capital for the pursuit of long-term goals.

In addition, the increasing secularization of society in general tends to shorten goal horizons. For example, the Protestant work ethic has traditionally espoused hard work combined with an ascetic lifestyle in order to attain a long-term goal of building wealth for future generations. Indeed, it was this work "ethic" that fueled the Industrial Revolution in eighteenth-century Europe: steam engines, built to power factory machinery in the late eighteenth century, still run smoothly today; these machines were built by individuals with both a long-term horizon and a commitment to quality in mind. Their construction contrasts sharply with contemporary designed-obsolescence manufacturing techniques.

Another implication of this growing substitution of a "corporate" culture for one based on religious belief is the disappearance of any meaningful *faith-based* moral stricture. This point is made eloquently by Donald T. Campbell (1986):

Rewarding and punishing reincarnations and afterlives promise individuals a net hedonic gain optimized over a longer period than their own immediate lives. . . . Belief in an afterlife was fundamental in protecting the production of protective goods against the erosion of individually optimizing free riding. . . . [If] in the past market mechanisms . . . have worked well, it is because of the helpful residue of such awed indoctrination and moral restraint. (p. 361)

Thus, the general adherence to some arbitrary moral stricture, whether based on religious tradition or otherwise, appears to be no longer a valid assumption in contemporary stakeholder relations. This point is echoed in a recent book by Amatai Etzioni (1988) who attempts to imbue rationalistic contemporary economic theory with a "moral dimension." He argues that the more stakeholders operate purely on the basis of economic self-interest, "the more the ability to sustain a market economy is undermined."

3. *Diminished sense of individual responsibility.* The regulatory environment in which business operates is being increasingly relied upon to explicitly enforce stakeholder contracts, thus diminishing the perceived importance of a moral code's role in this regard. Stakeholders are relying on government agencies, such as the SEC and the Environmental Protection Agency (EPA) to regulate generally accepted ethical norms. As a result, stakeholders feel a diminished responsibility to make ethical choices for themselves: "If it's legal, then it's ethical" is a temptingly simple ethos by which agents may judge their behavior. Undoubtedly, government regulations are designed to enforce generally accepted ethical procedures. Such a simple ethos, however, assumes that government agencies are able to adequately regulate all areas of business behavior and foresee all possible moral contingencies. Given the multiplicity and ephemeral nature of many implicit contracts in business, this is clearly an unreasonable assumption, particularly when one considers the high degree of informational asymmetry that is generally present.

This generally increasing reliance on explicit contractual enforcement via government fiat has been paralleled by an increasing reliance on the legal system to enforce contracts. For example, Earl Fry (1989) characterizes the United States as suffering from a "Litigious Affliction." He argues that "too many people and corporations are resolving their differences in the adversarial-structured legal system" (p. 44); stakeholders are endeavoring to substitute the explicit legal system for an implicit business ethic.

As discussed in Chapter 2, however, there are two fundamental caveats to a corporate culture founded primarily on the rule of law: cost and enforceability. A litigious business environment is expensive in a direct sense with legal fees and lost work time; however, it is also expensive in an indirect way. As Fry observes, "U.S. schools are currently graduating 10 lawyers for each engineer, whereas Japanese schools are graduating 10 engineers for each lawyer" (p. 44). Thus, an ever-expanding legal system exerts both a financial and a human drain on an economy's resources.

In addition to cost, there is the problem of enforceability. For example, recent evidence has demonstrated that the mere existence of laws prohibiting insider trading will not prevent insiders from trading illegally. With no moral code, illegal trading activities are undertaken whenever the probability of getting caught seems remote. If the threat of legal action is the sole restraint on opportunistic behavior, then this threat must be perceived as imminent. Monitoring costs, therefore, become significant, not to mention the distasteful specter of a "Big Brother"–type infringement into what many regard as a constitutional right to privacy. Consequently, for reasons of both expense and enforceability, a business environment characterized by an abundance of civil lawsuits would seem to be a poor substitute for one based on voluntary adherence to a moral code.

A HISTORICAL PERSPECTIVE

One might question our discussion so far by noting that ethical scandals are by no means unique to the business world of today. Economic history provides many examples of unethical behavior between stakeholders. The South-Sea Bubble, an incident in the early eighteenth century in which unscrupulous brokers sold shares in a fictitious company to unsuspecting investors, provides an early example of contractual failure between stakeholders in a diversely held company. More recently, one of the primary factors contributing to the Great Crash of 1929 was the unethically excessive use of margin lending by brokerage houses. Unethical behavior, therefore, is clearly not unique to present-day financial markets.

There is, however, a discernible difference between past and present views on ethical violations in business. Even though many instances of unethical behavior have occurred throughout business history, there has also been a general consensus on the need for some form of moral code governing business dealings. But, in contemporary aesthetic markets, there appears to be no general consensus on this point. In addition, even among advocates of some form of moral code, there is widespread disagreement as to what form this code should take (Milton Friedman's "the social responsibility of business is to increase its profits" versus Norman Bowie's "the primary objective . . . is to provide meaningful work for employees"). This profound and irremedial disagreement provides further evidence for the managerial paradigm shift—from modern to aesthetic—predicted here.

The current debate surrounding business ethics, therefore, is not simply whether stakeholders should act ethically or be value neutral, but rather whether a universal moral code exists by which stakeholders can judge their actions. If morality is strictly relative, then who is to say what is ethical versus unethical? If there is no generally accepted moral code governing stakeholder behavior, then an ethic of trust or honesty—as an implicit contractual enforcement mechanism—becomes impotent.

In short, trust, and ethics generally, lies beyond the finance paradigm because for trust to work it must have intrinsic value to agents: agents must honor trust for trust's sake, not for the sake of some anticipated future material gain. If only the latter applies, then trust becomes as fragile as the economic concept of reputation defined in Chapter 2. But, as was made clear earlier, a rational agent within the Technical Universe of the finance paradigm is strictly one who pursues material objectives only. In essence, therefore, with the deconstruction of the Enlightenment, the challenge that modern business faced was one of rationalizing trust or fairness or any moral concept as an objective *in itself.* The management paradigm of the Technical Universe cannot escape the epistemological fallout resulting from the collapse of Enlightenment morality. The Technical and Moral Universes are two dimensions within the same modernist rubric; both universes rest fundamentally on modernist instrumental rationality and logic, so neither universe is immune from the aesthetic deconstruction of these paradigms.

TEST CASE: PEPSI/BURMA

And what of our test case? Could not the management of Pepsi have employed the modernist principles of utilitarianism or ISCT in order to make its decision of whether to pull out of Burma?

If Pepsi's management were to apply ISCT, then it would analyze its operations in Burma to see if any "hypernorms" (i.e., moral absolutes) were being violated. Donaldson and Dunfee (1994) describe these hypernorms as:

• Core human rights, including those to personal freedom, physical security and well-being, political participation, informed consent, and ownership of property, the right to subsistence; and

• The obligation to respect the dignity of each human person. (Fritszche, 1997, p. 44)

A rigid application of this hypernorm principle could well have led Pepsi to pull out of Burma. Burma is a military dictatorship in which the Western notions of democratic human rights and freedom are not honored.

But I see three problems with Pepsi using ISCT's hypernorm principle to make this kind of decision. The first problem is ideological and was discussed above, namely, By what absolute authority does ISCT claim validity for these absolute moral principles born of modernist philosophy? Human rights are an invention of eighteenth-century Enlightenment philosophy and are continually open to amendment: What about animal rights, environmental rights, the rights of the as yet unborn, the rights of the dead? Similarly, the Western notion of individual freedom is likewise an Enlightenment invention: What exactly is it, and is it a "good" thing that we in the West should foist on everyone else? Even within the modernist period, the notion of freedom has oscillated wildly. Consider, for example, Hegel's (1942) notion of individual freedom: "[I]n duty the individual finds his liberation . . . from dependence on mere natural impulse. . . . In duty the individual acquires his substantive freedom" (p. 149). How different this is to the contemporary Western liberal notion of individual freedom.

In addition to this ideological problem, I see two practical problems that Pepsi would face in applying ISCT. First, consider the practical defense that Western multinationals use to defend their operations in countries that may not adhere to these Western hypernorms, namely, the defense that if the firm were to pull out, it would just make the situation of the native employees worse in terms of these hypernorms—example, a pullout would render the indigenous employess unemployed, financially destitute, homeless to the extent that the multinational was providing housing, unskilled to the extent that the multinational was training them, and uneducated to the extent that the multinational may have been providing educational opportunities. This argument may not have applied to Pepsi in Burma, but it was used with conviction in the 1980s by some companies operating in South Africa. And it is used convincingly today by several multinationals including Nike, Levi-Strauss, and British Petroleum. All of these companies devote significant resources to Westernizing the lives of their Third World employees. Once again, in evaluating the activities of these firms the incoherences of the modernist ethical project show through: Should these firms stay in, or should they pull out? Why should ISCT's hypernorms (whatever exactly they are) be the last word on this? Once again, we are back with the deafening silence. Whether in the form of ISCT or otherwise, from whence does the moral "ought" of modernity derive?

The second practical consideration is simple economic survival. Pulling out of Burma may not seriously impede Pepsi's ability to survive, but what about China? China currently fails to adhere to ISCT's hypernorms, so should all Western companies pull out? As regards Westernizing China, would it not make more sense for these Western firms to expand their influence, both economic and moral, in China? Anyway, simply in terms of practical economics, can these Western multinationals afford to turn their backs on a market of over 1 billion people? Maybe Pepsi, Coke, and others can afford the luxury of applying ISCT in Burma, but China is quite another matter. Note that Levi-Strauss, a company that strives to maintain an image as a paragon of corporate virtue, chose recently (April 1998) to reverse its earlier decision to pull out of China for human rights reasons. So Levi-Strauss, the world's largest clothing manufacturer, is now back in China. In announcing these decisions, whether it was to pull out or stay in, Levi always claimed the highest moral justification, which once again illustrates the elasticity of modernist ethical principles such as ISCT. Depending on which hypernorms are emphasized, and how they are defined, ISCT can be adapted to justify any decision that, at root, is probably economically motivated. It would seem that for many companies the Moral Universe is simply a public relations facade that gives a socially acceptable gloss to business decisions that exist firmly within the Technical Universe.

Indeed, as our discussion has indicated, morality for the modern corporation is very often a luxury that is jettisoned as soon as hard-core economic considerations arise. But, in some way, could not ethics be directly integrated into these hard-core economic criteria? For example, going back to the NPV rule of the Technical Universe, could not this be adapted to accommodate a modernist ethical principle? Just such an accommodation was attempted recently by Marjorie Stanley (1993). She proposes an ethically constrained capital budgeting model:

Applying ethically constrained sensitivity analysis in the capital budgeting procedure, the financial manager would endeavor to determine not only whether or not the net present value is positive, but whether or not the net present value is positive when cash flows are constrained by selected ethical criteria. (p. 101)

But she does not explain exactly what *form* these "selected ethical criteria" would take and who would select them. Would they be deontological or consequentialist or—as with rule utilitarianism—some combination of the two? How would these constraints be integrated into a numerically based evaluation criterion such as the NPV? Can managers realistically assign a dollar value to hypernorms, assuming, that is, that they wish to recognize them? If a hypernorm really is a hypernorm, then would it not rightfully take precedence over any technical decision criterion? Once again, the conceptual impasse between finance and modernist ethics endures. The "ought" of modernity remains epistemologically unjustified. The deafening silence holds sway.

Chapter 4

The Moral Firm

Big organizations do not have simple objectives, and the job of managers is to make balances and tradeoffs among objectives.
—John Kay, "We're All Postmodern Now"

The previous chapter identified the deafening silence of the Moral Universe as a failure to justify the moral "ought" of modernity. This question of justifying the ought of the moral manager is crucial to any justification of the Moral Universe of modernity. Perhaps the most extensive attempt to answer this question to date has come from an amalgamation of the technician with this Moral Universe. Specifically, an attempt has been made to justify ethics on some sort of strategic economic grounds. The manager is seen as part of some stakeholder nexus, and ethics is a means of nurturing this nexus. In the context of business, therefore, the modernist project has attempted to find justification for the ought of the Enlightenment by raising the material goals of the technician to the status of a dominant ontology. Ethics plays a strategic role in economics: one ought to act ethically insofar as it serves one's material economic goals. If this project works—if the union of the two modernist business universes of the moralist and the technician is successful—then this success would negate the central thesis of this book: The modernist project would succeed, the epistemological crisis predicted here would have been avoided, and the aesthetic manager would be superfluous.

In this chapter, I investigate this integration of the modern notion of the manager as technician with the moral manager. To what extent does invoking ethics as strategic economics yield any meaningful concept of ethics? And to what extent does such an integration and invocation remedy the internal deconstruction of the Technical Universe discussed earlier?

THE ECONOMICS OF "STRATEGIC" ETHICS

In Chapter 2, I described the firm in the Technical Universe as a complex network of contractual relations between various interest groups, or stakeholders. Within this network, agents pursue their self-interest, which is defined strictly in terms of individualistic, and opportunistic, wealth maximization. In order to function, the financial milieu must be able to reliably enforce this myriad of contractual relations. Many of these contracts are implicit, and therefore some means of implicit contractual enforcement is crucial.

The only means of implicit contractual enforcement that lies strictly within the Technical Universe of financial-economic theory is reputation. Specifically, given certain conditions, agents will honor implicit contractual arrangements to maintain reputations that will enable them to participate in future contracts. The problem with reputation is that it requires the existence of a certain environment. If this environment does not prevail, then agents will not value their reputations, and opportunism will hold sway, resulting in, at a minimum, inefficiencies (Jensen and Meckling's [1976] "residual loss") or, at worst, a total collapse of financial markets. As an implicit contractual enforcement mechanism, therefore, reputation is quite fragile (Diamond, 1989; Kreps and Wilson, 1982, Milgrom and Roberts, 1982; Rasmusen, 1989). Indeed, I concluded in Chapter 2 that reputation, as the sole means of contractual enforcement, is not enough. Quite simply, financial markets cannot function well and may not function at all without another means of contractual enforcement.

One candidate for this alternative means of contractual enforcement is *trust*. What if agents could simply trust each other to honor contractual agreements? Any rational justification of trust, or of ethics in general, must address the question, Why should I be trustworthy? One way of answering this question is to do so while remaining *within* the six axioms of financial-economic rationality: You should be trustworthy because it is in your long-term material interests to be so. This answer is often abbreviated as, good ethics is good business. Thus, one approach to financial ethics is to study the optimality of ethical behavior in financial contracting models. Within this approach, the six axioms remain entirely intact; ethics becomes a strategy within instrumental rationality for the pursuit of a material substantive-rationality goal.

This strategic concept of ethics is thus very similar to the economic concept of reputation discussed earlier. As we saw in Chapter 2, by behaving consistently in certain ways a firm or agent builds a reputation for trustworthiness; his reputation may have real economic value. For example, a firm that has built a reputation among lenders for a predisposition to make timely debt repayments may be charged a lower interest rate than a firm that has not built such a reputation (Diamond, 1989; John and Nachman,

1985). To the extent that honoring debt contracts may be construed as ethical behavior, then it follows that ethical behavior may have real economic worth. Swanda (1990), for example, notes that "[t]he value of the firm's moral character . . . can result in a market value of the firm that is greater than the firm's net assets" (p. 752). He conjectures that "[e]ven in the short run one can argue that the firm with an excellent ethical reputation can have a special economic advantage" (p. 753). Swanda characterizes this ethical reputation as both an asset and a source of income, as a stock and a flow:

> While morality as a resource cannot be considered in the same context as tangible assets or goods, it can be considered, however, as a highly valuable but volatile asset, one which reflects the perception of the community. . . . In this sense, it will use outflows of resources to establish *stocks* of morality in order to encourage various publics to hold the firm in trust. (p. 757)

Viewing ethical behavior in this strategic light brooks the question of whether agents merely act ethically as a means to an economic end or whether they act ethically simply because they view it as the "right" thing to do. The notion of strategic ethics invoked here implies that ethics is viewed as a means to an end.

A priori, one might think that business ethicists—not to mention moral philosophers—would find this definition of ethics somewhat distasteful in that it tends to corrupt the idea of ethics as a motivation in and of itself. Several leading business ethicists, however, appear to support—perhaps inadvertently—this strategic notion of ethical behavior in business. For example in his recent text *Competing with Integrity in International Business* (1993), Richard De George makes the following statements:

> Competing with integrity does not imply either a reluctance to compete or an inability to compete aggressively. . . . In fact, it demands precisely the institutional discipline that often gives a competitive edge. Competing *successfully* with integrity is in fact the *aim* and the norm of individuals who compete with integrity. (p. 7; my emphasis)

The ultimate objective or "aim" is success, and the moral value of "integrity" is construed as a means to that ultimate end: ethics is strategic. Here De George seems to be implying that the underlying motivation is and should be economic rather than moral. This is "ethics-for profits' sake" rather than "ethics for ethics' sake." In other passages, De George gives further support for this strategic invocation of ethics. When discussing "reputation" for example, he defines "reputation" in economic terms very similar to those used by Swanda: "A reputation as a reliable, ethical company justifiably commands a premium from those who use the company's products or services" (p. 7). Later we are told that "[e]thical action is compatible with profit and success. One might even claim that, to some extent, ethical action explains the success of IBM and Johnson & Johnson" (p. 8). Once again, economic rationales are applied to "sell" business ethics.

A similar justification for ethics can be found in the most recent work of another prominent business ethicist, Robert Solomon, in *The New World of Business: Ethics and Free Enterprise in the Global 1990's* (1994). In the preface, Solomon states that "ethics is not a burden or a business disadvantage but the very ground rules of business as such and the key to business success" (p. xv). So once again ethics is a means to an end, and the end is economic: ethics is construed as the "key to business success." In the book's introduction, Solomon states that "whether or not a corporation designates a portion of its yearly giving to the Environmental Defense Fund or the Sierra Club, it is no doubt keenly aware that being green is a good way to bring in the green" (p. 5)—again implying subtly that such decisions are— and by implication, therefore should be—economically motivated rather than ethically motivated.

Robert Black (1994) provides another example of an ethicist viewing ethics as primarily strategic: "[E]thical behavior will enhance and maintain customer confidence. . . . businesses who do not depend upon ongoing customer relations for continuing revenues need not attend so closely to ethical practices" (p. 361). The action may appear moral, but the motivation is clearly material. Honoring contracts in order to foster "ongoing customer relations for continuing revenues" is economics, not ethics. Another recent example is supplied by LaRue Hosmer (1994): "Let us assume that you accept for now the thesis of this article that acting in ways that can be considered to be 'right' and 'just' and 'fair' is absolutely essential to the long-term competitive success of the firm" (p. 200). Once again, the argument resembles more closely strategic economics than it does moral philosophy.

On the empirical side, two recent studies find evidence that strategic motives underlie what on the surface appear to be ethically motivated decisions. Craig Smith (1994) identifies an economic motivation behind corporate philanthropy: "[T]he strategic use of philanthropy has begun to give companies a powerful competitive edge" (p. 105). As mentioned earlier, Baneish and Chatov (1993) reach similar conclusions. In their study, the content of 160 corporate codes of conduct are analyzed in relation to the firm's business environment; the authors find that "managers choose code content so as to reduce the expected cost of adverse legal or regulatory action" (p. 29). They go on to conclude that "[o]ur findings are consistent with code adoptions and development as good *business* decisions" (p. 29; my emphasis).

From a methodological perspective, the development of a discipline of "financial ethics" along these *strategic* lines will not entail any significant modification to conventional financial contracting models. Indeed, the sizable body of agency theory literature relating to reputation effects in finance lends itself directly to this strategic analysis of ethics. Here we are ignoring motivation and defining ethics purely in terms of the observable act. For example, we may define agents' predisposition to timely debt repayment as "ethical" in the sense that these agents are honoring their contractual obligations. Within the "strategic approach," however, we ignore whether this timely debt repayment was *motivated* by a genuine desire on the part of the agent to be honorable or whether such behavior was merely economically optimal at that time.

Caution must be exercised, therefore, when interpreting the motivation behind apparently benevolent corporate actions such as cooperation, charitable giving, or the development of corporate credos or codes of conduct. The crucial factor here is not observable action but rather the underlying motivation. Indeed, given the superficial nature of this strategic approach to financial ethics, is this really ethics at all or merely strategic economics? By defining ethics in this way, are we diluting the concept of ethics to such an extent that it becomes merely a semantic modification to economic strategy? Are agents who build reputations for trustworthiness because it is in their material self-interest to do so really in any meaningful way ethical? What will these agents do when trustworthiness is not in their material self-interest? Is Robert Frank (1988) correct when he argues that a truly ethical act implies a motivation in which "satisfaction from doing the right thing must not be premised on the fact that material gains may follow; rather it must be intrinsic to the act itself" (p. 254)?

In essence, therefore, the problems with invoking ethics in this strategic role are twofold. First, from a philosophical perspective it seems questionable whether this type of "cooperation in the interests of personal material gain" is really ethics. Second, even if we accept this as ethics, it would seem to be a very tenuous and fragile behavioral trait. Just like reputation in the last chapter, its ability to enforce contracts would be dependent entirely on the agent's belief that such behavior results in personal material gain.

For example, Eric Noreen (1988) recognizes the value of religion or ethical rules as contractual enforcement mechanisms; but these strictures appear to lie beyond finance's "six axioms," and therefore adherence to them is hard to "rationalize." Thus, Noreen concludes that "[b]ehavioral norms (or ethical rules) are clearly a most fragile enforcement mechanism" (p. 367): Opportunistic agents have no rational a priori reason to abide by them.

It may be generally recognized that all agents would benefit from cooperation, but, as Noreen observes, any finite cadre of agents who choose to adopt this cooperative strategy, in the midst of a majority of opportunists, are clearly placing themselves in a very precarious position. In other words, to label the equilibria engendered by the finance paradigm as second-best implies that there is some feasible first-best alternative. But the implied first-best alternative, in which all agents trust one another, surely is logically insupportable since defection in such an environment is sooner or later the most profitable strategy (game theorists call this sooner-or-later point the *endgame*, where defection becomes the dominant strategy). Michael Jensen and William Meckling (1976), in their seminal article "Theory of The Firm," come to a similar conclusion:

[F]inding that agency costs are non-zero (i.e., that there are costs associated with the separation of ownership and control in the corporation) and concluding therefrom that the agency relationship is non-optimal, wasteful or inefficient is equivalent in every sense to comparing a world in which iron ore is a scarce commodity (and therefore costly) to a world in which it is freely available at zero resource cost, and concluding that the first world is "non-optimal"—a perfect example of . . . [a] " 'Nirvana' form of analysis." (p. 328)

But is the notion of a robust cooperative equilibrium so far-fetched that it warrants such dismissive treatment? Robert Frank thinks not. He undertakes just such a " 'Nirvana' form of analysis." In his book *Passions within Reason* (1988), Frank makes an innovative attempt to overcome the dilemma of opportunism while staying essentially within the finance paradigm's rationality construct. Through his "commitment model," Frank argues that acting in one's material self-interest need not be antithetical to acting ethically:

The commitment model is a tentative first step in the construction of a theory of unopportunistic behavior. It challenges the self-interest model's portrayal of human nature in its own terms by accepting the fundamental premise that material incentives ultimately govern behavior. Its point of departure is the observation that persons *directly* motivated to pursue self-interest are often for that very reason doomed to fail. They fail because they are unable to solve commitment problems. (p. 258)

Frank claims that inherently trustworthy agents will inadvertently betray their predisposition through emotional signals, namely, facial expressions and body language. Conversely, the shifty eyes and other uncontrollable emotional signals of opportunists will reveal their underlying motives to the principal. Thus, to paraphrase the title of Frank's book, our uncontrollable "Passions" betray our "Reason."

Frank's commitment model is an innovative attempt to combine economics and ethics so as to avoid the "Sirens' Song" of opportunism. However, the model has two basic flaws. First, emotional signals presumably require face-to-face interaction if they are to enforce contracts. Indeed, in supporting the reliability of emotional signals, Frank refers to one-on-one laboratory sessions of 30 minutes' duration in which interviewers determined the honesty of interviewees. In the contemporary business environment, however, any contractual enforcement mechanism requiring this degree of intimacy has serious limitations; computerization of stakeholder interactions has dramatically reduced the frequency with which individuals deal with each other on a face-to-face basis.

The second flaw in Frank's model is more fundamental. Frank invokes ethics as something beyond rationality. Agents do not choose to become ethical through some logical thought process. Frank merely argues that an agent who is a priori ethical may be no worse off materially than an opportunistic agent. Frank remains within the aforementioned sixth axiom: Unlimited material gain defines completely the agent's objective function. Ethics is merely a means to an end, and the end is material. As with strategic ethics, therefore, his commitment model casts ethics in a role that is both trivial and fragile. It is fragile because the justification of ethics in a material universe rests on the validity of nonmimickable emotional signals. It is trivial because ethics functions only as a tool for the accumulation of personal wealth.

Frank's commitment model is appealing in that ethics appears to find some logical justification within the existing economic rubric. In this regard his model is very similar to the one proposed by Gauthier in *Morals by Agreement* (1988), outlined earlier; in both cases, some form of ethic arises naturally in a competitive market system as agents realize the economic advantages of cooperation. But despite the logical eloquence of these models, they fail to overcome the fundamental dilemma of the strategic approach to ethics. They fail to rationalize ethics as an objective in and of itself.

What in essence is needed to counter Jensen and Meckling's " 'Nirvana' form of analysis" argument, therefore, is some rationalization of trustworthy behavior as an objective *in and of itself*. Even though trustworthy agents may suffer economically, they may consistently offer trust if such behavior has intrinsic value to them. Jones and Quinn (1993) argue that such agents may in fact *not* suffer economically. In an argument similar to that made by Frank, they suggest that "the number of opportunities expands for the person who is intrinsically honest" (p. 7). Thus, an intrinsically honest agent *might* reap economic rewards sufficient to make this an economically optimal strategy. But to make this argument Frank, Gauthier, and Jones and Quinn have to fall back on either emotional signals or reputation. They fail to address the following critical question: What rational mechanism would induce an agent to be intrinsically honest in the face of prisoner's dilemma-type scenarios, that is, in the face of real economic costs? Given the tenuous effectiveness of emotional signals or reputation, economic rationality clearly cannot answer this question: the dominant strategy for an economically rational agent is, sooner or later, opportunism. To rationalize intrinsic honesty, therefore, our focus must shift away from the material payoffs accruing to the agent and toward the agent's fundamental concept of rationality itself. We must, in essence, move beyond economic rationality toward a broadened rationality construct that, albeit a nirvana to some, is no less real. I shall do this in Chapter 5.

A FAILURE TO RATIONALIZE ETHICS

The fundamental weakness of these economic approaches to ethics, therefore, is that they fail to rationalize ethical behavior beyond the pursuit of personal economic gain. This would be fine if economic theory indicated that pseudoethical behavior generally leads to personal economic gain. But economic theory does not indicate this: the prisoners' dilemma, as outlined in Chapter 2, is pervasive. As regards Gauthier and Frank, for example, these models fail to explain why an agent will rationally act ethically. Gauthier's model explains why agents may honor trust some of the time, but his rationale is essentially that of the economic reputation effect discussed earlier: The underlying *motivation* for these agents' actions is economic, not moral. *Morals by agreement* are not morals at all but, rather, a cooperative strategy for economic gain that will presumably be dropped by the agent as soon as it is no longer economically optimal (i.e., in game theory parlance, when the *endgame* is reached). I am not alone in this view. To quote Thomas Donaldson in *The Ethics of International Business* (1989): "[D]o the conclusions generated by self-interested man in the Hobbesian state of nature or in the maximization models used by Gauthier add up to real morality? I am persuaded that they do not" (p. 28).

A similar criticism can be made of Frank's "rationalization" for ethical behavior. Frank gives no *reason* for why an agent would choose to be ethical. In his equilibrium, honest agents and opportunistic agents perform equally well, so presumably in choosing which path to follow, an agent may flip a coin—heads, I'm ethical; tails, I'm not! In short, in Frank's commitment model, some agents simply *are* ethical, and some are not. Frank, like Gauthier, does not *rationalize* ethics.

This failure stems, in large part, from the conceptual limitations of these game-theoretic-type approaches. Modernity tends to view business within the rubric of a game; consequently, the modernist conception of business—whether domestic or international—is provided by the mathematics of strategic game theory. For example, Gauthier's influential book on international business ethics, *Morals by Agreement* (1988), is based entirely on a game-theoretic conception of business.

THE VALUE BASE OF GAME THEORY

Is game theory really a clear methodological lens, or is its use to model business interaction more a case of looking through a glass darkly? In aesthetic vernacular, what is game theory's context? Certainly, game theory's ability to grapple analytically with the complexities of human interaction has made it a valuable tool in contemporary economic theory. But the human interaction modeled in economic game theory has been limited to a relatively simple wealth maximization–type behavior. Was our earlier, game theory–based critique of Enlightenment philosophy really fair, or is game theory really too conceptually narrow to accommodate a truly ethical agent?

Game theory has undoubtedly provided economists with a tool for tackling one of the most pervasive and intractable problems in economics, namely, the modeling of human interaction; game theory has proved particularly popular because it facilitates such modeling in an analytically rigorous manner, thus enabling economists to continue in their quest for scientific accuracy. For example, as noted earlier, in the introduction to his recent book *Games and Information* (1989), Rasmusen notes that "during the 1980s, game theory has become dramatically more important to mainstream economics. Indeed, it seems to be swallowing up microeconomics" (p. 13).

But game theory's analytical rigor comes at a price. Modeling human behavior in this manner requires that the parameters governing human motivation and belief be defined very precisely. The very essence of game theory necessitates human behavior being fully defined by some form of mathematically amenable objective function. Traditionally in economics this objective function defines individuals as narrowly self-interested and goal driven. Game theorists talk in terms of "payoffs," and generally the objective of each player in the game is simply to maximize his or her payoff with no regard to the possible consequences of this behavior on other players. Remember, Hausman and McPherson (1993) comment: "[Game theory] does not rule out altruism or sympathy . . . but it does rule out a collective perspective, a perspective that considers what *we* should do and what the consequences will be for *us*" (p. 718).

But, as we saw in Part I, there is an interesting irony here. Modern economics may have embraced self-interest, but the models built on this assumption do not reflect the economic desirability of self-interest. Indeed, these models invariably demonstrate that individual self-interest is self-defeating, both from the standpoint of the individuals involved and from the standpoint of the economy in aggregate. In short, to use the jargon of game theory, these self-interest–driven equilibria are invariably *second-best*.

By viewing human interaction through the lens of this narrow rationality construct, therefore, game theory has inadvertently strengthened the case for some broadened rationality concept. This is perhaps best illustrated by the agency theory models of financial economics. Even though agents are sufficiently sophisticated to know that such behavior is self-defeating, the nature of the rationality assumption precludes agents from overcoming prisoner's dilemma–type scenarios in which the desirable outcome can never be reached "rationally." The very concept of a "game," implying as it does competitiveness and winners and losers, weights the dice against any morally inclusive notion of rationality. Through constructs such as agency theory, game theory eloquently demonstrates the strategic need for ethics; but it is methodologically ill equipped to accommodate the ethics rubric.

Perhaps ethical agents are not really playing the types of games depicted by traditional game theory. These agents are not amenable to full description in terms merely of payoff functions and information sets. In essence they are involved in a different, more complex and multifaceted game that takes into consideration such "externalities" (more game-theoretic lingo) as human character, duty, justice, compassion, and moral courage. In virtue ethics theory, for example, to be discussed at length in Part III, the notion of self-interest is one totally alien to conventional economic theory. MacIntyre (1988) summarizes this more classical notion of self-interest as follows:

[Aristotelian agents] . . . can certainly be said always to act in their own interests as they understand them, but the interest of an individual is always his or her interest *qua* wife or *qua* host or *qua* some other role. . . . [T]here is not the same contrast between what is to one's own interest and what is to the interest of others as that which is conveyed by modern uses of "self-interest" and cognate terms. (p. 20)

Conventional game theorists would be very hard-pressed to fit this notion of self-interest into any existing model. Indeed, the whole notion of payoff seems inappropriate here since motivation stems from some sense of connectedness and community rather than from some expectation of future economic gain. Here the depth and interdependence of the motivations and the behavior of the agents go beyond mathematical enumeration, which brings to mind Aristotle's (1991) dictum:

Our discussion will be adequate if it achieves clarity within the limits of the subject matter. For precision cannot be expected in the treatment of all subjects alike, any more than it can be expected in all manufactured articles. . . . Therefore, in a discussion of such subjects (the noble, just and good) . . . we must be satisfied to indicate the truth with a rough and general sketch. . . . For a well schooled man is one who searches for that degree of precision in each kind of study which the nature of the subject at hand admits. (pp. 12–27)

Indeed, it is perhaps dangerous to confuse the contrived environments of game theory with real life. In a very fundamental way, real life is not a game. But although game theory is undoubtedly a numerically based modeling tool and—as with all such tools—is limited in its ability to model ethics, it does at least illustrate very clearly the shortcomings of self-interested behavior. In order to reach first-best (i.e., optimal) equilibria, some form of cooperative behavior is essential. The widespread adoption of game theory as the dominant methodology in business theory, therefore, should not be viewed in an entirely negative light. Albeit limited in its ability to accommodate the ethics rubric, game theory does at least illustrate clearly a strategic need for ethics. This is certainly more than can be said for the earlier classical models of economics, which tended to assume away the market imperfections and human attributes that give ethics meaning and purpose.

Indeed, the notion of narrow self-interest being self-defeating is by no means new to moral philosophy; game theory has merely demonstrated this in a particularly rigorous manner. Metaphorically speaking, through its demonstration of the limitations of narrow self-interest, modern game theory has led economists to the waters of moral enlightenment. But game theory alone will not be methodologically sufficient to enable economists to drink of these waters. For this to occur, a richer rubric is required, perhaps one that transcends mathematical enumeration. Before considering such a rubric in the next chapter, however, I would like to further illustrate the complexities of applying modernist ethics to business by looking at a specific finance decision criterion, namely, the abandonment versus continuation decision of capital budgeting. This discussion will have a connection with the ongoing review of the Pepsi/Burma test case since, as mentioned earlier, the latter decision can be viewed through the technician's lens as one of capital budgeting.

TEST CASE: ETHICS IN CAPITAL BUDGETING

Let's go back to the earlier "referendum" example of the project manager endeavoring to choose between locating a petrochemical plant in China or California. A defender of the Technical Universe might argue that any "moral" considerations concerning the environmental impact of the project are irrelevant. The financial manager is purely a technician and should simply apply the standard financial evaluation criteria, such as net present value. This, so our defender of the Technical Universe would argue, is a value-free criterion.

But on closer scrutiny, something like the NPV criterion is clearly not value free. Its application is based on the moral value judgments inherent in the finance paradigm, namely, that the objective of the firm (whatever that is) is to maximize the firm's stock price. As any business ethicist will readily point out, this objective is not a law of nature, nor is it a value-free prerogative.

Thus, even an area of finance as apparently technical as capital budgeting *always* entails moral judgment. Furthermore, the validity or justification of the moral judgment centers not on the action taken but on the motivation underlying the action. At root, therefore, the ethicality of our project manager's decision depends not on where she locates the petrochemical plant but rather on the rational judgment used (i.e., on the motivation) for locating it there. Indeed, for either action there could be several motivations. Let's take a closer look at these motivations. This closer look will reveal just how complex and value laden even the most apparently technical of financial decisions can be.

THE CONTINUATION VERSUS ABANDONMENT DECISION

Agents who abide by the NPV rule are endeavoring to maximize firm value and thus are honoring their fiduciary duty to shareholders. If the firm is taken as the relevant universe, then firm value maximization is consistent with utilitarianism. Given that no deception or unfairness is involved, such a motivation seems readily universalizable vis-à-vis Kant. An agent who abides by the NPV rule under these circumstances, therefore, will be acting ethically. But note that the motivation is strictly economic—strictly within the finance paradigm.

From the perspective of ethics, an agent who acts opportunistically is not motivated by a desire to maximize firm value and is therefore acting unethically from a utilitarian perspective. Given that opportunism may be deceptive, depending upon whether stakeholders expect the agent to act opportunistically, and that such behavior invariably incurs agency costs, it is not a behavioral principle that is readily universalizable.

What if the very nature of the project itself is ethically questionable, such as building the aforementioned petrochemical plant in China with minimal emission controls? Or what if there exist latent costs, such as possible environmental damage, that are not reflected in this standard NPV analysis? Perhaps management rationally continues with an unprofitable project to avoid the negative signaling implications of a project abandonment. The ethics of signaling is complex. Once again, the *motivation* of the agent is the determining factor. Continuing the negative-NPV project in order to avoid the reputation costs associated with an abandonment announcement does appear to involve deception. By not abandoning the project, the manager is depriving the market of information concerning the project's poor performance. But is it deception for the greater good? Because they believe the NPV rule to be misspecified, insiders are suppressing information concerning the fact that the project has a negative NPV. But, in doing this, are insiders merely protecting outsiders from themselves? The project is currently losing the firm money, but a negative signal in the form of an abandonment announcement will lose the firm even more money. Is the deception thus excusable on the utilitarian grounds that it is in the interests of firm value maximization?

More specifically, is the continuation of this project really deceptive? The answer to this question depends upon the expectations of stakeholders. If stakeholders believe and desire that managers abide by the NPV rule, then the agent's choice to continue a negative-NPV project is deceptive. But if stakeholders believe and desire that managers choose whichever action maximizes firm value, then the agent's continuation choice is clearly not deceptive: it is consistent with stakeholders' expectations and wishes.

Alternatively, by delaying the abandonment announcement, are insiders merely buying time for current shareholders to liquidate their holdings at the expense of future shareholders? In this case the abandonment delay represents an agency cost borne by future stakeholders, namely, those with a stake in the firm when the true worth of the project is revealed.

The apparently deceptive nature of the action could make it unethical from a Kantian perspective. The fact that the deception is perhaps in the interests of firm value maximization, however, may render the action ethical in terms of utilitarianism.

The fact that management involves deception does not, in and of itself, render it unethical. To determine the ethicality of the action, the motives behind the deception must be evaluated. An agency problem betrays unethical behavior because the underlying motive is invariably opportunistic. A "deceptive" signal betrays nothing concerning the underlying motivation for the signal. If management believes the NPV rule to be misspecified and thus continues the negative-NPV project in order to maximize firm value qua the RANPV, then the motivation is ethical in the sense that the ultimate objective is firm value maximization. But clearly, because it involves self-deception and serves no greater good, the continuation of an unprofitable project for egocentric reasons is unethical. As Iris Murdoch (1971) sagaciously observes, "[I]n the moral life, the enemy is the . . . ego" (p. 52).

In short, what this illustrates is that even the most apparently "cut-and-dry" type of financial decision may conceal a variety of motivations. All of these motivations have some ethical implications, and the implications are not always readily discernible. Consider, for example, deception. Generally deception is unethical, as in the case of agency problems caused by opportunism, but a possible exception might be a deceptive signal, such as continuing an apparently unprofitable project, that management chooses to emit with shareholders' interests in mind. Even the most "coldly" technical of financial decisions, therefore, such as the continuation versus abandonment decision, may contain a variety of ethical implications.

Of course, in addition to the above motivations, the agent may continue or abandon the project on purely *ethical* grounds. For example, an unprofitable project may be continued because the agent believes that its immediate abandonment will cause severe distress to certain stakeholders: delaying the closure of a factory in order to give employees time to search for alternative employment. Conversely, a profitable project may be abandoned because the agent believes that the nature of the project itself is unethical—for example, the building of the aforementioned petrochemical plant in China. But again, here we are left with this awkward impasse between what seems financially optimal versus what seems ethically justifiable. Enlightenment-based, modernist moral philosophy is simply incapable of bridging this gap between two rival conceptual universes.

THE SOURCE OF THE FAILURE

What is the root cause of the failure of the modernist project? Why does this approach not enable us either to clearly identify the ethical alternative or to justify choosing this alternative over, say, profit maximization?

The root of the problem does not lie simply in our choice of methodology: Game theory merely reflects symptoms of the problems of the modernist technical approach; it does not *cause* the problems. Nor does the root of the problem lie in our methods of application, such as shareholder referendums or corporate credos. Indeed, as we'll see in the next chapter, a corporate credo can be very successful.

No, the problem lies deeper. The problem lies not in finance or economics or game theory but in philosophy.

As with any approach to business ethics, the technical approach relies for its conceptual foundation on moral philosophy. If this foundation is unsound, then the whole application—whether to business ethics, finance ethics, or just applied ethics in general—collapses. As we discussed earlier, the philosophical foundation for the modernist approach—whether deontological or consequentialist—was the Enlightenment. The Enlightenment project, undertaken largely in eighteenth-and nineteenth-century Europe, was in essence an attempt to found ethics on logic and instrumental rationality. It was an attempt to release ethics from religious dogma and to move it into the age of reason. But, as several twentieth-century philosophers have argued, this project failed. Perhaps one of the most comprehensive arguments to that effect is MacIntyre's in *After Virtue* (1984a). In evaluating the Enlightenment project, he concludes:

> The project of providing a rational vindication of morality had decisively failed; and from henceforward the morality of our predecessor culture—and subsequently of our own—lacked any public, shared rationale of justification. In a world of secular rationality religion could no longer provide such a shared background and foundation for moral discourse and action; and the failure of philosophy to provide what religion could no longer furnish was an important cause of philosophy losing its central cultural role and becoming a marginal, narrowly academic subject. (p. 50)

Thus, the failure of modernity stems fundamentally from a lack of any sound philosophical foundation. It fails in its ultimate aim of "rationalizing" ethics. It fails to provide a *motivation* for ethical behavior and so fails to answer the fundamental question, Why should I be ethical? Consider the definition of ethics:

> Ethics concerns behavior. It is the "grammar of behavior." More specifically, ethics concerns the justification for the *motivation* underlying individual action when that action impacts the actions and beliefs of other individuals.

Thus, ethics cuts deep in the sense that it concerns not merely action but also the *motivation* underlying the action. That is why this book takes as its focus the very concept of what constitutes rational behavior within the firm. Simply conducting referendums or imposing codes essentially treats a symptom of the schism between modernist ethics and business but fails to address the cause.

This failure to address ethics at the motivational level is understandable when one considers the complexity involved. Actions are observable; motivations are not. In the arena of corporate governance, therefore, it is far simpler to control and constrain action than it is to sculpt motivation. But then if we don't address motivation, then we are not addressing ethics in any substantive sense.

This really is the normative challenge faced by any aesthetic notion of morality. Given that we have justified ethics in business, we must now find a way to motivate managers to be ethical. Rather than merely imposing some external—and irrational—pseudoethical constraint via a code of conduct, or simply passing the buck through a referendum, we must *endogenize* (i.e., internalize) ethics in business. If moral philosophy comprised the Enlightenment school only, then the absence of ethics in business may be justifiable on the grounds that ethical behavior simply cannot be *rationalized*, that is, cannot be given any ultimate meaning in a secular world; and this is the view shared by many contemporary philosophers and sociologists who are usually somewhat loosely labeled as the aestheticists. Solomon, in *A Brief History of Philosophy* (1996), describes this school as one that has placed moral philosophy in a "holding pattern." Like all new movements in moral philosophy, aestheticists reject all past attempts to justify ethics. But, unlike previous philosophical schools, aestheticists do not generally suggest an alternative; aestheticism is thus often labeled as a philosophy of moral despair.

Fortunately for our purposes, however, twentieth-century moral philosophy has spawned another school that views ethics in a quite different light. This is the *virtue ethics school*, and it makes no attempt to quantify ethics, or even rationalize ethics, in an economic context. Ironically, however, it may provide the key to accommodating ethics in the aesthetic world of business.

It is thus to virtue ethics theory that I would like now to turn. Here the focus will shift away from the actions chosen by managers and toward the very character and motivations of the managers themselves. A quite different rationality concept will be invoked—a concept that lies beyond the existing business ethics paradigm. Before moving on to virtue ethics and the aesthetic manager, however, I would like briefly to summarize the argument so far.

This chapter takes a critical look at the more traditional approaches to business ethics, namely, ethical theories based on deontological and consequentialist theories. In essence, deontological theories focus on the development of rules of conduct, irrespective of the consequences of abiding by these rules. A common example of the business application of deontology is a rule-based corporate code of conduct.

Conversely, consequentialist-based ethical approaches focus primarily on the consequences of actions. They endeavor to identify as correct that action that will maximize overall aggregate economic welfare.

The focus of these approaches on "actions" and "consequences" makes them amenable to evaluation through game theory. The conclusion is drawn that these traditional approaches to ethics fail to accomplish any meaningful integration of ethics with business theory. This failure stems from an inability to rationalize ethics as a motivation. Ethics remains a constraint in a wealth maximization–type rationality construct.

Another implication of this chapter is that game theory itself is not value neutral. In essence, by viewing business interaction through the lens of game theory, one presupposes an environment characterized by the individualistic pursuit of some payoff. Albeit very popular in contemporary economic discourse, an integration of ethics and business may require a view of business not encapsulated by the game-theoretic rubric.

A likely reason for the popularity of game theory in business is its widespread use by financial economists. It is hardly surprising, therefore, that the subject area of finance remains firmly entrenched within the Technical Universe. Indeed, the deconstruction of the Technical and Moral Universes, and by implication the deconstruction of modernity, is at its most dramatic and traumatic within the field of finance. I would like to devote the remainder of this chapter, therefore, to a discussion of the implications of this book's aesthetic critique for the theory and practice of financial management. Absent the certainties of modernism, how can the traditional financial objectives of the firm be meaningfully viewed?

AS A CORPORATE OBJECTIVE, IS STOCK PRICE MAXIMIZATION IMMORAL?

In a fascinating recent article, "Whose Wealth to Maximize: A Survey of Alternative Views on Corporate Objective" (1997), S. J. Chang continues the ongoing discussion in financial economics on the justification—in particular, the moral justification—of assuming that the objective of the firm is solely or primarily that of shareholder wealth maximization. Chang reviews various critiques of, and alternatives to, shareholder wealth maximization as a corporate objective. He concludes that, given the complex nature of contemporary business, shareholder wealth maximization may be something of an "oversimplification" (p. 10): "[J]ust as our policy formulation is a trial-and-error process of self-correcting value judgements, our evaluation of corporate objective should by no means be static or immutable" (p. 10). With this closing statement, Chang challenges financial economists to look afresh at what has indeed been viewed as static and immutable, namely, shareholder wealth maximization as *the* objective of the firm in finance. To give some examples from recent finance texts: "*The* goal of the firm, and therefore of all managers and employees, is to maximize the wealth of the owners for whom it is being operated" (Gitman, 1998, p. 4), or, "In this text we designate the goal of the firm to be *maximization of shareholder wealth*" (Keown et al., 1998, p. 2), or, "Most of the time we assume that the financial manager acts to increase the value of the shareholders' investment in the firm" (Brealey and Myers, 1991, p. 5), or, "[M]anagement's primary goal is stockholder wealth maximization" (Weston et al., in Chang, 1997, p. 2).

The corporate finance text of A. A. Berle, Jr., and Gardiner C. Means, *The Modern Corporation and Private Property*, originally published in 1932, is often cited as the origin of this traditional acceptance of shareholder wealth maximization as the corporate objective:

Taking this doctrine [i.e., shareholder wealth maximization] back into the womb of equity, whence it sprang, the foundation becomes plain. Wherever one man or a group of men entrusted another man or group with the management of property, the second group became fiduciaries. As such they were obliged to act conscionably, which meant in fidelity to the interests of the persons whose wealth they had undertaken to handle. (p. 336)

Chang's critique, therefore, clearly challenges the conventional wisdom in finance concerning the objective of the firm. Specifically, two questions present themselves:

1. Given shareholder wealth maximization's traditional acceptance within finance as the corporate objective, why is it necessary to modify it now?
2. Given that it is necessary, how can this modification be accomplished without compromising the veracity of finance theory and pedagogy?

Many finance educators that I have talked to express puzzlement and doubt about the need to question shareholder wealth maximization as the corporate objective *within finance*. They understand why business ethicists and others would question it, but they are doubtful about the need for finance educators to enter into this debate. They often point out that the idea of shareholder wealth maximization as *the* objective of the firm has been a linchpin in corporate finance since the inception of the discipline. So why, they understandably ask, should it be coming under particular scrutiny now?

The current scrutiny is just one more manifestation of the broad epistemological shift outlined in this book. Given that the general trend within this shift is toward a rejection of absolutes, and a questioning—a deconstruction—of any statement that lays claim to some unitary truth, statements in finance regarding some unified goal of the firm clearly fall into this category and are thus ripe for critique. Consider, for example, the typical finance text statement given earlier: "Management's primary goal is stockholder wealth maximization." A deconstruction would address the following questions: Given that the term "management" includes a collection of individuals (several hundred individuals in the average contemporary multinational corporation), to what extent is it meaningful to attribute to them a single unified goal? The use of the phrase "management's primary goal" implies that there are other goals (absent goals): What are these other goals, and why is this particular one singled out as being absolutely dominant? As with management, can "stockholders" be reasonably viewed as a single unified whole? Why the use of the word "maximization" as opposed to the "fair return" stipulated in Johnson & Johnson's credo, mentioned earlier? Thus, a deconstruction looks to reveal the hidden or subliminal meaning (the trace) that is contained implicitly in the explicit statement. Another manifestation of this epistemological shift is, of course, the rapid growth of the discipline of business ethics. In broad terms, the conflict between business ethics and corporate finance can be seen as a manifestation of the clash between modernism and postmodernism. Finance as an academic discipline is modernist: It traditionally models itself after the natural sciences and thus pursues some "goal" of "absolute truth" through the application of logic and mathematics. Business ethics, on the other hand, with its origins largely in philosophy, shares no such aspirations: To the extent that at least some of its progenitors embrace postmodernism, it can accommodate multiple goals and multiple truths regarding the nature and purpose of business. For example, many business ethicists would be quite comfortable with the idea that business has no—and should have no—single unified or primary objective and that it is not—and should not be—trying to maximize any particular quantifiable value. Such loose and ethereal views on business, however, will understandably be very unpalatable to a scientifically minded, modernism-imbued, financial economist.

From an educational perspective, as courses in business ethics become an accepted part of the undergraduate and graduate curricula, students (and instructors) find themselves faced with several apparently contradictory views on the purpose of business. Of course, everyone agrees that business should ultimately be socially beneficial, but there is widespread disagreement on how this translates into a day-to-day objective for managers. Understandably, financial economists tend to lean on an invisible hand–type argument whereby a focus on profits or stock price will lead ultimately to maximum social benefit. Contrarily, business ethicists tend to turn this logic on its head and argue that a direct quest for social benefit on the part of managers will have the likely side effect of financial success.

This stark contrast is confirmed by even the most cursory glance at business ethics texts. The airing of such criticism within business schools has led inevitably to some soul-searching among those of us who are exposed—

whether as students or as teachers—to both corporate finance and business ethics. Also, even strictly within the discipline of financial economics, the growing acceptance of an agency theory–type view of the firm, and a focus on individual interaction and motivation, and the resulting focus on behavior such as signaling and reputation building, has led finance theorists and educators toward a "softer" behavioral focus that would have appeared entirely incongruous to a more traditional, pre–agency theory, notion of corporate finance. To attain a consistent view of corporate objective, therefore, we need some reconciliation between the business disciplines.

This reconciliation can be addressed quite easily in finance texts. All that is required is some subtle fine-tuning of the ubiquitous statement of corporate objective found therein. This fine-tuning will not compromise the relevance or rigor of the remainder of the text; indeed, by clarifying corporate objective, and avoiding blatant contradictions with other business disciplines, it will add to both relevance and rigor. Thus, this fine-tuning need in no way compromise the rigor of the specific techniques discussed throughout the typical finance text (e.g., capital budgeting, ratio analysis, working capital management, etc.). Indeed, more careful wording in these sweeping chapter-one-type statements about the nature and purpose of business will actually strengthen the text by removing the obvious ambiguities in the current confused discussion of firm objectives, agency theory, and business ethics that appear in many finance textbooks at present. To this end, when making statements about corporate objective, authors and educators should heed the following six guidelines:

1. The prevailing descriptive view of the firm in finance is that supplied by agency theory: The firm is a complex web of principal-agent relations. Any prescriptive statement that implies some unified firm objective is clearly inconsistent with this view. It is the individual agents who have objectives, and even these individuals may have more than one conflicting objective. Indeed, the whole essence of agency theory is that the firm is a cauldron of aspirational conflict, not a unified decision node. In light of this, the notion of a firm as something that can have a single unified objective is clearly a misnomer. For example, Jensen and Meckling (1976) define the firm "as a nexus for a set of contracting relations among individuals" (p. 311). They go on to make the following observations:

Viewed in this way, it makes little or no sense to try to distinguish those things which are "inside" the firm from those things that are "outside" of it. There is in a very real sense only a multitude of complex relations (i.e. contracts) between the legal fiction (the firm) and the owners of labor, material and capital inputs and the consumers of output. . . . In this sense the "behavior" of the firm is like the behavior of the market; i.e., the outcome of a complex equilibrium process. (p. 311)

Therefore, avoid the phrase "the objective of the firm." If, by the use of this, one means the objective of management, then state this explicitly.

2. Another descriptive contribution of agency theory has been to show the extent to which the structure of a corporation is the result of the need to control individual opportunism. Indeed, agency theory implies that a normative goal of the firm is to minimize agency costs. Any explicit statement of corporate objective should recognize this.

3. Avoid any hierarchical ranking of corporate objective. For example, Chang (1997) notes that in their finance text Weston et al. state that "management's primary goal is stockholder wealth maximization" (p. 12). But why *must* this be the primary goal? The use of the word "primary" places this statement in flat contradiction to much business and business ethics theory and is entirely unnecessary. Why not state shareholder wealth maximization as one important goal of management? This would in no way compromise the veracity of finance theory; it would merely recognize the intrinsic importance of other managerial objectives such as product quality, employee welfare, community service, and integrity (note that these other objectives need not conflict with shareholder wealth maximization, but neither need they be viewed as strictly subservient to, and instrumental to, the maximization of shareholder wealth maximization). For example, the NPV rule of finance theory is based on the premise that capital investments should be judged on the basis of their contribution to equity market value. But even financial theorists accept that this approach should not be accepted blindly and should be just one input into a capital budgeting decision (Myers, 1984). And in the case of financial practice, no financial manager would make a capital budgeting decision purely on the basis of an NPV or similar analysis; other considerations—whether termed strategic or ethical or otherwise—always play a major role.

4. When making sweeping normative statements of corporate objective, remember that actual corporate credos and mission statements practically never give priority to the interests of stockholders. If we are to put any credence in the actual pronouncements of corporate practitioners, therefore, it seems odd to flatly contradict them in finance textbooks. Clearly, stockholders hold a unique claim on corporate cash flow, but they do not hold the only claim. In their recent business ethics text, for example, Buchholz and Rosenthal (1998) argue that "there is no justification for shareholders holding such an important position . . . and having first priority as regards corporate activity. . . . [T]he idea that shareholders are the group that takes the greatest risk and thus deserves special treatment is a fiction" (p. 169). Also, given the increasing multiplicity of hybrid securities in contemporary financial markets, any succinct definition of "stockholder" is difficult. In statements of corporate objective, therefore, avoid placing stockholders on a pedestal of absolute priority.

5. Use the term "stock price" or "equity market value" in preference to "shareholder wealth." This will make clear that stock price does more than merely measure the wealth of stockholders. In a statement of corporate

objective, make clear that stock price, at least in the long term, also reflects the extent to which the firm is serving the interests of other groups such as employees, customers, environmentalists, human rights activists, and others.

6. In deference to the postmodern cultural shift mentioned above, adopt a literal and linguistic style that avoids absolutes. For example, rather than saying, "Management should pursue stockholder wealth maximization," say, "Management should consider the impact of any decision on stock price." The two statements are essentially similar, but the latter avoids the implication that the pursuit of stockholders' wealth ad infinitum is the be all and end all of corporate activity.

Here, for example, is a concise statement of corporate objective that is consistent with these six guidelines:

Corporations exist to directly benefit all those individuals who comprise the corporation, thereby indirectly benefiting society as a whole. One measure of the extent to which the corporation is furthering these interests is its stock price. Explicitly, stock price measures the wealth of one particular group, namely, stockholders. But implicitly, stock price measures the extent to which management's decisions are furthering the aggregate interests of all corporate participants: If employees are unhappy at work, this will be eventually reflected in stock price; if customers are dissatisfied with the firm's product or service, this will be eventually reflected in stock price; if an environmental group is upset by the firm's production methods, this will—if the environmental group is something like Greenpeace—be reflected quite quickly in stock price. Stock price, therefore, represents a broad assessment by many participants of corporate worth.

Stock price is not a perfect measure. It is susceptible to dramatic short-run fluctuation that may have nothing to do with the firm itself. It is susceptible also to short-run manipulation by speculators or corporate insiders. Some argue that there are moral values, which a corporation should pursue, that cannot be priced and so cannot be reflected in stock price.

Even given these caveats, however, stock price provides an invaluable quantitative insight into the performance of management and the social worth of a corporation. Thus, even though it is often not clear exactly what the impact of a given decision will be, management should always consider the likely impact of any decision on stock price.

I have tried to keep this statement of corporate objective as concise as possible, and of course it could be greatly expanded upon. But it does at least give some justification for financial management's focus on stock price, while aligning this focus with the broader social role of business. As such, the above represents a first step toward some consistent view of corporate objective across the business disciplines. It also answers Chang's (1997) closing challenge that "our evaluation of corporate objective should by no means be static or immutable" (p. 10).

IMPLICATIONS OF THE MODERNIST CRISIS FOR FINANCE

It is noteworthy from the discussion of corporate objective in finance that although most business subject areas, such as marketing, accounting, and management, have in recent years been expanded to accommodate ethics, no such expansion has yet occurred in financial economics. Marketing ethics, accounting ethics, and management ethics are now established disciplines, but "finance ethics" has yet to appear.

Some might argue that this is inevitable since finance is essentially a technical subject. But even the most cursory review of the actual concepts covered by contemporary finance theory shows this presumption to be false. The majority of finance theory concerns behavior. Indeed, the most recent and predominant theories in finance—such as agency theory, signaling theory, and theories of the firm—are all at root *behavioral* theories. These theories rest on assumptions about how people choose one action over another, assumptions about what constitutes reasonable behavior.

These assumptions are just that—assumptions; they are not statements of fact. If we assume, as financial economists frequently do, that agents endeavor to maximize their personal wealth in whatever way they can, *ad infinitum*, then we are making certain value judgments about these individuals. To date, finance has been reluctant to recognize these value judgments. Specifically, finance texts have ignored the fact that these *are* value judgments. Such texts tend to view wealth maximization–type behavior as an inevitable law of nature. They ignore the ample evidence from psychology, from philosophy, and indeed from the other business disciplines that human behavior is both complex and highly suggestible. Thus, statements concerning how people act are often taken by those people as moral judgments on how they *should* act. Albeit unrecognized to date, finance theory does possess an implicit moral agenda.

For example, in my capacity as a finance lecturer, when I stand up week in and week out in front of my finance classes and tell all those young, impressionable faces that the *fundamental* assumption of finance is that people do whatever they can get away with in order to maximize their own personal wealth, I am—whether I wish to consciously admit it or not—sanctioning such behavior. In essence, in addition to teaching finance, I am—albeit inadvertently—teaching moral philosophy. Or more precisely, I am teaching one particular, rather narrow moral philosophy.

I think it's high time that we in finance recognized this. We must recognize that we teach values, as well as facts. It is true that most introductory finance texts now mention ethics in Chapter 1; some even attempt to mention ethics in other chapters. But these attempts are always peripheral to the main thrust of the book. For example, a text may discuss social responsibility in Chapter 1 but then implicitly assume unequivocal shareholder wealth maximization from Chapter 2 onward. These peripheral types of attempt to introduce ethics into finance may actually do more harm than good. They tend to portray ethics as some sort of inconsistent and ephemeral side issue. They often give the impression of paying lip service to a passing fad, and as such, they denigrate ethics.

A "Forum on Financial Ethics," which occurred recently at the Financial Management Association's annual meeting, probably represents the first time that an ostensibly finance organization has devoted serious attention to the topic of ethics. Did this attention represent merely the payment of lip service to a passing fad, or does it augur a radical expansion in the traditional conceptual boundaries of financial economics? What exactly would the discipline of "finance ethics" comprise that could distinguish it from accounting ethics, marketing ethics, and indeed business ethics in general? Is there any existing or even potential avenue worthy of serious intellectual inquiry relating to ethics that could be identified as specifically financial? Would finance ethics have anything unique to contribute to practicing financial managers above and beyond the usual applications of business ethics in corporate credos and the like? In short, could and should finance ethics become a distinct and circumscribed discipline?

Traditionally, ethics has been viewed as something fundamentally external to financial economics. At most, ethics is a constraint appended to a utility maximization–type objective function. The purpose of this book is to *endogenize* ethics within financial economics, to make ethics an integral part of the objective function, rather than merely some externally imposed constraint.

Ethics concerns behavior. It is the "grammar of behavior." More specifically, ethics concerns the justification for the motivation underlying individual action when that action impacts the actions and beliefs of other individuals. A logical place to begin this project, therefore, is with the behavioral models of finance. It is this area of financial economics that provides the most fertile ground for an accommodation of ethics.

In recent years a major research concern in financial economics has been the reconciliation of observed behavior with the predictions of the perfect-markets, utility maximization models that have traditionally supplied the dominant paradigm in finance. Behavioral finance has made significant progress in this regard. Concepts such as informational asymmetry and signaling have done much to bring financial theory closer to financial practice. The broad contribution of behavioral finance has been to explicitly model the market imperfections that earlier models in finance simply assumed away. A whole range of market imperfections have been identified; indeed, few if any areas of business theory have escaped scrutiny; the theory of the firm itself has, in effect, been recast. The firm has become a structure whose efficiency depends upon its ability to mitigate the costs associated with financial contracting, generally referred to as agency costs (Jensen and Meckling, 1976; Thakor, 1989).

But there is one area in which behavioral finance has so far made only a very limited contribution, namely, in modeling the more complex behavior often observed in real business interaction. It is apparent to many business practitioners that a predisposition among agents toward trustworthiness and honesty can play a vital role in financial contracting (Dobson, 1993; Noreen, 1988). Yet concepts such as trust sit very uneasily—if at all—within the existing notion of rationality in finance. The behavioral models of finance have tended to retain a very narrow and simplistic view of what constitutes rational behavior. Rationality is defined exclusively in terms of personal material gain.

The focus of research has been in modeling complex financial environments, with very little consideration given to the agent within the environment. For reasons of mathematical convenience, these agents are assumed to be simply wealth-maximizing automatons. But in actual financial environments, behavior is clearly more complex and multifaceted than this. It is not merely anecdotal evidence from practitioners that suggests a broadened notion of rationality. The history of moral philosophy itself is one of differing, often conflicting, rationalities. Alasdair MacIntyre (1988), for example, provides extensive historical evidence to support his contention that "rationality itself, whether theoretical or practical, is a concept with a history: indeed, since there are a diversity of traditions of enquiry, with histories, there are . . . rationalities rather than rationality" (p. 9).

MacIntyre (1984a) isolates three "central features of the modern economic order," namely, "individualism . . . acquisitiveness and its elevation of the values of the market to a central social place" (p. 254). He notes that the preeminence of these values is not, and has never been, universally accepted. In financial economics, however, the tacit assumption has been that such values as acquisitiveness and individualism are inviolable laws of nature. A certain rigid notion of rationality in which individual agents opportunistically pursue personal material gain has formed the bedrock of finance theory.

In Part III I explore an expanded, ethically inclusive notion of rational behavior in finance. Modernist business ethics and financial economics are both concerned with business, but they tend to view business from quite different perspectives. Financial economics adopts a very narrow view of behavior in which rational agents opportunistically and exclusively pursue personal material wealth maximization. I suggest that financial economics could benefit from broadening its conception of business activity along lines suggested by business ethics theory. The benefits would be twofold. First, such a conceptual broadening would make the rationality assumptions of finance theory more descriptively accurate. Second, it would make these rationality assumptions more prescriptively desirable from both an economic and a moral perspective. The feasibility of such a conceptual broadening has been enhanced by recent developments in moral philosophy, namely, those relating to virtue ethics theory.

Furthermore, there is increasing evidence that human behavior, even in a financial context, is far more complex and multifaceted than financial theorists have recognized. The behavioral assumptions that form the foundation of finance have been criticized on two broad fronts. First, from a descriptive perspective, the empirical validity of finance's simple personal wealth maximization assumption has been questioned. Second, arguments have been made to the effect that the descriptive accuracy of economic rationality is inseparable from its prescriptive desirability. Agents change their behavior when confronted with role models or assumptions about how other agents behave. In other words "is" inevitably implies "ought."

A recognition that the descriptive and prescriptive aspects of human rationality are inseparable draws the rationality assumptions of finance theory into the domain of ethics. These questions of how agents "do" behave, how agents "should" behave, and the extent to which "do" and "should" are connected extend our inquiry inevitably beyond the boundaries of traditional finance theory. *Finance ethics* is born.

But in general discourse, the term "finance ethics" often evokes wry smiles and chuckles. "Isn't that an oxymoron?" will often be the sardonic retort. Such cynicism is perhaps not surprising in light of the continual "scandals" that have rocked both domestic and overseas financial markets in recent years, not to mention the questionable practices of many business organizations and the (handsomely remunerated) executives therein. Indeed, from a pedagogical perspective—with ethics having permeated the disciplines of accounting, marketing, and management—finance survives as the last bastion of a "value-free" business discipline. Finance has traditionally been regarded as value free because it was seen as dealing with purely the technical aspects of business enterprise: such issues as the optimal mix of debt and equity financing, dividend policy, the evaluation of alternative investment projects, and more recently, the valuation of options, futures, swaps, and other derivative securities. Such questions are essentially technical in nature and would appear to render little scope for ethical evaluation.

But beneath this technical facade financial economics remains, at heart, a social science. With the advent of agency theory, the purview of this discipline has been recognized as rightfully and inevitably extending beyond these technical subject areas to encompass the firm as a *human* organization. Until comparatively recently, this social aspect tended to be assumed away by the aforementioned "perfect-markets" assumptions. But within the last two decades, financial theory has been experiencing—indeed, is still experiencing—something of a paradigm shift: a shift away from purely technical finance and toward behavioral finance. By the term "behavioral finance" I mean an explicit recognition of the importance of human behavior in the financial milieu. As the perfect-and-frictionless-markets-type assumptions are increasingly relaxed, the *contractual* nature of financial interaction is revealed. These contractual models are being built around agents who are unable to perfectly and costlessly enter into contractual relations with other agents (i.e., agency theory).

For example, the notion that not all market participants are equally well informed would seem intuitively obvious. Until recently, however, the perfect-and-frictionless-markets assumptions made the gross simplification of invoking omniscient agents. Relaxing this omniscience assumption has enabled finance to recognize the power of information to drive behavior. Behavior is to a large extent determined by conceptions of who knows what when in a given contractual situation. Who knows what when is in turn largely determined by agents' ability to suppress negative information and *signal* positive information. Such signals may take the form of dividend payment policies or the timing of earnings announcements. Managers of firms with superior earnings prospects, for example, may go to great lengths and some expense to credibly signal this fact to outside investors by committing their firm to a relatively high dividend payout.

General acceptance by financial theorists of the firm as a contractual nexus, therefore, has opened a Pandora's box of potential contractual problems between principals and agents in the corporate domain whose various claims cannot be explicitly enforced. These *agency problems* appear to threaten the efficiency with which the corporation can perform its role as a conduit through which real and financial resources are allocated.

Agency theory is gaining increasing momentum in financial discourse and represents a dramatic conceptual shift in the discipline of financial economics. From a descriptive perspective, this shift has enabled finance to make significant advances in its ability to model and explain the operations of financial markets. In essence, agency theory rests on the conceptual foundation of markets as collections of individual interest groups, each pursuing its own self-interest and each dependent—to a greater or lesser degree—on the beliefs and actions of other groups. This new wave of behavioral financial theory, as opposed to strictly technical finance, places human beliefs and motivations at center stage. Questions of psychology and philosophy—such as "What motivates individuals?" and "What should motivate individuals?"—are rapidly becoming relevant, indeed unavoidable, in finance.

Far from an oxymoron, therefore, a congruence of finance and ethics is becoming increasingly clear as an inevitable consequence of finance theory's broadened conceptual stance. Far from an aberration, the concept of finance ethics arises naturally as a means of answering behavioral questions raised by agency theory. Once the ethereal and malleable nature of human rationality is recognized, the descriptive question of what the agent actually does and the normative question of what the agent should do become inseparable.

Given this recognition, the question "Should finance consider ethics?" becomes exposed as the real nonsequitur. To the extent that it must be premised by some conception of what motivates and constrains human behavior, finance always considers ethics, albeit inadvertently to date. Finance has its own implicit ethical value base. The meaningful question, therefore, is not "Should finance consider ethics?" but rather "What *type* of ethic should finance consider?"

SO WHY DOES FINANCE NEED ETHICS?

Returning to this basic question, we can now see that the question itself is misspecified. Through its assumptions regarding rationality, finance already has ethics. More specifically, finance already has an implicit value base. The problem is that this "ethic" does not appear to be very ethical. A more appropriate question, therefore, would be "Is finance ethical?" or "Is the implicit value base upon which finance theory rests ethically justifiable?"

Both business ethics and financial economics are concerned with business and with the activities of agents within business. But what this book demonstrates is that a broad conceptual chasm currently exists between these two disciplines.

The rational agent in finance is one who pursues personal material advantage ad infinitum, with no consideration given to the impacts that this behavior may have on other agents. Similarly, the firm is viewed merely as a conduit through which agents may pursue these material ends with the minimum of conflict with other, self-regarding agents. These "conflicts" of interest between agents are generally termed "agency problems," and thus the optimal firm in finance is a contractual nexus that minimizes these agency costs.

In finance theory, therefore, the focus has tended to be on *instrumental rationality* rather than on *substantive rationality*. That is to say, the focus has been on how the agent may consistently order and pursue certain material objectives, rather than any critical consideration of what the objectives should be.

Contrarily, business ethicists devote considerable attention to issues surrounding substantive rationality. "What *should* be the objective of the agent?" and "What *should* be the objective of the firm?" are perhaps the central questions of business ethics. Indeed, nowhere are these substantive questions addressed more directly than in one new area of ethics theory, namely, virtue ethics.

Virtue ethics takes as its primary focus the character and motivations of the agent and the notion of the firm as a nurturing community rather than merely a contractual nexus. As one promising avenue for the integration of finance and ethics, virtue ethics theory will be discussed in greater detail in Part III.

This chapter has identified the schism that exists between financial economics and ethics. The next two chapters will provide both economic and moral justifications for removing this schism.

In addition to its economic shortcomings, the concept of rationality in finance can be criticized from a moral perspective. As a philosophy of behavior, opportunism is morally insupportable. Also, from a descriptive perspective, it cannot be defended on the empirical grounds that it reflects behavior in practice accurately: Real behavior is far more complex than straightforward opportunism. Attempts to argue that some form of strategic ethics occurs naturally within the finance paradigm can be criticized on the grounds that such behavior does not represent any substantive notion of ethics. Strategic ethics, that is, apparently ethical behavior in the interests of personal economic gain, does not rationalize ethics in the motivational sense. Such behavior is only superficially ethical and is better classified as strategic economics. Finally, any notion that financial practitioners may be able to sidestep ethical issues by passing on moral responsibility to other stakeholders is dismissed as infeasible and inappropriate.

In summary, accepting a need for an integration of ethics and finance broaches the question of how best to achieve such an integration. Conventional business ethics theories, that is, theories based on the Enlightenment moral philosophies, provide approaches that can generally be distilled into two conceptual paradigms. First, the focus can be on developing rules of behavior that can be applied through corporate credos or organizational codes of conduct. Second, the focus can be on choosing those actions that will be most beneficial to all stakeholders. A characteristic of both these approaches is their focus on the actions of the agent in a given contractual situation. Thus, the implications of imbuing agents in finance with these types of behavior can be readily illustrated through game theory, although game theory itself is shown to possess its own implicit value bias. Also, the practical example of capital budgeting is used to illustrate the moral complexities of financial decision making and the difficulty of applying these moral criteria in any systematic way. The fundamental weakness of these modernist approaches is identified as the philosophical failure to justify ethics. Once again, therefore, we are left with the problem of rationalizing ethics in business.

Part III

The Aesthetic Manager

The highest and strongest drives, when they break out passionately and drive the individual far above the average and the flats of the herd conscience, wreck the self-confidence of the community. . . . Hence just these drives are branded and slandered most. High and independent spirituality, the will to stand alone, even a powerful reason are experienced as dangers; everything that elevates an individual above the herd and intimidates the neighbor is henceforth called *evil*; and the fair, modest, conforming mentality, the *mediocrity* of desires attains moral designations and honors.

—Friedrich Nietzsche, *Beyond Good and Evil*

Chapter 5

The Manager as Artisan

Design, which by another name is called drawing . . . is the font and body of painting and sculpture and architecture and of every other kind of painting and the root of all sciences.
—Michelangelo, from correspondence with Francisco
de Hollanda, as quoted in "Master of His Arts"

Michelangelo was of course a great artist, but he was also recognized as a practical craftsman and as an astute businessman, as was Leonardo da Vinci. The complete separation of the roles of art, craft, and business is a strictly modern phenomenon: As mentioned earlier, ancient Greek and Old English made no distinction between the words "art" and "craft." Like Michelangelo, the manager as artisan that I wish to conjure in this chapter is in every sense a "Renaissance" individual. An individual who sees every aspect of life, business, or otherwise as fundamentally an aesthetic pursuit. An individual who cultivates Nietzsche's "highest and strongest drives" and cultivates them through the virtues. But more on this later.

What I endeavored to show in Parts I and II are the internal inconsistencies and incoherences in the conceptions of the manager as technician and moralist. These inconsistencies and incoherences have become increasingly apparent in the latter part of the twentieth century because of the epistemological shifts under way in both the fields of financial economics and moral philosophy. In the twenty-first century, the void left by the deconstruction of the Technical and Moral Universes will be increasingly filled by the manager as aesthete. But exactly what form will this manager as aesthete take?

I have labeled the "aesthetic manager" as such because the primary characteristic of this individual will be the absence of modernity; the character and behavior of this individual will not be ruled by the dictates of modern economics or modern ethics. Indeed, the moral rules or dogma, and the strict logic of the instrumental rationality of modernity, will be noticeably absent from the character and behavior of this individual. But then, what will this individual pursue, and by what means will this pursuit be undertaken?

The term "aestheticism" here does not so much express something beyond modernity, either chronologically or conceptually; but more it expresses something in which modernity is absent. Thus, the aesthetic manager as aesthete is someone who is rid of the identity of modernism. Since we currently live in an age characterized by modernity, we must look back in time to find a metaphysical universe devoid of modernity: To find the aesthetic manager, we must in fact seek out the premodern manager. This is why in the introduction to this book I use the term "artisan" to label the manager as aesthete; this is a premodern term, and it labels a certain type of individual. An artisan is an individual engaged in business, but the individual's conception of business, and in particular the individual's conception of the *good* of business, is very different to that of the modern manager.

The artisan views business as an art or craft in which the primary pursuit is of a certain type of excellence. In *The World According to Drucker* (1998), Jack Beatty notes that in his prolific career Peter Drucker has developed a similar theme: "Drucker discusses economic life in terms of value, integrity, character . . . but rarely money. He defends profit, but as if it were broccoli: a distasteful obligation of managers who would rather be reading Kierkegaard" (p. 19). Beatty goes on to note that "the manager for Drucker is the cultural hero of the 20th century" (p. 19). Thus, the goal is not material gain or adherence to some rationality founded moral dogma. Indeed, as the term "art" implies, the aesthetic manager pursues primarily nothing that is materially measurable or empirically observable. That is not to say that this pursuit is nonmoral, for this excellence is also *the good*. This pursuit may also be characterized by the generation of substantial material wealth. But neither morality nor material wealth defines this excellence or good. So what exactly is it?

I mentioned that to find the aesthetic manager empirically we must look to the premodern manager, and indeed it is in the metaphysics of the premoderns that a definition of our excellence or good can be found. Fortunately for our purposes, this premodern metaphysic has been made more comprehendible to us moderns by the resurgence of classical Greek philosophy in the latter half of the twentieth century. This resurgence is undoubtedly due in no small measure to the epistemological crises of modernity described above; the resurgence generally comes under the nomenclature of "virtue ethics." This label is perhaps unfortunate because in fact virtue ethics has nothing to do with modern conceptions of either virtue or ethics: in modernity virtue is frequently linked with female celibacy, whereas in classical usage it relates broadly to excellences (*arête*) in human character; the term "ethics" in modernity is linked to various rules or mores of social custom and obligation, whereas the premoderns had no equivalent word; other labels have been proposed by virtue ethicists, such as the ethics of excellence or the aesthetics of living, but unfortunately "virtue ethics" has stuck. So in the interests of consistency I will use the term "virtue ethics" below. Thus, our aesthetic manager is now being relabeled the virtuous manager, and the Aesthetic Universe defined in the introduction of this book is now defined as the metaphysic of virtue ethics.

So to describe the essence of the manager of the aesthetic era we look to the managers, craftsmen, and artisans of the premodern era; so we return again to a preindustrial, prefactory, village-based business concept, albeit one based on remote-access computer technology rather than the potter's wheel or spinning loom. The aesthetic manager may work with different tools than the premodern, but the essential view of human activity as an artistic pursuit or craft, as an excellence, will be rekindled in the aesthetic business era.

Virtue ethics theory represents an avenue by which to make this transition from modernism to aestheticism in a business context. Virtue ethics theory can thus be viewed as a type of translation mechanism. The progenitors of virtue ethics, and I am thinking particularly here of Alasdair MacIntyre, have made the notion of the absence of modernity comprehendible to those of us who are unavoidably part of modernity. Thus, as with all aestheticists, virtue ethicists deconstruct modernity, but in addition, virtue ethicists construct an alternative, or perhaps not so much an alternative but merely the view that remains once the obfuscations of modernity are removed. Those of us inhabiting the twentieth century are all moderns and are thus all subject to the delusions and prejudices of modernity, but virtue ethics gives us a window into a different metaphysic. In essence, virtue ethics is the translation of the premodern/aesthetic into a form intelligible to modernity. It is thus to virtue ethics that I turn in the remainder of this book. Virtue ethics will provide the medium or the prism through which, from the dark glass of modernity, the aesthetic manager may be glimpsed.

THE ROLE OF VIRTUE ETHICS/AESTHETICS IN BUSINESS

One defining characteristic of the aesthetic manager, emphasized particularly in virtue ethics theory, is a holistic approach to decision making. In modernist approaches, the economic and the moral are seen as entirely separable. A manager can make, for example, a capital budgeting decision, either on the basis of economic criteria such as the NPV or on the basis of moral criteria such as ISCT. But these two methods are entirely epistemologically separate; there is a dualism here so familiar to modernity. The internal crises in the universes of the technician and the moralist are reflected in the deconstructions of the ontological foundations of these concepts as intellectual modes of inquiry; specifically, what is being deconstructed are those prejudices and illusions that defined the dualism between the economic notion of the manager as technician and the modern philosophical notion of the manager as moralist. The aesthetic critique reveals these two heretofore separate ontologies as just two fragile and contextual metaphysical stances. This realization within the academic cloisters of economics and ethics is leading, first, to radical self-doubt and, second, to radical reorientation among—in the current context—business management theorists and practitioners. In essence, what financial economics and moral philosophy are experiencing are true Kuhnian paradigm shifts. Interestingly, the nature of these paradigm shifts is not dissimilar in that they both reflect a conceptual holism unfamiliar to modernism—characterized as modernism is by identification and compartmentalization—but very familiar to aestheticism in general and virtue ethics theory in particular.

The first step in explaining the role of virtue ethics in business, therefore, is to understand the paradigm shifts in both moral philosophy and financial economics that provided the metaphysical void necessary for the accommodation of virtue. So what exactly were these paradigm shifts as they relate to the rise of the aesthetic manager?

In essence, both shifts concern changing conceptions of rationality: of what it is to be human. Part I of this book made clear that the Technical Universe conjures human behavior with reference to a very narrow and rigid rationality construct. But what the history of moral philosophy makes clear is that the concept of rationality can be defined in several different ways. The Aristotelian concept of practical rationality, for example, includes the pursuit of moral excellence as integral to the very notion of rationality itself. D. S. Hutchinson (1986) emphasizes the broad-based characteristic of this Aristotelian approach to rationality thus: "We can discover what the standards are for human conduct by discovering what it is reasonable to do" (p. 51). Similarly, MacIntyre, in *Whose Justice? Which Rationality?* (1988), challenges the very core of the modernist concept of rationality as natural by arguing that there is no absolute rationality: "[R]ationality itself, whether theoretical or practical, is a concept with a history: indeed, since there are a diversity of traditions of enquiry, with histories, there are . . . rationalities rather than rationality" (p. 9). That which is deemed rational, according to MacIntyre, is entirely dependent upon cultural tradition:

It is an illusion to suppose that there is some neutral standing ground, some locus for rationality as such, which can afford rational resources sufficient for enquiry independent of all traditions. Those who have maintained otherwise either have covertly been adopting the standpoint of a tradition and deceiving themselves and perhaps others into supposing that theirs was just a neutral standing ground or else have simply been in error. (p. 367)

This chapter is clearly placing the practical rationality of virtue ethics within a particular context, within a particular tradition, namely, the context of a business management paradigm. Thus, here I use virtue ethics as a conceptual tool—or rather as the conceptual tool—with which to construct the aesthetic manager from the deconstruction of the modern technical and moral manager.

To some the link between virtue ethics and aestheticism may seem opaque. But note that both rely entirely on the notion of context: the mantra of business aestheticism as conjured here could be that everything is contextual and non absolute; similarly in virtue ethics, whether any particular action is moral depends centrally on the context in which that action is taken, both the physical context and the motivational context of the individual. To use one of Aristotle's examples, the act of getting drunk at a party could be the manifestation of a virtue (humor, magnanimity, kindness, conviviality) or a vice (intemperance, gluttony, overindulgence); which it is depends entirely on context. So what exactly are the defining characteristics of virtue ethics as a conceptual foundation for our aesthetic manager?

THE PRESENCE OF VIRTUE ETHICS

Virtue ethics is concerned primarily with the pursuit of a certain type of morally inclusive excellence. Aristotle called it *eudaimonia,* which can be roughly translated as "happiness" or "human flourishing." For present purposes, this approach to ethics can be thought of as exhibiting four basic attributes. Its primary attribute is a strong emphasis on the importance of certain generally accepted *virtues* or excellences of character; indeed, it is through honing and perfecting these virtues that an individual becomes truly ethical. Second, a strong emphasis is placed on the existence of an active *community* that nurtures these virtues. Third, virtue ethics theory makes clear that in the moral life one cannot rely merely on rules or guidelines; in addition, an ability to exercise *sound moral judgment* is requisite. Finally, the successful identification and emulation of moral *exemplars,* or role models, are essential for the dissemination of morality within the aforementioned nurturing community.

The remainder of this section will describe virtue ethics from these four perspectives: the role of the virtues, the role of community, the role of moral judgment, and the role of exemplars.

THE ROLE OF THE VIRTUES

An essential feature of rationality within virtue ethics is that rather than focusing on the material goals of the agent, it focuses on the character and motivations of the agent and on the agent's ability to pursue a certain very particular type of excellence. A characteristic of this excellence is that its pursuit necessitates adherence to certain virtues or traits of character.

These virtues place emphasis on the motivation for an action and entail the exercise of sound judgment. "Virtue lies in the reasons for which one acts rather than in the type of action one performs" (Annas, 1995, p. 250). There exist many lists of virtues. Socrates lists the four cardinal virtues as wisdom, courage, temperance, and justice. Nietzsche (1982) supplies an alternative list: "*Honest* towards ourselves and whoever *else* is a friend to us; *courageous* towards the enemy; *generous* toward the defeated; *polite*—always; this is what the four cardinal virtues want us to be" (p. 556). Michael Slote (1992) splits the virtues into two broad categories, namely, self-regarding and other-regarding:

When, furthermore, we look at the whole range of traits commonly recognized as virtues, we once again see that self-regarding and other-regarding considerations are both capable of underlying the kind of high regard that leads us to regard various traits as virtues. *Justice, kindness, probity, and generosity* are chiefly admired for what they lead those who possess these traits to do in their relations with other people, but *prudence, sagacity, circumspection, equanimity, and fortitude* are esteemed primarily under their self-regarding aspect, and still other traits—notably *self-control, courage, and (perhaps) wisdom in practical affairs*—are in substantial measure admired both for what they do for their possessors and for what they lead their possessors to do with regard to other people. (p. 9; emphasis mine)

A simple generic definition of "virtue" is supplied by MacIntyre (1984a): "A virtue is an acquired human quality the possession and exercise of which tends to enable us to achieve those goods which are internal" (p. 191). He distinguishes between internal and external goods as follows:

It is characteristic of what I have called external goods that when achieved they are always some individual's property or possession. Moreover characteristically they are such that the more someone has of them, the less there is for other people. . . . External goods are therefore characteristically objects of competition in which there must be losers as well as winners. *Internal* goods are indeed the outcome of competition to excel, but it is characteristic of them that their achievement is a good for the whole community who participate in the practice. (pp. 190–191; emphasis mine)

The pursuit of external goods, therefore, is no longer recognized as the ultimate end of human endeavor, but rather as a means to the achievement of excellence. Martha Nussbaum (1991) defines this excellence as "the end of all desires, the final reason why we do whatever we do; and it is thus inclusive of everything that has intrinsic worth [i.e., internal goods], lacking in nothing that would make a life more valuable or more complete" (p. 38). MacIntyre (1984a) concludes that virtues therefore are to be understood as those dispositions that will not only sustain practices and enable us to achieve the goods internal to practices, but which will also sustain us in the relevant kind of quest for the good, by enabling us to overcome the harms, dangers, temptations and distractions which we encounter, and which will furnish us with increasing self-knowledge and increasing knowledge of the good. (p. 450)

In a specifically business context, Kenneth Goodpaster (1994) lists five key virtues:

(1) *Prudence*—neither too short-term nor too long-term in time horizon; (2) *Temperance*—neither too narrowly materialistic (want-driven) nor too broadly dispassionate (idea-driven); (3) *Courage*—neither reckless nor too risk-averse; (4) *Justice*—neither too anarchic regarding law nor too compliant; (5) *Loyalty*—neither too shareholder-driven (private sector thinking) nor too driven by other stakeholders (public sector thinking). (pp. 54–55)

Clearly, to achieve excellence through the exercise of these virtues of character requires a sense of moderation. Thus, managers who are said to be "weathering the storm" or "sticking to their guns" may well be exercising the virtue of courage. But so might a manager who "knows when to call it quits." It is the reason or judgment underlying the action that will determine whether the agent is truly courageous. Thus, a virtue is not a maximum or a minimum. Unlike the modernist rationality of maximization and instrumentality, aesthetic rationality concerns fundamentally moderation, balance, and judgment in the exercise of virtue.

What of business vices? In characterizing Ivan Boesky, the financial anti-hero of the 1980s "greed decade," Manuel Velasquez (1998) lists the following vices: "Boesky is described as being 'greedy,' 'sick,' 'aggressive,' 'fiendish,' and 'ruthless.' Because what he said of himself did not match his secret dealings, some said he 'lacked integrity' others that he was 'hypocritical' and 'dishonest' " (p. 131).

The crucial difference, therefore, between modernist approaches to business ethics and the approach adopted in virtue ethics theory is that the latter focuses on the character and motivations of the agent and on the agent's ability to pursue excellence through virtuous acts. Sherwin Klein (1988) succinctly distinguishes between what I term the "modernist approach" to business ethics and the new "virtue ethics" approach by labeling them as "action-based" and "agent-based," respectively—the former tending to focus on moral rules that can be generally applied to contractual situations (e.g., Kantianism and utilitarianism), whereas virtue ethics concerns the aspirations of the agent and the agent's ability to exercise the moral virtues.

Virtue ethics implies also a certain openness of mind and flexibility on the part of the agent. The virtuous agent, in his or her pursuit of *eudaimonia*, is not following any set script or rule book. For the artisan-cum-aesthetic manager, life is one of open-minded pursuit, rather than dogged adherence to any dogma. As poet G. K. Chesterton and Zen philosopher Alan Watts both emphasize, *humor* and *a sense of innocent wonder* are both key virtues. Thus, unlike the shareholder wealth maximization–driven technician, or the moral dogma–driven moralist, the aesthetic manager will follow no set master script. For this individual the goal is aesthetic, and as such, it is not really a goal at all but more of a journey, a *tao*. The aesthetic manager realizes that one never arrives: aesthetic excellence through the exercise of virtue is not something one ever achieves, one merely pursues. But one cannot undertake this pursuit in isolation.

THE ROLE OF COMMUNITY

Virtue ethics theory also has implications for the role of the firm as a social organization. For the virtues to flourish requires a conducive infrastructure: "[O]ne cannot think for oneself if one thinks entirely by oneself . . . [I]t is only by participation in a rational practice-based community that one becomes rational" (MacIntyre, 1988, p. 396). Thus, rationality in virtue ethics is a shared rationality with a shared conception of what is ultimately desirable in all human endeavor. This shared conception must be supported by, and indeed be the raison d'être of, the organizations and institutions that control and direct human activity. This infrastructure is an aspect of what was known in the city-states of ancient Greece as the *polis*: "the form of social order whose shared mode of life already expresses the collective answer or answers of its citizens to the question 'What is the best mode of life for human beings?' " (*ibid.*, p. 133). Such an infrastructure is essential for virtue ethics:

Aristotle is articulating at the level of theoretical enquiry a thought inherited from the poets when he argues in Book I of the *Politics* (1252b28–1253a39) that a human being separated from the *polis* is thereby deprived of some of the essential attributes of a human being. . . . A human being stands to the *polis* as a part to its whole. . . . For the *polis* is human community perfected and completed by achieving its *telos*. (pp. 96–97)

The virtue ethics approach thus casts the firm or professional organization in a role that is far more active and intrusive than Jensen and Meckling's "contractual nexus" or Merton Miller's "wealth creating machine." The firm becomes a nurturing community, a *polis*. "Corporations are real communities . . . and therefore the perfect place to start understanding the nature of the virtues" (Solomon, 1992, p. 325). Robert Solomon emphasizes the link between virtue ethics and this expanded role of the firm as a nurturing community: "It [virtue ethics] is an Aristotelian ethics precisely because it is membership in a community, a community with collective goals and a stated mission—to produce quality goods and/or services and to make a profit for the stockholders" (p. 321). Within the rubric of virtue ethics theory, therefore, the goals and aspirations of the individual are nurtured and directed by the business organizations and institutions of which that individual forms a part.

THE ROLE OF MORAL JUDGMENT

Another significant aspect of virtue ethics is its rejection of a rule-based approach to moral education. Acting ethically in a given situation is less a function of rule adherence and more a function of exercising sound moral judgment. MacIntyre (1984a) makes this very clear:

What can never be done is to reduce what has to be learned in order to excel at such a type of activity to the application of rules. There will of course at any particular stage in the historical development of such a form of activity be a stock of maxims which are used to characterize what is taken at that stage to be the best practice so far. But knowing how to apply these maxims is itself a capacity which cannot be specified by further rules, and the greatest achievements in each area at each stage always exhibit a freedom to violate the present established maxims, so that achievement proceeds both by rule-keeping and by rule-breaking. And there are never any rules to prescribe when it is the one rather than the other that we must do if we are to pursue excellence. (p. 31)

This does not mean that, for example, derivatives traders should ignore exchange standards or codes of conduct, but rather that these should be viewed not as the entire professional ethic but as the foundation from which to pursue the professional ideal in this activity. This professional ideal will be defined in terms of the internal goods specific to the practice of derivatives trading. But more on this later.

THE ROLE OF MORAL EXEMPLARS

The role of exemplars is critical for the application of virtue ethics because it is from these individuals that the virtues are disseminated throughout the business or profession. Thus, in virtue ethics, ethics is something that is *learned* through observation of others' behavior. This point is made clearly by Dennis Gioia (1992) who draws on his personal experience as vehicle recall coordinator for Ford Motor Company. Gioia participated directly in the decision to keep the Ford Pinto on the road in the face of mounting evidence concerning the faulty fuel-tank design, which eventually resulted in over 500 burn deaths in rear-end collisions (Hoffman and Moore, 1990, p. 586). While analyzing his experience at Ford, Gioia concludes that "codes of ethics . . . are too often cast at a level of generality that can not be associated with any specific script" (p. 388), where a script is some generally accepted decision procedure within the firm. Gioia suggests that management must be exposed to "*learning* or training that concentrates on exposure to information or *models* that explicitly display a focus on ethical considerations" (p. 388, emphasis added). One approach designed to provide managers with this practical exposure to the resolution of ethical dilemmas within the firm is the *Critical Incident Technique*, or CIT.

This technique reflects two central features of virtue ethics, namely (1) the idea that ethics can be learned through personal narrative and (2) the need for role models or what Peter Dean (1992) terms "exemplary performers" (p. 289). It is from observation of how these individuals handle ethically charged decisions that other members of the organization learn practical ethics. Dean emphasizes the practical nature of the CIT, originally developed by the U.S. Air Force during World War II:

In its simplest form, the technique involves bringing together professionals familiar enough with the job area under study to be able to share "real life" examples of both effective and ineffective job performance, or in this case ethical and unethical decisions. (p. 287)

Through a series of workshops, the experiences of these professionals are relayed to other employees to demonstrate the effective *application* of a professional code of ethics. Once a code of ethics is established, the behavior of experienced and exemplary individuals is then tapped to perfect the delicate balance between the pursuit of material objectives and the pursuit of moral objectives that tends to appear in day-to-day managerial decisions. Most noteworthy in the current context, Dean emphasizes that the mere adherence to some set of rules or guidelines is insufficient: "The Critical Incident Technique facilitates the identification of those behaviors that distinguish really outstanding accomplishments, from those that achieve minimum standards only. . . . Further, *if outstanding decisions are labelled as such, they are more likely to be emulated*" (p. 288; emphasis mine).

Thus, once again, ethics is cast as an objective rather than as a constraint. The *moral minimalism* of traditional approaches to ethics, in which some ethical rule was merely one more constraint to be circumvented in the pursuit of material gain, is clearly inconsistent with the CIT. This technique illustrates, therefore, one way in which the practical implications of virtue ethics theory can be successfully applied in an organizational context.

In a similar vein, in his recent article on "good works," Michael Pritchard (1992) concludes that "beyond discussing codes of ethics, principles of right and wrong, dilemmas . . . and moral disaster stories, we need stories of a different sort—*stories of good professionals whose lives might inspire emulation*" (p. 170; emphasis mine). A recent resurgence in recognition of the critical importance of moral exemplars is supplied by cognitive science in its invocation of "exemplar theory." Alvin Goldman (1993) summarizes the theory as follows:

Moral theorists often assume that people's usage of moral terms is underpinned by some sort of rules or principles they learn to associate with those terms: rules governing honesty, for example, or fairness. The exemplar theory suggests, however, that what moral learning consists in may not be (primarily) the learning of rules but the acquisition of pertinent exemplars or examples. This would accord with the observable fact that people, especially children, have an easier time assimilating the import of parables, myths, and fables than abstract principles. *A morally suitable role model may be didactically more effective than a set of behavioral maxims.* (p. 341; emphasis mine)

So through exemplars, community, and enlightened judgment, virtue ethics gives the aesthetic manager a certain nonmaterial goal—a goal that is not a goal—namely, its own particular brand of excellence. But in order to begin to pursue this goal, we must recognize two fundamental tenets of this approach. First, the pursuit of this ideal cannot be undertaken in isolation: in the vernacular of virtue ethics, the aesthetic manager must view business as a *practice*. Second, within this practice, *internal* goods are pursued over and above all else. Barry Schwartz (1990) identifies three basic attributes of business as a practice:

1. It must establish its own standards of excellence, and indeed be partly defined by those standards.

2. It is teleological, that is, goal directed. Each practice establishes a set of goods or ends that is internal or specific to it and inextricably connected to engaging in the practice itself. In other words, to be engaging in the practice is to be pursuing these internal goods.

3. It is organic. In the course of engaging in the practice, people change it, systematically extending both their own powers to achieve its goods and their conception of what its goods are.

Similarly, the internal goods to be pursued within this practice may also be identified by three basic attributes:

1. They are unique to a particular activity. For example, in the context of the game of chess, MacIntyre (1984a) defines the internal goods as "those goods specific to chess, . . . the achievement of a certain highly particular kind of analytical skill, strategic imagination and competitive intensity" (p. 188). Thus, such goals as fame, power, and money are not internal goods because they are not unique to a particular activity.

2. They are not limited in supply. Thus my achievement of the internal good of job satisfaction, or analytical skill, in no way limits your ability to attain this or other internal goods. Once again, this criterion excludes fame, power, and money.

3. They are intangible in the sense that they do not readily lend themselves to simple definition, quantification, or mathematical enumeration. This may explain their relative absence from professional codes of conduct, and from explicit performance measurement criteria. It's hard enough to define such goods as "analytical skill or strategic imagination," let alone to measure them.

For existing managers, therefore, a process of reeducation may be necessary if this virtue-based notion of management is to take hold. In essence, managers must be educated into a broader conception of self-interest. They must be enlightened to the inherent superiority of internal goods over external goods and to the connected view of themselves, not as atomistic individuals but as part of an aesthetic "practice." Thus, rather than being conceptualized in purely economic terms, self-interest must be equated with broader considerations of judgment and harmony.

The virtue-enlightened aesthetic manager is released from the illusory conflict between acting in one's own self-interest and acting ethically; since professional fulfillment and flourishing is obtainable only through the pursuit of moral excellence within a professional community, the professional's concept of self-interest becomes a concept within which ethics takes center stage. Diane Swanson (1997) describes what she calls "discovery leadership," which bears a strong resemblance to our manager as aesthete:

"Discovery leadership" refers to an executive style of decision making that is congruent with a particular state of ego-development and sense of self. Discovery executives seek to serve the social good or the life-affirming economic and ecological values in the restated principles of corporate social responsibility. This executive type possesses the moral motivation of respect for others and an accompanying ethical awareness of the many value-defined duties relevant to business and society interactions. . . . In discovery leadership, the egoistic opportunism associated with economic self-interest is discarded in favor of a broadened other-oriented interest in serving life-affirming values of the stakeholder community. (pp. 108–109)

In short, the aesthetic manager is one who pursues the excellences or internal goods specific to his or her business as practice. This concept does not contradict the economic axioms of instrumental rationality, outlined in Part I; it merely subsumes these into a deeper concept of substantive rationality, what Aristotle termed "practical rationality." Indeed, as discussed briefly at the beginning of this chapter, it is this broadened notion of rationality at the heart of virtue ethics—namely, practical rationality—that characterizes and in large part defines the aesthetic manager. Thus, to clarify the aesthetic manager we must clarify this notion of practical rationality, particularly as it relates to business decision making. In what ways, specifically, would the behavior of our aesthetic practically rational manager differ from that of the instrumentally rational technician or the modern moralist?

PRACTICAL RATIONALITY AS A FOUNDATION FOR THE AESTHETIC MANAGER

In contrasting instrumental and practical rationality, the central issue is not whether agents act according to their own self-interest or whether they act in some way altruistically but, rather whether they view their own self-interest in a narrow sense—as invoked by modernity—or in a broader Homeric sense.

Invoking practical rationality as the substantive rationality premise for business management may justifiably cause some concern among theorists who value the analytical rigor afforded by a simple behavioral premise of instrumental rationality. But the idea of mathematical precision in modeling rationality, even such a precise application as economic rationality, has always been illusory. Consider, for example, the concept of *utility of wealth* introduced in Part I. As discussed there, we may say that this utility increases with increasing wealth and decreases with increasing risk (agents are assumed to be risk averse), but even though the functional relationship may be approximated by a lognormal or similar utility function, this function can never be measured with precision for any one individual or individuals in aggregate. Rather than a sacrifice, therefore, any loss of quantitative rigor engendered by practical rationality may simply represent the weighing of another of modernism's mathematically convenient but unrealistic conceptual anchors, namely, the concept of business behavior as an exclusively descriptive and mathematically precise science.

This qualitative broadening need not be at the expense of mathematical rigor where the latter is correctly applied. Clearly, such rigor has a valuable role to play even within the context of rationality, namely, in modeling instrumental rationality. But when it comes to assumptions concerning substantive rationality, even financial economists must recognize the value judgments inherent in their wealth maximization premise—specifically, as discussed above, the extent to which positive behavioral assumptions may become normative behavioral prerogatives: the implicit normative agenda. In essence, the aesthetic manager must search continually for the ideal balance—the Aristotelian mean—between the qualitative and quantitative analytical extremes. Thus, the aesthetic manager as aesthete does not reject analytical rigor, rather—unlike in the Technical Universe where analytical rigor defines the entire management rubric—for the aesthetic manager analytical rigor is viewed as just one context of management. This conceptual broadening will have implications for all managerial roles. Even the most apparently technical of decisions will now be evaluated in this broadened metaphysical light. Consider, for example, the corporate capital budgeting decision.

CAPITAL BUDGETING REVISITED

So far in this book capital budgeting has been discussed in the context of the Pepsi/Burma test case, which concerns PepsiCo's decision of whether or not to divest its assets in Burma. Capital budgeting methods such as the NPV rule discussed in Chapter 1, although analytically rigorous, are in no way antithetical to our aesthetic manager. This manager as aesthete will still employ capital budgeting methods but will view these as just one means of making a decision such as whether to pull out of Burma. The manager will recognize the aesthetic value judgments that underlie the analytics of capital budgeting: judgments such as the time frame assumed, the assumptions underlying cash flow estimates and discount rate estimates, and the assumptions of time value of money and reinvestment. All these value judgments underlie this type of analysis. They will be recognized by the aesthetic manager as forming the context of the analysis, and this context will be taken as just one possible context from which to make a decision.

The aesthetic manager will recognize that in making a capital budgeting decision, or indeed in making any ostensibly financial decision, there exists a set goal, or *telos*, namely, the identification and completion of investment projects that enhance the value of the firm as a contributor to the aesthetic enrichment of the broader community of which this firm as a microcommunity forms a part. The means by which this goal is achieved continually evolve as new techniques for capital budgeting develop through the interaction of financial theory and practice. The unique goods internal to capital budgeting are the intrinsic satisfaction that managers derive from applying— to the best of their ability—the tools supplied by financial theory, such as the NPV rule. Thus, the manager as aesthete pursues excellence in the practice of capital budgeting. Given that this excellence is defined in terms of identifying and completing profitable investment projects, the manager will also be pursuing a *telos* that is generally consistent with economic firm value maximization.

Consider the difference between this aesthetic manager and the opportunist of the Technical Universe. The latter, in pursuing external goods such as personal wealth and power, may underinvest, may choose inefficiently risky projects, or may be driven by ego or material self-interest to delay the abandonment of unprofitable projects. Contrarily, the practically rational manager as aesthete, in pursuing the goods internal to the practice of capital budgeting, would take none of these actions. To underinvest or risk shift or delay the abandonment of unprofitable projects would be inconsistent with the end of this particular practice and would consequently preclude the agent from acquiring the goods internal to the practice.

An aesthetic manager, therefore, can be viewed as someone involved in a variety of practices of which capital budgeting is just one. Each practice is supported by a unique body of knowledge that the manager attempts to apply in the pursuit of the goods internal to that practice. The good manager in a moral sense and the good manager in an economic sense thus converge: excellence for both entails a commitment to the communal goods of the practice over and above any personal material considerations. But note well that this manager as aesthete is in no way an altruist: this individual is pursuing self-interest as he or she perceives it; the essential difference is that, unlike the economic opportunist, this agent's pursuit of self-interest is in accord with the pursuit of the internal goods of the practice.

So the aesthetic manager's prerogative, albeit complex and multifaceted, is in no way a purely chaotic, unstructured, and futile one; this manager is just no longer laboring under the illusion that decisions can be made purely on the basis of technical or moral criteria. In pursuing these elusive internal goods of practical rationality, the aesthetic manager recognizes the need to exercise pure judgment in weighing the many considerations—economic, moral, and aesthetic—that go into sound decision making. More precisely, the aesthetic manager merely realizes that any decision criterion, even something as apparently cut and dry as the NPV rule, is in reality at root just another aesthetic context from which to view the art of business.

PRACTICAL RATIONALITY AND GAME THEORY

Perhaps the most definitive characteristic of practical rationality, which distinguishes it categorically from modernist instrumental rationality, is practical rationality's accommodation of community interest as part of self-interest; rationality becomes a concept capable of accommodating a sense of communal purpose. But, from a conventional business methodology standpoint, this sense of communal purpose presents a problem. The conventional tool for modeling human interaction is game theory. The problem here is that the methodology of game theory does not lend itself to any notions of communal rationality; game theory focuses exclusively on the preferences of individual agents acting as individuals. In an overview of some laboratory studies of the descriptive and prescriptive abilities of financial-economic game theory, Richard Thaler (1988) concludes thus:

The conclusion that subjects' utility functions have arguments other than money is reconfirmed. . . . We have seen that game theory is unsatisfactory as a positive model of behavior. It is also lacking as a prescriptive tool. While none of the subjects in . . . [the laboratory] experiments came very close to using the game-theoretic strategies, those who most closely approximated this strategy did not make the most money. (p. 202)

It appears, therefore, that any rigorous development of our manager as aesthete along lines suggested by practical rationality will necessitate first the rejection of game theory, at least conventional economic game theory, and the adoption of some new tool for modeling human interaction. Exactly what form this new tool will take remains for future research. I suspect, however, that we may find a limit to the degree to which the theoretical modeling of any type of nontechnical management paradigm can be meaningfully pursued along rigorous, mathematically oriented, game-theoretic lines. The view of corporate culture as a competitive game, although illuminating in some respects, must be recognized as just one view. The manager as aesthete provides another view.

For example, in concluding their seminal work on the theory of the firm, Jensen and Meckling (1976) note that "whatever its shortcomings, the corporation has thus far survived the market test against potential alternatives" (p. 357). This statement has since been further vindicated by recent developments in eastern Europe and the republics that once comprised the Soviet Union. We exit the twentieth century with the market system increasingly omnipresent, auguring a global corporate culture. Thus, when viewed within the economic or technical universe, the story of the firm as a competitive enterprise is undoubtedly a story of success.

From the virtue ethics or aesthetic perspective, however, there are other universes or contexts. These contexts may not be as amenable to the logic of game theory, but they are no less real. Indeed, some would argue that they are more real and, in a moral sense at least, in some way superior. In the Aristotelian moral philosophy that forms the foundation of virtue ethics, for example, the superiority of this nonmaterial universe is absolute because humanity's *telos* exists within it. Success in the economic sphere is merely a prerequisite for entry into the aesthetic universe.

This aesthetic context is, according to Aristotle, obscured by the economic paradigm where excellence is equated with efficiency in achieving solely material ends. The latter is a paradigm that is oblivious to the intrinsic value of the aesthetic universe: In economic game theory, there is no virtue, no internal good, no craftsmanship or excellence, save in the name of effectiveness, no communal purpose. In the competitive game of economic self-interest, truth and the good become subservient to profit. Individuals, businesses, and even ostensibly noneconomic institutions such as universities all shift their allegiance from truth and good to profit:

In the *Republic*, Plato implicitly and explicitly argues that materialism is the source of many of our moral ills. If one's value system is essentially materialistic, it encourages us to cheat, lie, steal, and the like, for if we can get away with such actions, we will be materialistically better off. (Klein, 1989, p. 62)

When Aristotle described life's ideal as one of intellectual pursuit or contemplative inquiry, he accepted that the material wealth of *his* society was sufficient for only a small fraction of its inhabitants to realize this ideal. In the nineteenth and twentieth centuries, wealth generated by the firm through the market system has freed the majority of humanity from the fetters of material servitude. But the victory has been Pyrrhic. To the extent that the aesthetic universe has been eclipsed in modernity by the game-theoretic economic universe, the fetters of material servitude have merely been replaced by those of artistic impoverishment. The tragedy of contemporary corporate culture is thus the tragedy of King Midas. In creating the means for unlimited material acquisition, we have prevented ourselves from acquiring those nonmaterial goods that we most desire.

Chapter 6

The Business Aesthetic

The Age of Unreason may become an Age of Greatness.
—Charles Handy, *The Age of Unreason*

Chapter 5 used virtue ethics to describe a business environment absent of modernity. I conjured the aesthetic manager as the virtuous individual. This individual would no longer be constrained to act purely in terms of the modernist notion of instrumental rationality but would rather act in accordance with a broader rationality rubric, namely, practical rationality. In essence, this aesthetic manager as virtuous individual would view business less as a competitive game and more as a communal quest—a quest for an Aristotelian type of all-inclusive excellence. Unlike in the Technical Universe of financial economics, material profit would no longer be the ultimate objective. Unlike in the Moral Universe of business ethics theory, behavior would not be proscribed by given rules or principles. Material profit, and moral principles, would still apply, but they would be inputs into a holistic quest for excellence. The extent to which any individual manager achieved this excellence would depend upon the nuanced application of various virtues of character. The "art" in the art of business thus becomes the ability to embrace any given decision with the correct balance of courage, temperance, prudence, justice, compassion, and other virtues. So, unlike the modern manager who tends to approach decisions in an instrumentally technical or moralist fashion, decision making for the aesthetic manager is primarily contextual and judgmental.

In this final chapter, I consider the implications of the aesthetic manager for the nature of business enterprise. How will this nature appear, given managers as virtuous individuals? More fundamentally, is this notion of the virtuous individual really applicable to an activity such as business? This latter question is addressed first and is answered by posing three additional questions. First, why does this question need to be asked in the first place; that is, why is it not obvious why the manager should be a virtuous individual? Second, what are the defining characteristics of virtue ethics that determine its applicability to business? Third, are these characteristics present in business, and if not now, then could they conceivably be in the future?

In answering these questions, I will draw heavily on the insights of Alasdair MacIntyre. Although generally recognized as a leading figure in the resurgence of virtue-based philosophy in the latter half of the twentieth century, MacIntyre's specific views on business are less well known. He is often dismissed in the business ethics literature as "antibusiness." What I will endeavor to show here, however, is that MacIntyre's perspective on business, and in particular his perspective on the modern business contexts of the Technical and Moral Universes, is more nuanced and enlightening than the antibusiness label suggests. I will argue that MacIntyre's antiquated view of business as a craft dovetails neatly with my invocation of the manager as an artisan. Once again, therefore, it is to the premodern that we must turn to define the aesthetic. And no one conjures the premodern better than MacIntyre. Indeed, to the extent that they both represent the absence of modernity, the premodern and the aesthetic are one. Whether in a medieval guild or a multinational corporation, the artisan is merely one who pursues excellence through the virtues over and above any modernist material or moral considerations. The reason why this notion of the artisan seems unfamiliar to us and thus requires justification is that—whether or not we attain the aesthetic distance to realize it—we are all products of modernity and so subject to its prejudices and distortions. The challenge that I face here is to use the language of modernity to describe the absence of modernity. Given that our conception of business is largely a product of modernity, the challenge of illuminating business specifically in a nonmodernist light is particularly acute.

VIRTUE IN BUSINESS? WHY DOES THIS QUESTION NEED TO BE ASKED?

I could answer glibly, "Why not ask it, since the nature of aesthetic inquiry is to question everything?" If this is sufficient justification, and it probably is, then we can move on; but I think a more pedantic justification is also compelling. Reference to the virtue ethics literature, when it relates to business activity, reveals that there is no consensus on the question of the applicability of the virtues to business. Robert Solomon (1992), for example, seems to have no problem with applying virtue ethics to business: "Corporations are real communities . . . and therefore the perfect place to start understanding the nature of the virtues" (p. 325). But Alasdair MacIntyre (1984a), on the other hand, argues forcefully that virtue ethics is entirely anathema to business, at least to modern business: "[T]he tradition of the virtues is at variance with central features of the modern economic order" (p. 254). Specifically, MacIntyre isolates three "central features of the modern economic order" that exclude it from the virtues. These are "individualism . . . acquisitiveness and its elevation of the values of the market to a central social place" (p. 254).

MacIntyre himself might be surprised by the frequency with which his name appears in the business ethics discourse. Although over a period spanning nearly 50 years he has written prolifically on the subject of ethics, he rarely addresses the subject of business ethics. Why, then, should we in business or in business ethics concern ourselves with his views? I think our interest in MacIntyre stems from our interest in virtue ethics, specifically our interest in the applicability of the virtues to business. When it comes to virtue ethics, MacIntyre is recognized as an authority, if not *the* authority. Even his fiercest detractors would, I hope, admit that he has been largely responsible for the resurrection of classical philosophy in the latter half of this century. His book *After Virtue* (1984a), in which he criticizes modernity and praises a classical virtue-based approach to ethics, is undoubtedly one of the most influential books on moral philosophy written this century. Indeed, as poststructuralism and aestheticism gain steam as a sociocultural force, its full influence is yet to be determined. If MacIntyre's critique of modernity proves correct, then much of modernist business theory—not to mention moral theory in general—would be discredited. Thus, interest in MacIntyre's thesis, from many quarters, is understandable.

On the rare occasions when MacIntyre does discuss business, it is invariably in a tangential fashion, using business to illustrate some point or other; for example, in "Utilitarianism and Cost-Benefit Analysis" (1977), which appeared in *Values in the Electric Power Industry*, a book of readings, MacIntyre uses a critique of the accepted financial practice of cost-benefit analysis as a tool for a broad critique of utilitarianism. Given this tangential approach, therefore, it is not surprising that his views on business are opaque and open to misinterpretation. This opacity is compounded by the fact that, as MacIntyre freely admits, his views have subtly changed and evolved over the past four decades. For example, in "Incommensurability, Truth, and the Conversation between Confucians and Aristotelians about the Virtues" (1991), MacIntyre notes the change in his views since writing his 1966 book *A Brief History of Ethics*. This intellectual drift is hardly unusual or surprising. What is perhaps more surprising is that his main philosophical thrust, that of a critique of modernity, has remained consistent throughout his career. This consistency is noted by Peter McMylor in his book *Alasdair MacIntyre: Critic of Modernity* (1994). McMylor begins by quoting from the first book that MacIntyre wrote (*Marxism: An Interpretation* [1953]) and noting that "[h]ere we see presented to the world for the first time many of MacIntyre's familiar themes and concerns: the anxiety about the division and fragmentation of everyday life in relation to a great moral scheme and an absolutely distinctive certainty that this is a modern 'bourgeois' phenomenon" (p. 3). Indeed, it is this critique of modernity, which lies at the heart of MacIntyre's work, that provides the key to a full understanding of his position on business.

MacIntyre's views are generally known through his two most popular works, namely, *After Virtue* (1984a) and *Whose Justice? Which Rationality?* (1988). Andrew Wicks (1997), for example, has recently provided a critique of MacIntyre's perspective on business, and the above are the only two works of MacIntyre's referenced by Wicks. Some of MacIntyre's more recent work, however, although not as well known, has clarified the sweeping critique of business offered briefly in the above books. In constructing what I hope will be a balanced account of MacIntyre's views on business, I draw heavily on these more recent works. Of course, what I will be providing below is "MacIntyre's view on business as I see it," which may or may not be entirely consistent with "MacIntyre's view on business as MacIntyre himself sees it." But then, from an aesthetic perspective, this is inevitable.

MACINTYRE'S POSITION ON BUSINESS

As I mentioned at the beginning of this chapter, among those who have ventured an opinion, MacIntyre is almost universally labeled as "antibusiness." But what exactly does this label mean? Wicks (1997), in his recent critique, for example, assigns this label thus: "According to their descriptions (Dobson, MacIntyre, and others) of business and ethics, the two realms are fundamentally different and inherently antagonistic" (p. 526). In essence, Wicks accuses MacIntyre of making a straw man–type argument. MacIntyre, according to Wicks, conjures business in a certain particular context; this is a Milton-Friedman-type context in which individualism, acquisitiveness, and market values are the dominant characteristics. Having labeled this business context as "business per se," in other words, having created the straw man, MacIntyre has no problem in identifying the schism between business and ethics. To discredit MacIntyre's view on business as Wicks sees it, Wicks cites several authors who argue that modern business can, and does, imbue itself with some ethic. In the current context the most notable of these is perhaps Robert Solomon (1992), who argues that not only can ethics exist in modern business, but specifically virtue ethics.

In short, Wicks's criticism of MacIntyre centers on the latter's definition of business. Wicks believes that MacIntyre misdefines a morally impoverished subcontext of business as the entire business context. As Wicks (1997) himself puts it, "MacIntyre paints with broad brush strokes, taking particular characteristics (such as individualism, acquisitiveness, and market values), generalizing narrow and extreme interpretations of them, and then imposing these qualities onto the landscape of business as essential characteristics of all managers and firms" (p. 524).

To his credit, Wicks's critique of MacIntyre is not entirely one-sided: Wicks does credit MacIntyre's "analysis" as "provocative and cause for serious reflection on current practices" (p. 524). Wicks thus distinguishes himself from other commentators who have dismissed MacIntyre outright by assigning labels to him of "relativist," or "communitarian," or both. For example, Keeley, in his review of Derek L. Phillips's book *Looking Backward: A Critical Appraisal of Communitarian Thought* (1993), notes that Phillips views MacIntyre as someone who pines for a return to classical Greek community: "Take the polis of ancient Athens, *the* model of community for MacIntyre" (Keeley, 1996, p. 550). Fortunately, in his recent work, MacIntyre has defended his position directly against the charges of relativism and communitarianism, so these types of labels are readily removable. For example, in "A Partial Response to My Critics" (1994), MacIntyre defends himself against the charge of relativism: "I had hoped that what I said about truth in enquiry in chapter 18 of *Whose Justice? Which Rationality?* would have made it adequately clear that I regard any attempt to eliminate the notion of truth from that of enquiry as bound to fail" (pp. 297–298). In the same article he defends himself also against the charge of communitarianism and against the charge that he idealizes classical Greek society. In the case of the former charge, he states: "[From contemporary communitarians] I have strongly dissociated myself whenever I have had an opportunity to do so" (p. 302). In the case of the latter charge, he states that "the truths of Thomistic Aristotelianism, as I have defended them, have to be detached from, and happily are detachable from, not only Aristotle's false assertions about women, but also his false assertions about the capacities of those engaged in productive labour" (p. 301).

The removal of Wicks's type of antibusiness label, however, requires a more nuanced approach. But I believe it is removable.

Wicks, as far as he goes, is correct. MacIntyre does believe that individualism, acquisitiveness, and market values define the context of modern business. Furthermore, MacIntyre does believe that these characteristics tend to preclude, or at best marginalize, ethics. What MacIntyre's more recent work makes very clear, however, is that he does not view this as the only conceivable or feasible business context; he recognizes that there are a variety of business contexts; these may be arrayed on a spectrum ranging from entirely morally impoverished to entirely morally enlightened. Where on this spectrum business lies at any given time and in any given place will depend upon the extent to which the surrounding culture adheres to the tenets of virtue ethics. If the culture nurtures the virtues by recognizing such concepts as practices and internal goods, then morally enlightened business activity will flourish. For example, in referring to the businesses of farming, fishing, architecture, and construction, MacIntyre (1994) states the following:

The aim internal to such productive crafts, when they are in good order, is never only to catch fish, or to produce beef or milk, or to build houses. It is to do so in a manner consonant with the excellences of the craft, so that not only is there a good product, but the craftsperson is perfected through and in her or his activity. . . . And it is in terms of this that the virtues receive their initial, if partial, definition. (p. 284)

If undertaken within the context of the virtues, therefore, business is an inherently moral pursuit. MacIntyre goes on to clarify his position by considering two fishing communities. The communities differ in terms of context. MacIntyre precedes his description of the crews by admitting, "My descriptions of these will be of ideal types, defining the extremes of a spectrum on which there are many points" (p. 284). He describes two types of fishing business as follows:

A fishing crew may be organized as a purely technical and economic means to a productive end, whose aim is only or overridingly to satisfy as profitably as possible some market's demand for fish. Just as those managing its organization aim at a high level of profits, so also the individual crew members aim at a high level of reward. . . . When however the level of reward is insufficiently high, then the individual whose motivations and values are of this kind will have from her or his own point of view the best of reasons for leaving this particular crew or even taking to another trade . . . management will from its point of view have no good reason not to fire crew members, and owners will have no good reason not to invest their money elsewhere. (p. 285)

MacIntyre then describes another fishing community:

Consider by contrast a crew whose members may well have initially joined for the sake of their wage or other share of the catch, but who have acquired from the rest of the crew an understanding of and devotion to excellence in fishing and to excellence in playing one's part as a member of such a crew. . . . So the interdependence of the members of a fishing crew in respect of skills, the achievement of goods and the acquisition of virtues will extend to an interdependence of the families of crew members and perhaps beyond them to the whole society of a fishing village. (p. 285)

In considering these two extremes of the business context spectrum, MacIntyre concludes that the first extreme characterizes modern business: "[M]uch modern industrial productive and service work is organized so as to exclude the features distinctive of a practice" (p. 286). Indeed, it is on this point, this empirical observation, that MacIntyre and I part company with modern critics such as Wicks. Wicks and those he cites believe that modern business exists in contexts more morally enlightened than that of

Macintyre's first fishing community. Why don't MacIntyre and I agree with him?

MacIntyre and I see modern business as a facet of modern culture, a culture characterized by the instrumentally rational pursuit of material goods. Attempts to imbue this culture with an ethic have, in our view, failed. This is the essence of our critique of modernity, outlined perhaps most clearly in MacIntyre's Gifford Lectures, which are reproduced in his book *Three Rival Versions of Moral Enquiry: Encyclopaedia, Genealogy, and Tradition* (1990). The moral impoverishment of contemporary business, therefore, is inevitable, given the moral impoverishment of modernity.

To summarize, labeling MacIntyre's position simply as antibusiness, although not entirely incorrect, is potentially misleading. A more fitting label, and one with which MacIntyre himself would, I think, have no qualms, would be "antimodernity." For MacIntyre, it is modernity that has corrupted business. In a virtue-based culture, business is an entirely moral pursuit. Virtue ethics is not antithetical to business activity; his description of the second fishing community makes that clear. Indeed, his description of these two extremes of the business context spectrum implies that the second community will be a more economically successful long-term business because it respects and nurtures the natural and human resources necessary for the fishing business to flourish. From an economic perspective, this is the essence of the difference between the two communities: While the first community exploits (in an economic sense) the natural resources as a means to the end of material profit, the second community sees material profit as one necessary means to the end of sustaining the community and pursuing excellence within the practice of fishing.

Thus, for MacIntyre it is not so much a matter of applying the virtues to business but rather a matter of applying business to the virtues: business simply reflects the enveloping cultural milieu; if that culture nurtures the virtues, then business within that culture will be virtuous.

So here it becomes clear how MacIntyre's comprehensive critique of modernity dovetails neatly with the central thesis of this book. In the preface I described this thesis as "business reflects culture": culture reflects business, and business reflects culture; the relation is not simply one of cause and effect; both affect each other in a continual symbiosis—hence, my prediction for the twenty-first century that the broad cultural rejection of modernity and consequent embrace of aestheticism will conjure the aesthetic manager. This is my *descriptive* prediction, which dovetails with MacIntyre's *prescriptive* prediction that a virtuous culture is necessary to conjure virtuous business. Thus, MacIntyre also recognizes this fundamental symbiosis between the nature of business activity and the encompassing cultural milieu.

MacIntyre's work also provides the key to why modernity—and so why modern business—is incapable of embracing the aesthetic value of virtue. MacIntyre's critique of modernity is not simply that modernity has chosen a moral context devoid of virtue. His critique goes deeper than this. The tragedy of modernity, according to MacIntyre, is that it fails to realize that it *is* a context. He sees this failure reflected in modern business:

Managers themselves and most writers about management conceive of themselves as morally neutral characters whose skills enable them to devise the most efficient means of achieving whatever end is proposed. Whether a given manager is effective or not is in the dominant view a quite different question from that of the morality of the ends which his effectiveness serves or fails to serve. Nonetheless there are strong grounds for rejecting the claim that effectiveness is a morally neutral value. (MacIntyre, 1984a, p. 74)

Thus, modern business is so immersed in its context of individualism, acquisitiveness, and market values that it does not even realize that this *is* a context.

In addition to agreeing with MacIntyre's critique of modernity, my own experience lends empirical support to his philosophy. My personal "context" is financial economics, I teach finance, and I read both academic and practitioner business literature. What I see is individualism, acquisitiveness, and the elevation of the values of competitive economic activity to the status of a natural law. To take just one recent, and typical, example: *Financial Practice and Education*, a leading finance publication that caters to both finance practitioners and educators, recently published an article entitled "Corporate Ethics and Shareholder Wealth Maximization" (Chambers, and Lacey, 1996). The central thrust of this article is that "shareholder wealth maximization serves as a conduit of ethics rather than a net determinant of ethical behavior. . . . Market values can price ethics just as they can price anything else" (p. 93). In essence, the presumption here is—as MacIntyre predicts—that modern business transcends any aesthetic context.

Thus, the context of modern business is further reflected in the behavioral assumptions made by financial economists. Hayne Leland and David Pyle (1977), for example, in their capital structure signaling model, state that "the entrepreneur is presumed to maximize his expected utility of wealth" (p. 373). Kose John and David Nachman (1985) directly transfer the traditional objective of the firm to managers when, in their agency model, they assume that management's "overall objective is to . . . invest in nonnegative NPV projects" (p. 867). Douglas Diamond (1989), in his model of reputation acquisition in debt markets, defines management's objective as an endeavor to "maximize discounted expected consumption over T periods" (p. 833). Evidence that financial economists view this wealth maximization rubric as inviolable and beyond context can be found in the seminal agency theory article of Michael Jensen and William Meckling (1976), discussed earlier. In this article they summarily dismiss any attempt to model agents with values other than those embraced by modernity as nothing more than

a " 'Nirvana' form of analysis" (p. 328). An overview of the behavioral assumptions of financial economics, therefore, fully supports MacIntyre's
claim of the material nature, and the conceptual narrowness, of the modern
business rubric. A rubric truly devoid of aesthetic value.

But MacIntyre does not merely deconstruct modernity. He also constructs an alternative, namely, a Thomistic interpretation of virtue ethics.
This alternative undoubtedly places business in a context alien to that in
which modern business resides. While modern business competes for external goods within markets, Thomistic business would strive for internal goods
within practice-based communities. This latter type of business, like Mac-
Intyre's second fishing community, may be a type of business with which
modernity has made us unfamiliar; but it is business nonetheless. Furthermore, it is a type of business that can flourish and still does flourish on
occasion, despite the encroachment of modernity. As MacIntyre (1994)
concludes: "Of course no fishing crew can ever completely ignore the economic dimensions of their enterprise. But we have enough experience of
members of crews preferring to endure the hardships of economic bad times
in their trade, when they could have earned far higher wages elsewhere, for
us to know that the subordination of economic goods to goods of practice
can be a rewarding reality" (pp. 285–286). Note that, in this enlightened
business community, competition, external goods, and markets would still
be characteristics; they would just no longer be the defining characteristics.
Profit would still be important and would still be pursued, but it would not
comprise the entire universe of managers' objectives.

Surely this view is not antibusiness. Contrary to the characterizations of
Wicks and others, MacIntyre is not conjuring "business and ethics . . . [as]
two realms [that] are fundamentally different and inherently antagonistic"
(Wicks, 1997, p. 526). MacIntyre and I merely conjure aesthetically impoverished modern business in that light. Furthermore, we identify the source
of this antagonism as modernity's delusion that it transcends all context. In
reality, its tenets of individualism, acquisitiveness, and disengaged reason
locate it at just one point on the spectrum of business contexts. Thus, for
MacIntyre, the tragedy of modern business is twofold. First, it exists within
a context that has failed to identify a foundational ethic. Second, it does not
even realize that it is a context.

The first step in clothing this naked emperor of modernity is to strip him
both of the delusion that he is already clothed and of the delusion that there
is such a thing as complete nakedness. A collection of MacIntyre's essays is
entitled *Against the Self-Image of the Age* (1984b); against the self-image of
his age, MacIntyre has seen the naked emperor.

Other recent support for MacIntyre's position within the business ethics
literature is supplied by Norwegian social historian Francis Sejersted (1996).
Sejersted summarizes an impressive body of Scandinavian management literature that questions the very foundation of much U.S.-based business

ethics, namely, the assumption that business management can in any way be a moral pursuit. In general, this literature concurs with MacIntyre's critique summarized above.

In short, despite its increasing popularity among philosophers, the applicability of virtue ethics theory to business has been questioned. Aesthetic glibness aside, any justification of the artisan manager as aesthete in business requires a satisfactory account of how this manager may be characterized as a meaningful individual actor in business. In the previous chapter I suggested that virtue ethics might provide just such a characterization. But given the context of virtue ethics, who exactly would this manager be, and how exactly would he or she make decisions in business?

CAN BUSINESS ACTIVITY BE REGARDED AS A PRACTICE?

If business is viewed in the standard financial-economic context of a competitive enterprise in which survival depends solely on an ability to accumulate material profits, namely, the Technical Universe, then there seems little room for virtue. In essence, far from pursuing internal goods within a practice, an individual engaged in business pursues solely external goods within a market.

But this view of business activity is too simplistic. It conjures economic "man" as one who pursues solely external goods competitively. This may indeed accurately describe the actions of many businesspeople; but I concur with MacIntyre and others who do not see why it necessarily has to be taken as the only plausible description of the motivations underlying business activity per se. Consider, as an alternative, the artisan conjured here who pursues the internal goods specific to some particular practice. Could not such individuals also thrive in business? An affirmative answer to this question rests on a further question, namely, whether a business-type activity can qualify as an Aristotelian practice. To address this question is to address the central question of whether virtue ethics is applicable to business. Consider the following scenario.

ACID TEST: DERIVATIVES TRADING

One of the most esoteric and fastest-expanding areas of business activity is derivatives trading, specifically the trading of options, futures, and swaps. Every day literally billions of dollars, yen, marks, and pounds change hands in these arcane transactions. The activity of derivatives traders has been described as a close approximation to pure capitalism in that it is a highly competitive and individualistic form of controlled chaos that centers entirely around money. Such an environment would seem to be an acid test for the virtues. Could the virtues flourish here?

They evidently did not flourish in the case of Nigel Leeson and Barings Bank. One of England's oldest and largest merchant banks, Barings was recently sold to a Dutch financial institution for one British pound sterling because of aggregate trading losses of $1.4 billion. These losses were sustained by a single trader, Nigel Leeson. Judging by characterizations of him from business associates, Leeson was someone intent on the accumulation of external goods. In many ways Leeson epitomizes the archetypal rational agent in economics: someone who pursues wealth with "if necessary, guile and deceit" (Noreen, 1988). But clearly such characteristics have not served Leeson, or his employer, particularly well: Leeson is currently serving a six-year prison term in Singapore, where the trading losses were incurred; his employer, Barings Bank, is bankrupt. Might a virtuous derivatives trader fare better?

Although outright speculation undoubtedly explains much derivatives activity, it does not explain the whole market. Take for example two of the most popular trading strategies employing derivatives, namely, portfolio insurance and index arbitrage. Without getting into the technicalities, the essential objective behind portfolio insurance is—as the name implies—to insure a portfolio against heavy losses. This is generally achieved by entering into derivatives positions that become profitable if the portfolio to be insured loses value. Similarly, the objective behind index arbitrage is not to maximize profits ad infinitum but, rather, to lock in a modest risk-free return. This is achieved by exploiting the "spread" between the value of a futures contract and the corresponding spot value.

Rather than simple wealth maximization, therefore, such strategies are better described as risk management. Furthermore, they involve the application of a substantial body of sophisticated knowledge that evolves through time. There is an excellence to pursue here, namely, the development of a trading strategy that successfully meets some risk-management goal. The activity is also communal: traders work in various groups that pursue certain common goals. For example, the traders in a "pit" on the London International Financial Futures Exchange (LIFFE) share the common goal of maintaining as liquid a market as possible for their particular contract; or the traders in a trading room of a financial institution share the common goal of meeting performance targets and designing contracts that meet the risk-management needs of clients. Indeed, the reason why Leeson was able to bankrupt Barings stems not from some inherent flaw in the activity of derivatives trading but rather from a specific failure in organizational structure at this particular bank (Brickley, Smith, and Zimmerman, 1995). In essence, Leeson viewed derivatives trading as a means solely to the acquisition of external goods. He possessed technical expertise, but he did not possess judgment. This judgment could only have come with a fundamental reconceptualization of the activity of derivatives trading. Leeson did not feel that he was engaged in the communal pursuit of the internal goods of the practice of derivatives trading. But could some business activity as inherently competitive, financial, and technical as derivatives trading ever be realistically viewed, by those engaged in it, as a practice?

Consider the three characteristics of a practice listed earlier. I see no reason why derivatives trading, correctly perceived, could not meet all three standards. First, it establishes its own standards of excellence in the design and successful implementation of the various trading strategies summarized above. Second, there are particular internal goods specific to derivatives trading. As always with the concept of internal goods, it is hard to find words to define them. Remember, in the context of chess, MacIntyre defines the internal goods as analytical skill, strategic imagination, and competitive intensity. One might reasonably question why these goods are unique to chess: Could they not equally be the goods of other practices? But I think what MacIntyre is getting at here is that the *type* of analytical skill pursued as an excellence in chess is unique to chess—just as, I would argue, the type of analytical skill necessary for excellence in derivatives trading is unique to derivatives trading. Third, derivatives trading is undoubtedly organic. These markets are continually changing, and new strategies and contracts are being developed all the time.

In short, I see no reason why the tenets of virtue ethics theory cannot be applied to even the most cold-bloodedly technical of business activities, namely, derivatives trading. The fact that this activity centers around money in no way excludes the virtues. Money is, in essence, simply a way of keeping score. Thus, a truly excellent derivatives trading organization would be one in which its members viewed themselves as engaged in the pursuit of the internal goods unique to the practice of derivatives trading—for example, the successful application of the theoretical tools of option-pricing theory or the ability to design a portfolio insurance strategy that meets as closely as possible the stated risk-management objectives. Thus, the complex financial nature of the derivatives industry, and the fact that it is financially competitive, in no way precludes the virtues. Indeed, it is perhaps the very complexity of the activity that more clearly defines the practice and the internal goods specific to it.

In summary, the tenets of virtue ethics theory are not anathema to business activity. Although business theory generally assumes that all agents are opportunists, there is no reason why such characteristics are essential for business. Thus, even though the behavioral assumptions of business theory may exclude the virtues, these virtues as character traits in business practice are in no way inconsistent with success. It is the character of the individual and the nature of the organization that will determine whether the virtues are embraced or excluded. Whether the organization happens to be one engaged in derivatives trading, capital budgeting, architecture, or politics is largely irrelevant.

SOME IMPLICATIONS FOR ECONOMIC THEORY

From strictly an economist's perspective, there is a certain irony here. Economists tend to view a business environment as ideal when it approximates that of perfect competition. This is the most economically efficient market in the sense that there is no financial slack, and all firms are producing where marginal cost equals marginal revenue and where total costs are minimized. It is a Darwinian-type economic environment in which only the economically fittest will endure. From the perspective of virtue ethics theory, however, this type of business environment is least desirable to the extent that it defines business activity purely in terms of external goods.

But of course we don't live in a world of perfect competition. And despite the protestations of free-market economists, most industries do not even approximate perfect competition. Most business environments are characterized by a few very large firms that are highly regulated and possess tremendous financial slack; as Amatai Etzioni (1991) notes, "[A]ll corporations allot some funds 'inefficiently.' . . . Hence, the real decision is whether to use the 'slack' that is practically always available, to advance aesthetic, prejudicial and selfish or—moral purposes" (p. 363). Thus, somewhat perversely, it is what economists would regard as the economic inefficiency of business activity that facilitates the virtues. By this I do not mean that economic inefficiency is in any way a sufficient condition for the virtues to flourish; a glance at contemporary Russia, for example, would rapidly dispel this notion. But what I do suspect is that a degree of economic inefficiency is a necessary condition for the virtues. For example, I see no room for the virtues in the Darwinian environment of perfect competition. That is not to say that in such an environment individuals might sometimes cooperate or honor agreements; there may indeed be simulacra of the virtues as suggested by David Gauthier in *Morals by Agreement* (1988). But with material survival so pressing, I do not see how the virtues could gain a foothold. Aristotle argued that there could be no virtue among slaves, and agents operating in such an environment are a type of slave: a Marxian "wage slave." Fortunately, however, for us and for the virtues, few of us operate under such conditions.

This conceptual incompatibility between economic theory and virtue theory may help explain the conflict outlined earlier between authors such as MacIntyre, Solomon, and Wicks. MacIntyre's reluctance to admit the virtues into business stems from his very modernistic view of business activity. For him business is all about individualism, acquisitiveness, and the values of the market—labels readily applicable to the agent of economic theory. Contrarily, Solomon (1994) talks of firms as "communities" in which ethics provide "the very ground rules of business" (1994, p. xv)—hardly a view familiar to economic theory.

Returning to MacIntyre's fishing communities. His choice of this industry to highlight the conflict between business and virtue was perhaps not arbitrary. Few industries have demonstrated more starkly the need for governmental intervention—to preserve species and habitats—in the face of shortsighted economic exploitation. For example, if MacIntyre's two fishing communities were to compete for the same fishing grounds, which in reality they would sooner or later be forced to do, it seems unlikely that his second virtuous "fishing community as long term enterprise" could survive the onslaught of the economic opportunists. It would be left to some omniscient, omnipotent, and omnipresent third party, namely, a government or an aesthetic enlightenment, to protect the former community from the enslavement of the free-market, Technical Universe opportunists. This highlights an important attribute of aesthetic business: it is sustainable. Unlike for John Maynard Keynes, for the manager as artisan, there *is* a long run!

DEFINING THE ARTISAN

To summarize the chapter so far, I address the question of whether virtue ethics theory is applicable to business. The question distills down to that of whether business can be viewed as a practice-based activity.With substantial assistance from MacIntyre, I conclude that virtue ethics is applicable to business. Business activity can successfully be construed as a type of practice in which internal goods may be pursued; thus, although modern business may tend to exclude the virtues, an aesthetic invocation of business embraces and nurtures them.

Consequently, a central theme of this book has been a broadening of the business paradigm to encompass another dimension, an aesthetic dimension: a dimension supplied by virtue ethics theory. To some extent this broadening is a reflection of the considerable cultural impact of the contemporary firm in the form of the transnational corporation. To some extent it is a reflection of increasing debate in the business, ethics, and business ethics literature concerning the essential nature of the firm: Is the firm an atomistic decision unit, a contractual nexus, or a nurturing community? But, most fundamentally, it is a reflection of the fact that the firm is a *human* organization, implying that, in addition to economic relationships, business should consist of moral relationships—what John Rawls (1971) refers to as a "social union." As economist Kenneth Arrow (1975) admits: "It can be argued that the presence of what are in a slightly old-fashioned terminology called virtues in fact plays a significant role in the operation of the economic system" (p. 109).

Rather than being an aberration, therefore, this book's invocation of the business management paradigm in a still broader arena of human interaction is perhaps an inevitable consequence of the increasing impact that the business or market rubric is having on intellectual and practical affairs. This increasing impact necessitates a more holistic conception of human endeavor in economic contexts as being concerned with the acquisition of both external goods *and* internal goods.

Part I of this book established the manager as technician's existence entirely within the universe of substance (i.e., that of external goods) and its complete ignorance of the universe of value (i.e., that of internal goods); thus, a recognition not only of the existence of internal goods but of their moral superiority leads inevitably to a rejection of this narrow view of economic rationality.

Earlier, I defined the aesthetic manager as artisan as one motivated primarily by a desire to achieve excellence. Here I coin this word in what I believe to be its true context, namely, in the context of Aristotelian excellence, conjuring the image of ethics as something toward which we strive rather than something that constrains us. As MacIntyre (1984a) notes: "[T]he whole point of ethics—both as a theoretical and practical discipline—is to enable man to pass from his present state to his true end" (p. 54).

The pursuit of internal goods, in preference to external goods, is what defines the artisan. Interestingly, the concept of the internal good is very similar to the concept of quality in the increasingly popular total quality management literature and to the concept of excellence in the in search of excellence–type management motivational literature. All these concepts have to do with the pursuit of some ethereal goal that is not external or finite but that is universally recognized and acclaimed as desirable. According to practical rationality, the pursuit of this quality/excellence/internal good entails adherence to certain behavioral ideals, commonly called the virtues.

Consider the four critical virtues enumerated by Socrates of wisdom, justice, courage, and temperance. Justice, for example, would include a sense of fairness, which would generally entail being honest and trustworthy. But note my tentative wording. I say "*would* generally entail being honest" rather than "*will* entail being honest" because in the pursuit of moral excellence there are no absolute ethical rules; there are times when circumstances may dictate that the ethical agent conceal the truth. For example, while experiencing negative cash flow, a chief financial officer (CFO) may choose to borrow funds in order to maintain timely dividend payments. Such action could be construed as deceptive in that the payment of dividends is generally taken by outsiders as a signal of a firm's ability to generate sufficient internal cash flow. But the CFO may genuinely believe that such deception is for the greater good; it is consistent with the pursuit of moral excellence. If the CFO is confident that the firm is only temporarily insolvent but is unsure of his ability to relay this confidence to investors, and if he believes that the announcement of a dividend omission would cause unnecessary concern—if not outright panic—among investors, then this deception is entirely ethical. His motivation is practically rational and virtuous, even though his action is arguably deceptive.

But what about a CFO who chooses the same action, namely, borrowing to maintain the dividend, but who has no expectation regarding the firm's future earning potential? Rather, the CFO's motivation is to maintain the stock price temporarily in order that she may exercise some stock options. Clearly, this agent's fundamental motivation is personal material gain. The deception is not motivated by the pursuit of moral excellence. This CFO is not exercising *sound moral judgment*. She is not exercising the virtues of justice or wisdom because, as the classical philosophers make very clear, a wise individual (i.e., one who has been exposed to the concept of moral excellence) will realize that it is only through virtuous behavior and the pursuit of internal goods that one can live the good life. And what is the good life?

Once again, this question brooks no simple answer. The good life is the life that any virtuous individual would choose. It involves adherence to the virtues and the pursuit of quality/excellence/internal goods. It entails placing virtue and moral excellence above external goods as a source of primary motivation in life. Only the agent who is so motivated and acts in this manner is able to flourish and achieve true happiness.

Thus, the pursuit of moral excellence is not self-sacrificing: it is entirely consistent with the pursuit of personal self-interest. A manager as artisan simply possesses a heightened concept of self-interest vis-à-vis the interests of the community (what Aristotle calls the *polis*)—a concept nurtured by aesthetic understanding (the virtue of wisdom) but not nurtured by the narrow materially opportunistic behavioral assumptions of the Technical Universe. An economic agent, that is, one motivated primarily by economic gain, may act in a trustworthy manner, but this has nothing to do with virtue since the *motivation* is not moral excellence. The moral agent, that is, one motivated primarily by the pursuit of moral excellence, will also generally act in a trustworthy manner and will therefore reap the economic— as well as the moral—benefits of a reputation.

As virtue ethics theory makes clear, however, the fact that ethics may pay financially cannot be the motivation behind our ethical actions. Even if ethics does not pay off in an economic sense, which clearly in some circumstances it doesn't, classical moral philosophy gives us ample reason to act ethically: short-term material gain through unethical behavior is inevitably at the expense of long-term happiness and the good life. The concept of the manager as *artisan* sheds additional light on the difference between the economically rational agent of modernity and the practically rational agent of virtue ethics. Consider Duska's (1992) statement that:

to be an agent in business is to be a professional. . . . One doesn't simply do what one is told, one has expertise, one reads and anticipates the needs and interests of the principal and operates for the principal's good. Managers, Financiers, Accountants, Ad Executives, Sales Representatives, are all agents. Agents are, qua agent, committed to good, i.e., the good of their client. (p. 164)

This invocation of the agent in business is clearly at odds with the individualistic wealth-maximizing opportunist of the Technical Universe. Agency theory certainly does not view the agent as possessing a "professional" attitude. Duska's notion of the agent as one "committed to good" is clearly more in line with practical rationality than it is with economic rationality. The practically rational manager can thus be viewed as the consummate professional, or the moral exemplar.

THE AESTHETIC FIRM AS A *POLIS*

> Perhaps the polis is, as Plato and Aristotle thought, the only form of community in which human beings can flourish, rather than merely endure.
>
> —Alasdair MacIntyre, *After Virtue*

As discussed in Chapter 5, practical rationality has implications for the role of the firm. The firm becomes a nurturing community with a unified mission, or *telos*, namely, to pursue internal goods. This is the essence of the classical Greek concept of the community as a unity, but as a unity of free-thinking individuals: a *polis*.

Given that this aesthetic pursuit of personal excellence is only possible within an organization that approximates a *polis*, business organizations must be constituted on this premise—the premise that the pursuit of external goods is always in some absolute sense inferior to the pursuit of internal goods. Indeed, the two will not always be compatible. Exercising the virtues could very well entail a material sacrifice; as MacIntyre (1984a) admits, "[P]ossession of the virtues may perfectly well hinder us in achieving external goods" (p. 196).

The manager in a multinational corporation, for example, may exercise the virtues of courage and justice by paying workers in a developing country the wage that he of she feels is just, rather than merely the minimum market-clearing wage as dictated by economic theory. The manager is exhibiting courage by taking an action that is not strictly in the interests of firm value maximization and may damage the firm's competitive position, at least in the short term. It might appear, therefore, that this manager, albeit virtuous, is not acting in the interests of shareholders. If we assume, however, that shareholders are also practically rational, and thus form part of the communal practice, or *polis*, then such virtuous actions on the part of the manager would be in the broadened interests of shareholders. Indeed, if the firm is truly to be a communal practice in the Aristotelian sense, then all stakeholders must be practically rational and thus are pursuing the same internal goods of excellence over and above the economic goods of effectiveness.

An appropriate institutional infrastructure is essential, therefore, in order to enlighten managers as to the superiority and ultimate desirability of the internal goods of the artisan, for as MacIntyre (1984a) warns: "We should therefore expect that, if in a particular society the pursuit of external goods were to become dominant, the concept of the virtues might suffer at first attrition and then perhaps something near total effacement" (p. 196).

An interesting analogy can be drawn between the role of the *polis* in directing human endeavor and recent research that highlights the importance of institutional infrastructure in guiding human activity (Romer, 1990). Douglas North (1991), for example, notes that "[t]he subjective perceptions (mental models) of entrepreneurs determine the choices they make" (p. 5). And it is the infrastructure, the *polis*, that helps sculpt these mental models: "It is the institutional framework that dictates the kind of knowledge perceived to having the maximum pay-off" (p. 10). The firm, therefore, as an attribute of the *polis* is instrumental to practical rationality. Its role is to guide and assist agents in their pursuit of the *telos*: the absolute Quality.

Broadening the role of the firm in this way prompts a definition of the firm that extends that which is implicit in the finance paradigm by recognizing the firm's role as an integral part of the organizational infrastructure, necessary for the pursuit of the *telos*:

> *Firms facilitate and nurture individual and collective material acquisition as a means to the attainment of excellence through virtue.*

Note that this definition invokes the firm as more than merely a contractual nexus or wealth-creating machine. As part of the *polis* the firm adopts a more active and nuturing role. As facilitator, the firm provides an external-good support for the pursuit of excellence through the exercise of the classical virtues. As a nurturer, the firm provides an organizational structure premised on the superiority of classical *phronesis* (practical intelligence informed by virtue) over *techne* (technical skill)—in other words, the superiority of internal goods over external goods.

Invoking the firm as a constituent of the *polis*—as a true corporate culture—clearly broadens its role considerably. Indeed, one likely criticism of this invocation of the firm is that despite its current size and power as reflected in the transnational corporation the firm—even as it exists in Japan— still remains a primarily *economic* organization. A great deal has been written about Japanese corporate culture as distinct from that in the West. Japanese corporations tend to provide lifetime employment and therefore adopt a paternal role. For example, a Japanese firm is often likened to an extended family, and therefore "company loyalty functions as the motivating force" (Bowie, 1991, p. 18). As such, the behavioral assumptions that underlie economic rationality may be even less appropriate in a Japanese setting.

Even if desirable, is it plausible to invoke the concepts of *polis* and *telos* in the contemporary world of liberal individualism? MacIntyre (1988) believes that it is: "[I]f at least those features of the *polis* which are minimally necessary for the exercise of justice and of practical rationality can be exhibited by forms of social order other than those of the *polis*, then the grounds for that charge of irrelevance may fail" (p. 99). Whether or not the charge fails will clearly depend to a large degree on the infrastructure in which individuals learn about and practice business. As North (1991) notes: "If the highest rates of return in a society are for piracy, then organizations will invest in knowledge and skills that will make them better pirates" (p. 4).

In an educational context, we must accept the "indoctrination" aspect of business education; that is, we accept that "is" implies "ought," and therefore economic rationality must be rejected on the grounds that it fails to recognize the Aesthetic Universe and hence virtue and indeed morality in general: Thus, we reject economic rationality not on the basis of its descriptive accuracy (albeit questionable) but rather on the basis of its prescriptive undesirability (of course, if "is" implies "ought," then the two become inseparable). If we further accept the ultimate desirability of an Aristotelian-type notion of rationality, with its accompanying notions of *telos* and *polis*, then we must accept the Theory of the Firm as more than merely a passive description of an organization and human activity therein. The Theory of the Firm becomes much more than this. It becomes moral dogma: a theory, not only of what the firm is but of what the firm *should* be. Norman Bowie (1991) argues (as do many other business ethicists) that "business education and research into business must take into account the ethical paradigm as well" (p. 19). Our discussion here implies that business education and business-ethics education are entirely inseparable. The contemporary flirtation with psychological egoism in the form of the intellectual hegemony of financial-economic rationality is misguided in the sense that it fails to identify the true *telos*. Aristotle (1991) identifies this as an educational failure: "[O]ne mark of educational failure will be a tendency on the part of individual citizens to identify as *the* good and *the* best some good which is merely an external by-product of those activities in which excellence is achieved—money or honor, for example" (p. 12).

Thus the failure of business education has been not so much a manifestation of a "closing of the American mind," as Allan Bloom (1987) suggests, but rather a misdirection of the American mind and indeed the minds of all those immersed in the corporate culture of modernity: a confusion of means and ends. This misdirection has led MacIntyre (1988), for example, to lament the modern student as "someone whose education has been as much a process of deprivation as of enrichment" (p. 400). In the current context, this enrichment entails merely the recognition of the firm as a human organization and the fact that those goods that are ultimately desirable in all human endeavor—whether they be defined as *eudaimonia*, quality, excellence, or internal goods—are only attainable through the exercise of moral virtue. Thus, the theory of the firm is an aesthetic theory because the firm is an aesthetic organization; and business is an art in the classical sense of a craft undertaken by a community of artisans. Consequently, rather than modeling itself after the physical sciences, the business school must be a fundamentally aesthetic and artistic institution.

In summary, modernism invokes the firm as solely a conduit through which agents pursue individual material wealth. Virtue ethics recognizes a more interactive role for the aesthetic firm as a nurturing community in which individuals may flourish aesthetically as well as materially. In addition to being a powerful economic force, as discussed earlier, this aesthetic firm will also be a powerful *moral* force. Individual virtue—by minimizing agency costs—supports the economic role of the firm, whereas the structure of the firm itself as a nurturing community encourages individual virtue. The relationship is reciprocal and long-term sustainable.

IMPLICATIONS OF VIRTUE FOR MODERNIST BUSINESS ETHICS

Anyone undertaking a keyword search of the business ethics literature ten years ago, or even five years ago, would only infrequently come across the word "virtue." If one were to undertake a similar search today, however, "virtue" would likely rank among the most common keywords. But, as has been made clear in this chapter, "the tradition of the virtues is at variance with central features of the modern economic order" (MacIntyre, 1984a, p. 254). Thus the fact that virtue has become popular within the modern business ethics discourse is not without paradox. In this section, I wish to explore this paradox by addressing two simple questions. First, Why is virtue finding such a powerful voice within the business ethics discourse? Second, What are the implications for the discipline of business ethics in general if it is viewed increasingly through the lens of virtue ethics theory?

In answer to the first question, business ethics is turning to virtue because—as revealed in Part II—attempts to apply other moral philosophies to business have largely failed. Conventional modernist business ethics is being exposed as a naked emperor: a discipline with no sound conceptual foundation. This phenomenon is just one more reflection of the deconstruction of the Moral Universe that has now manifested itself in business ethics theory. The growing use of the virtue rubric in business ethics is an attempt to fill the void left by the deconstruction of modernity, a deconstruction that has revealed the Aesthetic Universe as that which remains once the obscuring layers of modernity are removed.

In answer to the second question, many of the business ethicists who are currently embracing virtue do not realize just what they are admitting into their discourse. Virtue ethics is not just one other ethics theory, like Kantianism or utilitarianism. It is a Trojan horse that, once admitted within the ontological walls of business ethics theory, will force the latter to question the very tenets of modern competitive business enterprise. Indeed, just as virtue ethics theory discredits much of modern moral philosophy, it may well discredit *all* of conventional business ethics theory.

NAKED EMPERORS

I turn now to a more detailed answer to the first question posed. In the Hans Christian Andersen story "The Emperor's New Clothes," while under the illusion that he is clothed in the finest of robes, the emperor parades through the streets of his kingdom stark naked. This odd state of affairs stems from the antics of two self-proclaimed tailors. Recognizing that all those in positions of authority are fundamentally insecure, the tailors tell the king that they are weaving robes with magic silk that will be invisible to anyone who is stupid or who is unqualified to hold his position. Not willing to admit to either of these faults, but believing that they may well be guilty of them, neither the king nor his courtiers are willing to admit that they cannot see the emperor's clothes. The myth is thus sustained and the more people who participate in the deception, the stronger the deception becomes. The enduring wisdom contained in this fairy tale is evidenced by the frequency with which the term "naked emperor" is used metaphorically to describe concepts that are, in reality, conceptually empty.

If the discipline of business ethics is indeed a naked emperor, then it is a discipline that—despite the protestations of its adherents—lacks any sound logical foundation in moral philosophy. Judge Richard Posner hints at this lack when he observes "moral philosophy as a weak field, a field in disarray, a field in which consensus is impossible to achieve in our society" (in Dunfee, 1988, p. 138). Recent evidence that business ethicists may feel somewhat "naked" can be gleaned from their reaction to Andrew Stark's (1993) infamous critique entitled "What's the Matter with Business Ethics" that appeared in the *Harvard Business Review*. From what I witnessed at the 1993 annual meeting of the Society for Business Ethics (SBE), in Atlanta, this one fairly innocuous article precipitated a feverish crisis of confidence among the business ethics fraternity. This crisis climaxed in a terse "letter to the editor" of the *Harvard Business Review* from the Society of Business Ethics. The letter expressed nothing short of moral outrage: "It is unfortunate that a distinguished journal allowed such an uninformed and largely unsubstantiated indictment of serious professionals and their field to be published in its pages" (Duska, 1993b, p. 10). It is surely unlikely that a similar critique of, say, finance or psychology would have engendered such an officious and defensive response.

Indeed, even some of the leading champions of business ethics recognize that it faces a real crisis of legitimacy: "Where does business ethics stand today? Despite the clamor for it, its legitimacy as an academic discipline is suspect. . . . Unless this question of legitimacy is addressed, and to some extent answered, the future of business ethics is not bright" (Bowie and Freeman, 1992, p. 17). It seems that many in the discipline of business ethics recognize this crisis and are, as Lambeth (1990) puts it, "[w]aiting for a New St. Benedict" (p. 97). Some feel that they have found this St. Benedict in the guise of virtue ethics theory. For example, Solomon (1992) argues that "[b]usiness ethicists have been looking for theory in the wrong place and, consequently, they have been finding and developing the wrong theories" (p. 319).

Solomon recognizes the impotence of business ethics as stemming from its inability to answer the fundamental question, Why should I be ethical? As MacIntyre (1984a) points out, conventional deontological and consequentialist moral philosophy (what he calls "post-Enlightenment" moral philosophy) has failed to answer this question. Thus, given that business ethics theory looks to moral philosophy for its epistemological foundation, business ethicists face a real problem of legitimacy. Attempts have been made to subvert and circumvent this problem by rejecting moral philosophy in favor of economic theory. Ethical action is given a strategic economic role and is justified on these grounds. An economic justification is given surreptitiously along the platitudinous lines of "Good ethics is good business." Thus, ethics becomes just another economic strategy within the Technical Universe.

To see this, one need look no further than the first few pages of many business ethics texts. In these texts, we have, as Gauthier (1988) defines them, "morals by agreement," which of course means that we don't have true morality at all but rather a means to strategic advantage through co-operation; we have strategic ethics rather than real ethics. The underlying motivation for the cooperation envisioned by Gauthier is strategic economic self-interest. This is why Donaldson (1989) criticizes Gauthier's justification for morality as being insufficient to instill moral behavior in an international environment where one agent is considerably more powerful than another: In such an environment, we need real ethics, such as justice or compassion, because strategic mutual benefit through cooperation may not apply.

As virtue ethics makes clear, the crucial factor here is not observable action, but rather the underlying motivation. It is the *motivation* for the action that determines whether the act is fundamentally ethical or economic. Business ethicists often seem to forget this; they confuse strategic cooperation with moral cooperation. For example, two recent books in the field appear to suffer from just such confusion. In *Competing with Integrity in International Business* (1993), Richard De George states that "competing successfully with integrity is in fact the aim and the norm of individuals who compete with integrity" (p. 7). And in *The New World of Business: Ethics and Free Enterprise in the Global 1990's* (1994), Solomon states that "ethics is not a burden or a business disadvantage but the very ground rules of business as such and the key to business success" (p. xv). The meaning of these statements clearly rests on what is meant by "success." If "success" means economic success, then this sounds a lot like an economic justification for ethics, that is, strategic ethics; we are back in the Technical Universe.

TROJAN HORSE

I turn now to the second question posed above concerning the impact of virtue ethics on conventional modernist business ethics theory. Business ethicists often introduce virtue ethics theory as merely an alternative to stakeholder theory or social contracts theory (e.g., Dunfee, 1995, p. 167). But such superficial treatment betrays a failure to grasp the full substance and depth of the virtue rubric.

For example, despite its fashionable appearance, the term "virtuous corporation" is thwart with ambiguity. A true and in-depth understanding of the virtue concept, as supplied for example by MacIntyre, reveals that it is a concept that may be fundamentally antithetical to competitive economic activity. Thus, individuals within a modern corporation, which by its very nature is engaged in the competitive acquisition of material wealth as its fundamental raison d'être, could only exercise some simulacra of the true virtues if limited conceptually by the parameters of the Technical or Moral Universes.

By introducing virtue into their dialogue, therefore, business ethicists may be getting more than they bargained for. On the surface, virtue may look fairly innocuous. But once one delves beneath the surface—once the Trojan horse is opened—one is faced with a view of the world that challenges the very tenets of contemporary Western corporate culture. That is, it challenges the premise of a culture built on the acquisition of external goods. But what exactly precludes individuals within a modern corporation from exercising the virtues? Why can we not have a modernist virtuous corporation?

As I have endeavored to show in this chapter, it is a modern corporation's focus on external goods—on the goods of effectiveness over and above the goods of excellence—that disqualifies it as a practice. A truly virtuous corporation simply could not have an ultimate goal of economic survival or economic success: "It is of the character of a virtue that in order that it be effective in producing the internal goods which are the rewards of the virtues it should be exercised without regard to consequences" (MacIntyre, 1984a, p. 198). This once again emphasizes the link between virtue ethics and the aesthetic manager as artisan. For the virtues to flourish, business must be fundamentally an aesthetic pursuit that transcends modernist means-ends reasoning. Without this transcendence, the business aesthetic outlined in this chapter will remain a chimera.

TEST CASE: PEPSI/BURMA—A FINAL WORD

In previous discussion of this test case in Parts I and II, I outlined the shortcomings of the technical and moral approaches to business decision making. In the case of the technical approach, these shortcomings stemmed largely from the narrow mechanistic view of business activity. For example, technical methodologies such as the net present value assume that all factors impacting a capital budgeting decision can be monetized and that the present discounted value of these future monetized values can be estimated accurately. Furthermore, even if we buy into the Technical Universe, that is to say, even if we accept that the firm is purely or primarily a money-making machine, we are still faced with the self-deconstruction of financial-economic theory, what I termed earlier the "finance paradox": specifically, the inability of instrumentally rational wealth-maximizing opportunists to rationally achieve their rationally chosen material goal.

In the case of modernist moral approaches to business, as reflected in conventional business ethics theory, a similar deconstruction is apparent. Any justification for business within the Moral Universe, whether in the form of integrated social contracts theory or some application of utilitarianism or Kantianism, rests on a single premise, namely, the ability to rationalize the moral "ought" embedded in all these principles. But as several astute observers have noted, and I am thinking here particularly of Nietzsche and MacIntyre, the modernist project has failed to find a rational-in-a-modernist-sense justification for its moral "ought." And the entire project, no matter how sophisticated its trimmings, rests on this justification. This is what I labeled earlier as modern moral philosophy's deafening silence.

In summary, both the Technical and Moral Universes, albeit the dominant universes of business in the twentieth century, are exposing themselves increasingly as fragile edifices built wholly on epistemological sand. These metaphysical universes are facing, to coin MacIntyre's (1984a) phrase, "epistemological crises":

We have already noticed that central to a tradition-constituted enquiry [e.g., the Technical or Moral Universe] at each stage in its development will be its current problematic, that agenda of unsolved problems and unresolved issues by reference to which its success or lack of it in making rational progress toward some further stage of development will be evaluated. At any point it may happen to any tradition-constituted enquiry that by its own standards of progress it ceases to make progress. Its hitherto trusted methods of enquiry have become sterile. Conflicts over rival answers to key questions can no longer be settled rationally. Moreover, it may indeed happen that the use of the methods of enquiry and of the forms of argument, by means of which rational progress had been achieved so far, begins to have the effect of increasingly disclosing new inadequacies, hitherto unrecognized incoherences, and new problems for the solution of which there seem to be insufficient or no resources within the established fabric of belief. . . . This kind of dissolution of historically founded certitudes is the mark of an epistemological crisis. (p. 362)

It is the recognition of this crisis in the Technical and Moral Universes that will result in the Aesthetic Universe becoming the dominant management paradigm of the twenty-first century. But how best can companies, and specifically senior-level managers within companies, handle this metaphysical shift? Does the transition from the moral manager or the manager as technician and toward the artisan necessarily have to be a difficult and costly one? From our earlier discussion, it seems to have been costly for Pepsi with its experiences in Burma, and it seems to have been costly for Royal Dutch–Shell with its experiences in Nigeria, but could these transition difficulties have been avoided? In short, as we enter the twenty-first century, how can firms best forearm themselves against the potentially disruptive effects of this epistemological crisis? This book's attempt to explain the epistemological crisis is a forewarning, and as the saying goes, to be forewarned is to be forearmed. But in these remaining pages, I attempt a more explicit forearming. I will give some practical examples of how a management culture can be enlightened to the Aesthetic Universe and how such an enlightenment could have helped Pepsi's management in its decision regarding operations in Burma. Management cultures can change and can be changed. The key for management is to recognize the cultural shift and so adapt to it proactively, rather than being forced to adapt ex-post facto when the firm faces a crisis wrought by some cultural clash, as in the aforementioned case of Shell. The responsibility for this proactive leadership falls on senior management; the cultural adjustment must be from the top down. As Paul Nystrom (1990) observes: "A corporation's top management sets the ethical tone for its employees" (p. 971). But how can top management best fulfill this obligation? It what follows I suggest an approach. I label it the "education approach."

THE EDUCATION APPROACH

The approach begins from this chapter's conclusion that the aesthetic manager as artisan represents a practical application of the tenets of virtue ethics theory. The successful transition to this virtue-based notion of the management paradigm rests crucially, therefore, on the ability of senior managers to convince other individuals within the organization that a personal and communal ethos based on a virtue ethics–type notion of aesthetic excellence is preferable to one based on material self-interest or moral dogma. In his recent book *Passions within Reason* (1988), discussed earlier, Robert Frank argues that a predisposition to act ethically will also serve the agents' material self-interest. Ethical agents will be identified as such and will therefore be able to enter contracts with a minimum of monitoring costs as compared to their unethical counterparts. Thus, in a direct economic sense, ethics pays. The applicability of Frank's "commitment model" is limited, however, by the fact that Frank views ethics as emotion based. Either an agent is predisposed to act ethically, or she is not. Frank tends to imply, therefore, that ethical attitudes are set by adulthood, whereas the education approach that I propose here relies on an ability to change ethical attitudes among adult managers. Thus, my education approach assumes centrally that ethical behavior may be the result of intellectual reflection, in addition to emotion.

In practical terms, the development of such a personal ethos among employees may be facilitated initially by the drafting of a corporate credo emphasizing the aesthetic ideals of virtue ethics. Note particularly that rather than casting ethics as a constraint on behavior, a virtue ethics–based corporate code emphasizes the role of moral excellence as an objective. Such a code provides no easy answers for practitioners faced with ethically charged decisions; judgment calls are always necessary; for example, Mark Pastin (1986) extols managers to "relentlessly emphasize that codes are merely guidelines, that rules have exceptions, and that the essence of ethics is independent thinking and question" (p. 474). What such an ethos will provide, however, is a framework of values by which to make these judgment calls. It will spell out that which is most desirable in all human endeavor. As Oliver Williams and Patrick Murphy (1990) note in their article supporting the application of virtue ethics to corporate marketing practices:

[T]he perspective of this ethical system [i.e., virtue ethics] is that all rules and principles are, at root, an attempt to preserve a human way of life; thus, our most fundamental task in ethics today is not primarily concerned with analyzing situations so that one can make the right decisions, but rather with reflecting on what constitutes the good life. . . . [B]eing an ethical person is not simply an analytical and rational matter. (p. 24)

A corporate ethos based on virtue ethics, therefore, requires a broad-brush approach rather than an enumeration of specific rules for each possible contingency. In essence, such an ethos places virtue above material gain. Johnson & Johnson Inc.'s "Credo," for example, reflects this. The credo begins with the following statement: "We believe our first responsibility is to the doctors, nurses and patients, to mothers and fathers and all others who use our products and services." The credo proceeds to enumerate responsibilities to employees and the community at large, and only toward the end of the credo are stockholders mentioned as deserving "a fair return." No specific moral guidelines are given for individual financial, marketing, or other decisions. But what is enumerated is a value system predicated on the classical aesthetic virtues of honesty, integrity, courage, justice, and a respect for human life and dignity *over and above* the need to return stockholders their "fair return." Similarly, Nike's credo talks about "trust, teamwork, honesty and mutual respect" and a "quest to enhance people's lives through sports and fitness"; no mention is made in Nike's credo of maximizing shareholder interests.

The existence of the credo at Johnson & Johnson enabled it to react quickly, decisively, and ethically to the crisis concerning cyanide-contaminated Tylenol capsules. As Williams and Murphy (1990) note, "[T]he firm's recall of the Tylenol capsules was a result of the culture in place at Johnson & Johnson" (p. 26). Procter & Gamble (P&G) reacted similarly to the Rely tampon crisis. At the first sign of health problems resulting from the use of this product, it immediately, without hesitation, demarketed a product that had taken 20 years to develop at a cost of $74 million (Hoffman and Moore, 1990, p. 636). As Edward G. Harness, chairman of the board of P&G, commented, "[P]rofitability and growth go hand in hand with fair treatment of employees, of customers, of consumers, and of the community" (p. 636).

Such behavior lies in sharp contrast to that of Dow Corning in the wake of revelations concerning the long-term effects of silicon breast implants and to the dithering of Union Carbide (UC) in the wake of the asphyxiation tragedy in Bhopal, India. (We might also add Pepsi's dithering in its decision of whether or not to sever all business ties with Burma, but more on this shortly.) In the case of Union Carbide, as John Ladd (1991) points out, Union Carbide lacked a corporate ethos or aesthetic with which to make complex decisions that involved both financial and moral aspects. He concludes that UC's behavior "reflected a perfectly commonplace and 'normal' preoccupation with matters of self-interest and of self-advancement to the exclusion of any consideration of the wider implications of their actions or non-actions and of their absence of concern for the safety and the welfare of others" (p. 89).

Although corporate codes of ethics may provide managers with a valuable framework for ethical decision making, they are not in and of themselves sufficient to ensure ethical conduct. As Dinah Payne and Cecily Raiborn (1990) observe, "[E]thics codes cannot simply be handed out to employees who are then expected to follow the standards. Training programs are essential to introduce the employees to the code" (p. 888). These training programs should focus on the pursuit of the ethical ideal through sound moral judgment. As guidance to this pursuit, Peter Dean (1992) identifies eight basic tenets or "virtues":

• Due care and concern for others in professional activities
• Respect where appropriate for confidentiality
• Fidelity to special responsibilities
• Avoidance of conflict of interest

- Willing compliance with the law
- Acting in good faith in negotiations
- Respect for human well-being
- Respect for the liberty and constitutional rights of others

Clearly, this list is not exhaustive. Indeed, each of these tenets is open to differing interpretation and potential conflict. For example, respect for confidentiality could conflict with a willingness to comply with the letter of the law. But then these potential conflicts and ambiguities are the very essence of the Aesthetic Universe. This is why the ability to exercise sound judgment is so critical and why knowledge of the virtues through the observation of exemplars within an organization that nurtures such knowledge is crucial.

As mentioned earlier, the importance of exemplars places particular responsibility on senior-level managers. In an extensive study of ten major corporations recently undertaken by the Business Roundtable (1988), the conclusion was reached that "with regard to corporate ethics, no point emerges more clearly than the crucial role of top management" (p. 4). The education approach emphasizes the educational role of senior management in establishing a virtue-based ethos within the organization. Once such an ethos is in place, its moral import filters down the corporate hierarchy to impact not only financial decisions but all aspects of corporate activity.

The actual steps involved in the initiation and perpetuation of such a value system within a specific firm are outlined in some detail by Michael R. Rion (1982), corporate responsibility director for Cummins Engine Inc., one of the world's largest diesel-engine manufacturers. Rion's division organized regular three-day workshops for groups of 18 to 24 middle-level, and upper-level managers. Attendance at these workshops was entirely optional, but Rion notes that the sessions were always oversubscribed, reflecting a keen interest among managers concerning these broader aesthetic aspects of the management function. Rion enumerates three learning goals. These progress logically from a broad recognition of the value of virtue to specific application of virtue ethics precepts in business decisions:

1. To increase recognition of ethical dimensions in management decisions.
2. To acquire concepts and methods for analysis of ethical issues.
3. To strengthen the capacity for practical resolution of ethical issues. (p. 14)

These goals are addressed sequentially in three sessions. The first session focuses on recognition. Through discussion of the importance of implicit contracts based on trust (Cornell and Shapiro, 1987), managers are led to a recognition of the value of virtue in corporate culture. Managers analyze their own personal motivations in relation to those of the corporation in accordance with Sherwin Klein's (1988) suggestion that "[c]orporate people . . . function according to a double standard—amorally as an official of an organization and morally as a private person" (p. 63). Through a discussion of virtue ethics, they realize that such schizophrenia is inappropriate: the aesthetic pursuit of excellence through virtue permeates both personal and professional life.

This leads finally to a discussion of the ultimate objective of the firm. The firm is recognized as Merton Miller's "wealth creation machine," but in light of virtue ethics, this wealth creation is seen as a means to an end rather than as an end in itself. The Aristotelian concept of *eudaimonia* (i.e., happiness through moral excellence) is revealed as the ultimate end of all human endeavor, and the firm is thus revealed as a human organization that facilitates this pursuit of moral excellence through material gain. The important conclusion of this first session is that the economic objectives of the firm serve the aesthetic objectives, and not vice versa.

The second session narrows the focus by applying the broad conclusions of the first session to the "ordering and analysis" of individual business decisions. Managers are made aware of the fact that there are no simple solutions to ethically charged decisions. In addition, they realize that practically *every* decision they make has an ethical dimension. For example, decisions such as receivables collection policy or project abandonment versus continuation, which at first blush might appear entirely economic, do in fact entail some moral deliberation: the decision by a project manager to abandon a pet project may entail the exercise of the virtues of courage and honesty. Similarly, for a derivatives trader to report a large position loss immediately may entail the pursuit of the internal goods derived from honesty and courage, in preference to the external goods of ego, image, and material reward. Indeed, it is the virtues that must provide the foundation from which managers order and analyze business decisions. Rion (1982) lists these virtues explicitly:

- Promise keeping
- Truth-telling
- Reparation (compensating for previous wrongful acts)
- Gratitude
- Justice
- Beneficence (doing good, preventing or removing evil)
- Nonmaleficence (refraining from doing evil)
- Morally virtuous self-development (p. 14)

The elucidation of these virtues leads naturally to a discussion of concepts such as the good and excellence in the context of business ethics. This, in turn, leads to a broadening of the discussion into aesthetic areas covered in the first session. The circle of logic, from the broad aesthetic of virtue to its specific application, is thus complete.

The third and final session focuses on morally and aesthetically enlightened business judgment. Managers are faced with a series of realistic scenarios in which they must exercise judgment in accordance with the conclusions drawn in the previous two sessions. Classic moral dilemmas such as whistle-blowing and information disclosure are thus addressed in a realistic setting. Managers realize that in many situations profits and ethics need not conflict: although opportunism may increase returns in the short run, morally restrained behavior will lead to greater long-run profitability through the acquisition of reputational capital. When profits and ethics do appear to conflict, the holistic business aesthetic—educated by the virtues—is shown to be a worldview that can resolve this conflict by exposing the true role of the firm within society.

Note the broad-brush characteristic of these workshops, consistent with virtue ethics. The whole process is one of edification, rather than sermonizing or the prescribing of specific rules of conduct. Managers are awakened to the concept of virtue and are thus prepared for the daunting task of weighing the aesthetic responsibilities and ideals of their firm against its economic constraints and objectives. In short, the aesthetic manager is born. This manager will have escaped the prejudices that bedevil the modern manager—the illusion of presence; the illusion of a single, quantifiable corporate objective; the illusion of some universal concept or context for business judgment. Fundamentally, the aesthetic manager will realize that the real governing principle of the business universe is chaos: business reality is nonrational and nonquantifiable and cannot be circumscribed by rationally based moral dogma. Thus, business decision making comes down to judgment. But not blind judgment. Rather, it is judgment based on an educated application of certain aesthetic values as outlined in virtue ethics theory: Courage must be tempered with prudence, prudence must be tempered with justice, justice must be tempered with compassion, and so on. The art of business alluded to in the title of this book comes down to the manager's judicious application of these virtues in business decisions—an application undertaken with an overarching vision of business as a practice-based activity in which internal goods or excellences are recognized as the aesthetic ideal.

In evaluating the success of this technique, Rion (1982) admits that "Cummins does not meet its goals with perfect accuracy and the problems of sustaining and implementing ethical management arise regularly" (p. 109). Thus, he recognizes that the practice of sound moral judgment in business decisions requires continual education and vigilance. But—as Dennis Gioia (1992) lucidly illustrated earlier with his experience in the Ford Motor Company's vehicle-recall division during the time of the Pinto gastank fiasco—the costs both moral and economic of a failure to provide such education and vigilance can be great.

IMPLICATIONS FOR PEPSI

What this discussion implies for PepsiCo is that Pepsi lacked an ethos. Not an ethos in the sense of a rigid code of conduct or corporate credo but an ethos in the sense of an overarching conception of excellence. Pepsi may have attempted to apply some technical criterion to its decision of whether or not to pull out of Burma, or it may have attempted to apply some moral criterion, but what Pepsi and other multinational corporations are going to increasingly discover in the twenty-first century is that these types of decisions can no longer be made with reference to any fixed modernist criteria, whether technical or moral; as this book has shown, these two metaphysical universes are facing increasingly irresolvable crises that are rendering them impotent as socially acceptable means of business decision making.

For example, if Pepsi had declared that its decision was based on whichever choice yielded the highest net present value, this would have been viewed as unconscionably cold-blooded and "technical" by many segments of society. Contrarily, if Pepsi had declared that its decision was based on strict adherence to the dictates of ISCT, or some other modernist moral dictum, then this would have been viewed by some other segments of society—and indeed perhaps by some of the same segments—as a breach of fiduciary responsibility to stockholders, bondholders, and other financial stakeholders. Also, as discussed in Part II, the ability of modern ethical precepts such as ISCT to provide sound business guidance is questionable. So given the deconstruction of the Technical and Moral Universes, how can Pepsi and other companies make decisions?

The central thesis of this book is that such decisions will have to be made on the basis of aesthetic judgment: judgment informed by the virtues or excellences of virtue ethics theory. As the discussion outlines, there are ways in which Pepsi's management could be educated into the virtues, into the ability to balance the various conflicting aspirations to the excellences of practical wisdom, temperance, courage, and justice. I label this type of judgment as aesthetic because there is no single answer, no rule, no dictum that can simply be applied; all decisions are contextual, and all require judgment.

In this Aesthetic Universe the rightness or wrongness of a managerial decision will not be based on the extent to which the decision maximizes some financial scorecard, whether that scorecard be earnings per share, stock price, economic value added, and so on. Nor will the rightness or wrongness of a decision be based on the extent to which the decision adhered to some moral dictum, whether ISCT, the Golden Rule, or utilitarianism among others. No, the rightness or wrongness of a decision will be based purely on the extent to which the decision is consistent with the overall corporate ethos: an ethos that reflects the business aesthetic. Thus, judgments of rightness or wrongness will not be based on abstract absolutes but rather on contextual judgments. The former type of judgment entails the application of some absolute contextless criterion, some "view from nowhere," but the whole essence of the aesthetic is that there is no absolute criterion, there is no view from nowhere. In the Aesthetic Universe, Pepsi's management may have decided to pull out of Burma, or they may have decided to stay in Burma. From this aesthetic perspective the important thing would not have been the resulting action of Pepsi but rather the motivation and the thought process behind the action. Was Pepsi's decision informed by the virtues? That is the critical question. That is the question that would determine whether Pepsi's managers were enlightened or whether they were still enslaved by the delusions of a now-defunct and socially unacceptable modernity.

So, from the perspective of the aesthetic manager, that is, from the perspective of the central argument of this book, what should Pepsi have done?

Pepsi should have developed an internal corporate ethos that would have enlightened managers to the art of aesthetic judgment. One way to achieve this would be along the lines of those methods used by Rion at Cummins Engine. Having been through this process of enlightenment, that is, having transformed themselves from technicians or moral managers into artisans, then Pepsi's decision makers would be ready to make decisions in the aesthetic business universe. Whether these managers as artisans would have chosen to pull out, and when they would have chosen to pull out, is impossible to say in retrospect; the context from which Pepsi had to decide has passed. No doubt, whatever decision they made would have been unpopular in some quarters; but they would have made a decision, and it would have been a decision based on sound judgment, that is, aesthetic judgment informed by the virtues. The decision, thus made, would have been firm and would have been eminently defensible in this aesthetic era.

As an old Zen proverb says, "Walk or sit, but don't dither." Pepsi's failure was that, in making this decision, it dithered. Initially, Pepsi denied any intention to pull out; then in April 1996, in an attempt to placate protestors prior to its annual general meeting, Pepsi announced a partial pullout in the form of divesting its 40 percent stake in a Burmese bottling operation while retaining franchise agreements for the sale of its syrup and use of its trademark. Not until January 1997 did Pepsi pull out of Burma completely. The lack of a corporate ethos at Pepsi meant that the grounds for decision oscillated between the Technical, Moral, and Aesthetic Universes, with this resulting confusion and hesitation.

In fairness to Pepsi, such confusion and hesitation are by no means unusual in contemporary decision making. Indeed, given the cultural confusion engendered by the collapse of modernism, such dithering is likely to be the norm among firms unenlightened to the aesthetic cultural shift currently under way; such firms are in essence attempting to simultaneously serve three different and incompatible epistemological masters. Such confusion will end only when the manager as artisan is recognized as the only valid management paradigm available to fill the void left as the Technical and Moral Universes deconstruct. Managers who recognize themselves as artisans, and who recognize business as an art, will flourish.

The key words of the modernist business universe of the past 150 years may have been those of "logic," "reason," "science," "technical expertise," "instrumental rationality," "wealth maximization," and "moral rectitude." But the key concepts of the aesthetic business era will be such things as "harmony," "balance," "sustainability," "aesthetic excellence," "judgment," "context," "compassion," "community," "beauty," and "art." Those corporate cultures that recognize this shift will flourish both financially and aesthetically; those that don't will founder and perish.

In the case of Burma, Pepsi foundered. In the case of Nigeria, Shell foundered. In the case of Vietnam, Nike foundered. The recent changes that managers at these firms have wrought, which were discussed at the beginning of this book, reflect an awakening within these corporate behemoths to the Aesthetic Universe. They reflect a recognition that corporate success in the twenty-first century, financial or otherwise, will be primarily a matter not of technical expertise or moral conformity but of aesthetic harmony.

A FINAL, FINAL WORD

Although I believe that this book is in many respects original, I also recognize that several other recent books have recognized this broad cultural shift toward the aesthetic. Not just books by academics or social commentators but also books by managers. For example, returning to Shell, in his recent book *The Living Company* (1997), Arie de Geus (who worked at Shell for 40 years) recognizes this shift: "The twin policies of managing for profit and maximizing shareholder value, at the expense of all other goals, are vestigial management traditions" (p. 15).

Many have labeled what I call the Aesthetic Universe as the postmodern or poststructural. For example, Terry Eagleton, in *The Illusions of Postmodernism* (1996), suggests that "[m]any a business executive is . . . a spontaneous postmodernist" (p. 133). But I have avoided the latter terms of "postmodernism" and "poststructualism" because of their frequent negative, nihilistic interpretation.

I do not see the coming dominance of the Aesthetic Universe as in any way negative or nihilistic, either for business or for culture generally. In fact, quite the opposite. As Charles Handy (1990) concludes at the end of his book *The Age of Unreason*: "The Age of Unreason may become an Age of Greatness" (p. 269). Just as Nietzsche saw the death of God as an awakening for Western culture, rather than as an apocalypse, so the death of the Technical and Moral Universes augurs an awakening for business culture. The birth of beautiful business.

Bibliography

Akaah, Ishmael P. 1989. "Differences in Research Ethics Judgements between Male and Female Marketing Professionals." *Journal of Business Ethics* 8, pp. 375–381.

Alchian, A. 1969. "Corporate Management and Property Rights." In H. Manne, ed., *Economic Policy and the Regulation of Corporate Securities*. Washington, D.C.: American Enterprise Institute for Public Policy Research, pp. 337–360.

Allen, F., and G. Faulhaber. 1989. "Signalling by Underpricing in the Initial Public Offering Market." *Journal of Financial Economics* 23, pp. 303–323.

Allen, Peter M. 1985. "Towards a New Science of Complex Systems." In S. Alda et al., eds., *The Science and Praxis of Complexity*. Tokyo: United Nations University, pp. 268–297.

———. 1988. "Evolution, Innovation and Economics." In G. Dosi, C. Freeman, R. Nelson, G. Silverberg, and L. Soele, eds., *Technical Change and Economic Theory*. London: Pinter Publishers, pp. 95–119.

Allmon, Dean E., and James Grant. 1990. "Real Estate Sales Agents and the Code of Ethics." *Journal of Business Ethics* 9, no. 10 (October), pp. 420–428.

Ambarish, R., K. John, and J. Williams. 1987. "Efficient Signalling with Dividends and Investments." *Journal of Finance* 42, no. 2 (June), pp. 321–344.

Annas, Julia. 1995. "Prudence and Morality in Ancient and Modern Ethics." *Ethics* 105, no. 2 (January), pp. 54–56.

Aristotle. 1991. *The Nicomachean Ethics*. Oxford, England: Oxford University Press.

Armstrong, Mary Beth, and John Dobson. 1994. "An Application of Virtue Ethics to the Accounting Profession." California Polytechnic State University working paper.

Arrow, Kenneth. 1975. "Gifts and Exchanges." In E. S. Phelps, ed., *Altruism, Morality, and Economic Theory*. New York: Russell Sage Foundation, pp. 105–115.

———. 1984. "The Economics of Agency." Stanford University research paper.

Ashton, T. S. 1966. *The Industrial Revolution 1760–1830.* London: Oxford University Press.

Axelrod, Robert. 1984. *The Evolution of Cooperation.* New York: Basic Books.

Baber, Harriet. 1994. "The Market for Feminist Epistemology." *The Monist* 77, no. 4 (October), pp. 403–423.

Ball, Donald, and Wendell H. McCulloch, Jr. 1990. *International Business: Introduction and Essentials,* 4th ed. Homewood, Ill.: BPI-Irwin.

Baneish, Messod D., and Robert Chatov. 1993. "Corporate Codes of Conduct: Economic Determinants and Legal Implications for Independent Auditors." *Journal of Accounting and Public Policy* 12, pp. 3–35.

Bannock, G., R. E. Baxter, and R. Rees. 1972. *The Dictionary of Economics.* London: Penguin Books.

Barach, J., and John B. Elstrott. 1988. "The Transactional Ethic: The Ethical Foundations of Free Enterprise Reconsidered." *Journal of Business Ethics* 7, no. 7, pp. 545–552.

Barnea, A., R. Haugen, and L. Senbet. 1980. "A Rationale for Debt Maturity Structure and Call Provisions in the Agency Theory Framework." *Journal of Finance* 35 (December), pp. 1223–1234.

Baron, C., and B. Holmstrom. 1980. "The Two Tiers of Informational Asymmetry." *Journal of Finance* 35 (September), pp. 496–502.

Bartlett, Christopher A., and Sumantra Ghoshal. 1989. *Managing across Borders.* Cambridge, Mass.: Harvard Business School Press.

Baumhart, Raymond C. 1961. "How Ethical Are Businessmen?" *Harvard Business Review* 10, no. 4, pp. 15–19.

Beatty, Jack. 1998. *The World According to Drucker: The Life and Work of the World's Greatest Management Thinker.* New York: Free Press.

Beatty, R., and J. Ritter. 1986. "Investment Banking, Reputation, and the Underpricing of IPO's." *Journal of Financial Economics* (March), pp. 213–232.

Bella, David, and Jonathan King. 1989. "Common Knowledge of the Second Kind." *Journal of Business Ethics* 8, pp. 415–430.

Bellah, Robert N., Richard Madsen, William M. Sullivan, Ann Swidler, and Steven M. Tipton. 1985. *Habits of the Heart: Individualism and Commitment in American Life.* New York: Harper and Row.

Beltramini, Richard F., Robert A. Peterson, and George Kozmetsky. 1984. "Concerns of College Students Regarding Business Ethics." *Journal of Business Ethics* 6, pp. 265–280.

Bentham, Jeremy. 1789. *An Introduction to the Principles of Morals and Legislation.* 1956. Reprint, Oxford: Oxford University Press.

Berle, A. A., Jr., and Gardiner C. Means. 1932. *The Modern Corporation and Private Property.* New York: Macmillan.

Bernstein, Peter. 1995. "Risk as a History of Ideas." *Financial Analysts Journal* (January–February), p. 4.

Betz, Michael, Lenahan O'Connel, and Jon Shepard. 1987. "Gender Differences in Proclivity for Unethical Behavior." *Journal of Business Ethics* 8, pp. 321–324.

Black, Robert. 1994. "John Commons on Customer Goodwill and the Economic Value of Business Ethics: Response to Professor Sen." *Business Ethics Quarterly* 4, no. 3, pp. 359–366.

Bloom, Allan. 1987. *The Closing of the American Mind*. New York: Simon and Schuster.

Bowen, Sally. 1998. "People Power Keeps Peru's Investors in Check." *Financial Times*, February 6, p. 6.

Bowie, Norman E. 1991. "Challenging the Egoistic Paradigm." *Business Ethics Quarterly* 1, pp. 1–21.

Bowie, Norman E., and R. Edward Freeman, eds. 1992. *Ethics and Agency Theory*. New York: Oxford University Press.

Brearley, Richard A., and Stewart C. Myers. 1991. *Principles of Corporate Finance*. New York: McGraw-Hill.

Brennan, Timothy J. 1989. "A Methodological Assessment of Multiple Utility Frameworks." *Economics and Philosophy* 5, pp. 197–199.

Brickley, James, Clifford Smith, and Jerold Zimmerman. 1995. "The Economics of Organizational Architecture." *Journal of Applied Corporate Finance* 8, no. 2 (Summer), pp. 19–31.

Brown, Vivienne. 1991. "Signifying Voices: Reading the 'Adam Smith Problem.' " *Economics and Philosophy* 7, pp. 187–220.

Buchanan, James M., and Viktor J. Vanberg. 1991. "The Market as a Creative Process." *Economics and Philosophy* 7, pp. 167–186.

Bucholz, Rogene A., and Sandra B. Rosenthal. 1998. *Business Ethics*. New York: Prentice-Hall.

Bull, C. 1983. "Implicit Contracts in the Absence of Enforcement and Risk Aversion." *American Economic Review* 73, no. 4 (September), p. 658.

Buller, Paul F., John J. Kohls, and Kenneth S. Anderson. 1997. "A Model for Addressing Cross-Cultural Ethical Conflicts." *Business and Society* 36, no. 2 (June), pp. 169–193.

Business Roundtable. 1988. *Corporate Ethics: A Prime Business Asset*. New York: Author.

Byron, W. J. 1988. "Twin Towers: A Philosophy and Theology of Business." *Journal of Business Ethics* 7, pp. 525–530.

Campbell, D. 1986. "Rationality and Utility from the Standpoint of Evolutionary Biology." *Journal of Business* 59, no. 4 (October), pp. 355–365.

Campbell, S., and C. Kracaw. 1986. "Why Do Financial Intermediaries Exist?" University of Pennsylvania working paper.

Carson, Thomas. 1993a. "Friedman's Theory of Corporate Social Responsibility." *Business and Professional Ethics Journal* 12, no. 1 (Spring), pp. 3–32.

———. 1993b. "Second Thoughts about Bluffing." *Business Ethics Quarterly* 3, no. 4, pp. 317–342.

Carter, R., and S. Manaster. 1990. "Initial Public Offerings and Underwriter Reputation." *Journal of Finance* 45, pp. 1045–1067.

Chakravarthy, B. 1986. "Measuring Strategic Performance." *Strategic Management Journal* 7, pp. 437–451.

Chambers, Donald R., and Nelson J. Lacey. 1996. "Corporate Ethics and Shareholder Wealth Maximization." *Financial Practice and Education* 3, no. 2 (Spring–Summer), pp. 93–96.

Chang, S. J. 1997. "Whose Wealth to Maximize: A Survey of Alternative Views on Corporate Objective." *Journal of Financial Education* 23 (Fall), pp. 1–13.

Chung, K. S., and R. L. Smith II. 1987. "Product Quality, Nonsalvageable Capital

Investment and the Cost of Financial Leverage." In Thomas E. Copeland, ed., *Modern Finance and Industrial Economics*. Oxford: Basil Blackwell, pp. 42–48.

Coase, R. H. 1937. "The Nature of the Firm." *Economica*, n.s., 4, pp. 386–405. Reprinted in *Readings in Price Theory*. Homewood, Ill.: Irwin, pp. 331–351.

Collins, N. W., S. K. Gilbert, and S. H. Nycum. 1988. *Women Leading: Making Tough Choices on the Fast Track*. New York: Stephen Greene Press/Viking.

Copeland, T. E., and J. F. Weston. 1983. *Financial Theory and Corporate Policy*. New York: Addison-Wesley.

———. 1988. *Financial Theory and Corporate Policy*, 3rd ed. New York: Addison-Wesley.

Cornell, B., and A. C. Shapiro. 1987. "Corporate Stakeholders and Corporate Finance." *Financial Management*, 16, no. 1 (Spring), pp. 5–14.

Cottril, Melville T. 1990. "Corporate Social Responsibility and the Marketplace." *Journal of Business Ethics* 9, no. 9, pp. 723–729.

Cozine, Robert. 1998. "More Top Shell Jobs for Women." *Financial Times*, January 13, p. 17.

Crockett, J., and I. Friend. 1986. "Corporate Dividend Payout Policy." University of Pennsylvania working paper.

Dann, L. 1980. "The Effect of Common Stock Repurchases on Securityholders Returns." *Journal of Financial Economics* 6 (June), pp. 297–330.

Dann, L., and W. Mikkelson. 1982. "Convertible Debt Issuance, Capital Structure Change and Financing-Related Information: Some New Evidence." Graduate School of Business working paper, University of Chicago.

Darrough, M. N. 1987. "Managerial Incentives for Short-Term Results: A Comment." *Journal of Finance* 42, no. 4 (September), pp. 1097–1102.

Darwin, Charles Robert. 1871. *The Descent of Man*. 1955. Reprint, Oxford: Oxford University Press.

Dawkins, Richard. 1972. *The Selfish Gene*. Oxford: Oxford University Press.

Dean, Peter J. 1992. "Making Codes of Ethics Real." *Journal of Business Ethics* 11, pp. 285–290.

DeAngelo, Harry, Linda DeAngelo, and Douglas J. Skinner. 1996. "Reversal of Fortune: Dividend Signaling and the Disappearance of Sustained Earnings Growth." *Journal of Financial Economics* 40, no. 3, pp. 341–372.

Dees, Gregory J. 1992. "Principals, Agents, and Ethics." In Norman E. Bowie and R. Edward Freeman, eds., *Ethics and Agency Theory*. New York: Oxford University Press.

De George, Richard T. 1990. *Business Ethics*, 3rd ed. New York: Macmillan.

———. 1993. *Competing with Integrity in International Business*. New York: Oxford University Press.

de Geus, Arie. 1997. *The Living Company*. Cambridge, Mass.: HBS Press.

DeJong, D., R. Forsythe, and R. J. Lundholm. 1985. "Ripoffs, Lemons, and Reputation Formation in Agency Relationships: A Laboratory Market Study." *Journal of Finance* 40, no. 3 (July), pp. 921–926.

DeJong, D., R. Forsythe, and W. Uecker. 1985. "Ripoffs, Lemons and Reputation Formation in Agency Relationships: A Laboratory Market Study." *Journal of Finance* 50, pp. 809–820.

Derry, Robin. 1996. "Toward a Feminist Firm: Comments on John Dobson and Judith White." *Business Ethics Quarterly* 6 (January), pp. 101–110.

Derry, Robin, and Ronald Green. 1989. "Ethical Theory in Business Ethics: A Critical Assessment." Paper presented at the annual meeting of the Business Ethics Society, Atlanta, Ga., August 26–29, 1992.

Diamond, Douglas W. 1989. "Reputation Acquisition in Debt Markets." *Journal of Political Economy* 97, pp. 828–861.

Dielman, T., and H. Oppenheimer. "An Examination of Investor Behavior during Periods of Large Dividend Changes." *Journal of Financial and Quantitative Analysis* 19, no. 2 (June), pp. 197–216.

Dienhart, John. 1995. "Rationality, Ethical Codes, and an Egalitarian Justification for Ethical Expertise." *Business Ethics Quarterly* 5, no. 3 (July), pp. 419–450.

Dobson, John. 1990. "The Role of Ethics in Global Corporate Culture." *Journal of Business Ethics* 9, pp. 481–488.

———. 1991. "Reconciling Financial Economics and Business Ethics." *Business and Professional Ethics Journal* 10, no. 4 (Winter), pp. 22–25.

———. 1992a. "Ethics in Financial Contracting." *Business and Professional Ethics Journal* 11, nos. 3–4 (Fall–Winter), pp. 93–128.

———. 1992b. "Ethics in the Transnational Corporation." *Journal of Business Ethics* 11, pp. 21–27.

———. 1992c. "The Importance of Corporate Reputation in Transnational Business." *School of Business Journal, San Francisco State University* 1, pp. 79–86.

———. 1993. "Financial Ethics: What Practitioners Really Need to Know." *Financial Analysts Journal* (November–December), pp. 16–18.

———. 1996. "The Feminine Firm: A Comment." *Business Ethics Quarterly* 6, no. 2, pp. 227–233.

———. 1997a. "Ethics in Finance II." *Financial Analysts Journal* (January–February), pp. 15–25.

———. 1997b. *Finance Ethics: The Rationality of Virtue.* Lanham, MD.: Rowman & Littlefield.

Dobson, John, and Mary Beth Armstrong. 1995. "Application of Virtue-Ethics Theory: A Lesson from Architecture." *Research on Accounting Ethics* 1, pp. 187–202.

Dobson, John, and Robert Dorsey. 1992. "Reputation, Information and Project Termination in Capital Budgeting." *Engineering Economist* 4, pp. 33–37.

Dobson John, and Uric B. Dufrene. 1993. "The Impacts of U.S. Presidential Elections on International Security Markets." *Global Finance Journal* 4, no. 1, pp. 39–47.

Dobson, John, and Cheryl MacLellan. 1996. "Women, Ethics, and MBAs." *Journal of Business Ethics* 4, pp. 18–20.

Dobson, John, and Kenneth Reiner. 1995. "The Rationality of Honesty in Debt Markets." *Managerial Finance*, pp. 20–36.

Dobson, John, and Judith White. 1995. "Toward the Feminine Firm." *Business Ethics Quarterly* 5, no. 3 (July), pp. 463–478.

Dolecheck, Maynard M., and Carolyn C. Dolecheck. 1989. "Ethics: Take It from the Top." *Business* (January–February–March), pp. 12–18.

Donaldson, T., and T. W. Dunfee. 1994. "Toward a Unified Conception of Business Ethics: Integrative Social Contracts Theory." *Academy of Management Review* 19, No. 2, pp. 252–284.

Donaldson, Thomas. 1989. *The Ethics of International Business.* New York: Oxford University Press.

Dunfee, W. Thomas. 1995. "Introduction to the Special Issue on Social Contracts and Business Ethics." *Business Ethics Quarterly* 5, no. 2 (April), pp. 4–8.

———. 1998. "The Marketplace of Morality: Small Steps toward a Theory of Moral Choice." *Business Ethics Quarterly* 8, no. 1 (January), pp. 127–146.

Dunfee, W. Thomas, and T. Donaldson. 1995. "Contractarian Business Ethics." *Business Ethics Quarterly* 5, no. 2 (April), pp. 173–186.

Dunkel, Arthur; 1991; quoted in *The Economist* (June 1–7), pp. 13–14.

Duska, Ronald F. 1992. "Why Be a Loyal Agent? A Systematic Ethical Analysis." In Norman E. Bowie and R. Edward Freeman, eds., *Ethics and Agency Theory*. New York: Oxford University Press, pp. 30–34.

———. 1993a. "Aristotle: A Pre-Modern Post-Modern?" *Business Ethics Quarterly* 3, no. 3, pp. 227–250.

———. 1993b. "To Whom It May Concern." Unpublished letter to the editor of the *Harvard Business Review* (July 12).

Dybvig, P. H., and C. S. Spatt. 1985. "Does It Pay to Maintain a Reputation?" Yale School of Organization and Management working paper.

Dyl, E., and M. Joehnk. 1979. "Sinking Funds and the Cost of Corporate Debt." *Journal of Finance* 34 (September), pp. 877–893.

Eagleton, Terry. 1996. *The Illusions of Postmodernism*. Oxford: Blackwell Publishers.

Edgeworth, Francis. 1881. *Mathematical Psychics*. London: Kegan Paul.

Eisenhardt, Kathleen M. 1989. "Agency Theory: An Assessment and Review." *Academy of Management Review* 14, pp. 57–74.

Ekins, Paul. 1989. "Trade and Self-Reliance." *The Ecologist* 19, no. 5, pp. 42–48.

Estes, Ralph. 1996. *Tyranny of the Bottom Line*. San Francisco: Berret-Koehler Publishers.

Etzioni, Amitai. 1988. *The Moral Dimension*. New York: Free Press.

———. 1991. "Reflections on Teaching Business Ethics." *Business Ethics Quarterly* 1, no. 4 (October), pp. 355–366.

Fama, E. 1980. "Agency Problems and the Theory of the Firm." *Journal of Political Economy* (April), pp. 288–307.

Fama, E. F., and M. C. Jensen. 1983. "Separation of Ownership and Control." *Journal of Law and Economics* 26 (June), pp. 301–325.

Flannery, M. 1986. "Asymmetric Information and Risky Debt Maturity Choice." *Journal of Finance* (March), pp. 19–38.

Foot, Philippa. 1967. *Theories of Ethics*. Oxford: Oxford University Press.

Francis, J. C. 1986. *Investments: Analysis and Management*. New York: McGraw-Hill.

Frank, Robert. 1988. *Passions within Reason*. New York: W. W. Norton.

Frank, R., T. Gilovich, and D. Regan. 1993. "Does Studying Economics Inhibit Cooperation?" *Journal of Economic Perspectives* 21 (Spring), pp. 92–98.

Freeman, R. E., ed. 1991. *Business Ethics: The State of the Art*. New York: Oxford University Press.

Friedman, Milton. 1970. "The Social Responsibility of Business Is to Increase Its Profits." *New York Times Magazine* (August), pp. 14–15. Reprinted in *Business Ethics*, by W. M. Hoffman and J. M. Moore. New York: McGraw-Hill, 1990, pp. 153–156.

Fritsche, David J. 1997. *Business Ethics*. New York: McGraw-Hill.

Fry, Earl H. 1989. "Is the United States a Declining Economic Power?" *Business in the Contemporary World* 1, no. 4 (Summer), 44.

Fuchsberg, Gilbert. 1992. "Female Enrollment Falls in Many Top MBA Programs." *Wall Street Journal*, September 25, p. B1.

Furubotn, E. G., and S. Pejovich. 1972. "Property Rights and Economic Theory." *Journal of Economic Literature* 17, pp. 1137–1160.

GATT (General Agreement on Tariffs and Trade). 1971. *Studies in International Trade, Industrial Pollution Control and International Trade.* Geneva: GATT.

"GATT's Last Chance." 1991. *The Economist*, p. 65.

Gauthier, David. 1988. *Morals by Agreement.* Oxford: Clarendon Press.

Gellerman, Saul. 1986. "Why 'Good' Managers Make Bad Ethical Choices." *Harvard Business Review* (July–August), pp. 85–90.

Getz, Kathleen A. 1990. "International Codes of Conduct: An Analysis of Ethical Reasoning." *Journal of Business Ethics* 9, no. 7 (July), pp. 124–128.

Ghorbade, Jai. 1991. "Ethics in MBA Programs: The Rhetoric, the Reality, and a Plan of Action." *Journal of Business Ethics* 10, pp. 891–905.

Gilligan, Carol. 1982. *In a Different Voice.* Cambridge: Harvard University Press.

Gilmore, J. Thomas. 1986. "A Framework for Responsible Business Behavior." *Business and Society Review*, no. 58 (Summer), pp. 31–34.

Gioia, Dennis A. 1992. "Pinto Fires and Personal Ethics: A Script Analysis of Missed Opportunities." *Journal of Business Ethics* 11, pp. 379–389.

Gitman, Lawrence J. 1998. *Principles of Managerial Finance.* New York: Addison-Wesley.

Goldman, Alvin I. 1993. "Ethics and Cognitive Science." *Ethics* 103, pp. 337–360.

Goldsmith, E. 1990. "The Uruguay Round." *The Ecologist* 20 (November–December), pp. 202–204.

Goodpaster, Kenneth E. 1991. "Business Ethics and Stakeholder Analysis." *Business Ethics Quarterly* 1, pp. 54–73.

———. 1994. "Work, Spirituality and the Moral Point of View." *International Journal of Value-Based Management* 7, no. 1, pp. 49–62.

Goodpaster, Kenneth E., and John B. Matthews. 1982. "Can a Corporation Have a Conscience?" *Harvard Business Review* (January–February), pp. 132–141.

Grossman, S. J., and O. D. Hart. 1982. "Corporate Financial Structure and Managerial Incentives." In John J. McCall, ed., *The Economics of Information.* Chicago: University of Chicago Press, pp. 107–140.

Haley, C. W., and L. D. Schall. 1979. *The Theory of Financial Decisions.* New York: McGraw-Hill.

Hall, B. 1986. *Who Owns Whom?* New York: Harper and Row.

Handy, Charles. 1990. *The Age of Unreason.* Cambridge, Mass.: HBS Press.

Harris, M., and A. Raviv. 1985. "A Sequential Signalling Model of Convertible Debt Call Policy." *Journal of Finance* 40 (December), pp. 1263–1282.

Hart, Oliver D. 1983. "Optimal Labour Contracts under Asymmetric Information: An Introduction." *Review of Economic Studies* (January), pp. 3–36.

Hasnas, John. 1998. "The Normative Theories of Business Ethics: A Guide for the Perplexed." *Business Ethics Quarterly* 8, no. 1 (January), pp. 19–42.

Hausman, Daniel M., and Michael S. McPherson. 1993. "Taking Ethics Seriously: Economics and Contemporary Moral Philosophy." *Journal of Economic Literature* 31 (June), pp. 671–731.

Hegel, G. W. F. 1942. *Philosophy of Right.* Trans. T. M. Knox. Oxford: Clarendon Press.

Heilbroner, R. C. 1982. "The Socialization of the Individual in Adam Smith." *History of Political Economy* 14, no. 3, pp. 741–793.

Hoffman, Michael W., and Jennifer Mills Moore. 1990. *Business Ethics.* New York: McGraw-Hill.

Hollis, Martin, and Steven Lukes. 1982. *Rationality and Relativism.* Oxford: Basil Blackwell.

Holmes, Stephen. 1990. "The Secret History of Self-Interest." In Jane J. Mansbridge, ed., *Beyond Self-Interest.* Chicago: University of Chicago Press, pp. 267–286.

Holmstrom, B. 1979. "Moral Hazard and Observability." *Bell Journal of Economics* 10 (Spring), pp. 74–91.

———. 1981. "Contractual Models for the Labor Market." *American Economic Review* (May), pp. 307–313.

Homer. c. 900 B.C. *The Odyssey.* Trans. R. Fitzgerald. 4th ed., 1975. Reprint, Garden City, N.J.: Anchor Press/Doubleday.

Hosmer, LaRue Tone. 1994. "Why Be Moral? A Different Rationale for Managers." *Business Ethics Quarterly* 4, no. 2, pp. 191–204.

Hu, Henry T. C. 1991. "New Financial Products, the Modern Process of Financial Innovation and the Puzzle of Shareholder Welfare." *Texas Law Review* 69 (May), pp. 1273–1317.

Hume, D. 1955. *Writings in Economics.* Ed. Eugene Rotwein. Madison: University of Wisconsin Press. (Quote in text is taken from the essay "An Enquiry Concerning the Principles of Morals," originally published in 1751.)

Hunt, Lester H. 1991. *Nietzsche and the Origin of Virtue.* London: Routledge.

Hutchinson, D. S. 1986. *The Virtues of Aristotle.* London: Routledge and Kegan Paul.

Ingersoll, J., Jr. 1977. "A Contingent Claims Valuation of Convertible Securities." *Journal of Financial Economics* 4 (May), pp. 289–322.

Jarrel, G., and S. Peltzman. 1985. "The Impact of Product Recalls on the Wealth of Sellers." *Journal of Political Economy* (June), pp. 512–536.

Jensen, M. C. 1989. "The Eclipse of the Public Corporation." *Harvard Business Review* (September–October), pp. 53–57.

Jensen, M. C., and W. H. Meckling. 1976. "Theory of the Firm: Managerial Behavior, Agency Costs and Ownership Structure." *Journal of Financial Economics* 3, no. 4 (October), pp. 305–360.

John, K., and A. Kalay. 1985. "Informational Content of Optimal Debt Contracts." In E. Altman and M. Subrahmansam, eds., *Recent Advances in Corporate Finance.* Homewood, Ill.: Irwin, pp. 133–161.

John, Kose, and David Nachman. 1985. "Risky Debt, Investment Incentives and Reputation in a Sequential Equilibrium." *Journal of Finance* 40, pp. 863–877.

John, K., and J. Williams. 1985. "Dividends, Dilution and Taxes." *Journal of Finance* 40 (September), pp. 1053–1070.

Johnson, Elmer W. 1997. "Corporate Soulcraft in the Age of Brutal Markets." *Business Ethics Quarterly* 7, no. 4 (October), pp. 109–124.

Jones, Thomas M., and Dennis P. Quinn. 1993. "Taking Ethics Seriously: The Competitive Advantage of Intrinsic Morality." University of Washington, unpublished working paper.

Kahneman, D., Jack L. Knetsch, and Richard H. Thaler. 1986. "Fairness and the Assumptions of Economics." *Journal of Business* 59, pp. 285–300.

Kalay, A. 1980. "Signalling, Information Content and the Reluctance to Cut Dividends." *Journal of Financial and Quantitative Analysis* 15 (November), pp. 855–863.

Kanodia, Chandra, Robert Bushman, and John Dickhaut. 1989. "Escalation Errors and the Sunk Cost Effect: An Explanation Based on Reputation and Information Asymmetries." *Journal of Accounting Research* 27, no. 1, pp. 59–77.

Kantrowitz, Barbara, Devra Rosenberg, Karen Springen, and Patricia King. 1992. "Giving Women the Business." *Newsweek*, November 16, p. 98.

Kavka, Gregory S. 1991. "Is Individual Choice Less Problematic Than Collective Choice?" *Economics and Philosophy* 7, pp. 143–165.

Keeley, Michael. 1996. "Community, the Joyful Sound." *Business Ethics Quarterly* 6, no. 4, pp. 549–560.

Kay, John. 1998. "We're All Postmodern Now." *Financial Times*, April 29, p. 12.

Kelvin, Lord Peter. 1896. *The Principles of Physics*. London: Kegan Paul.

Keohane, Kieran. 1989. "Toxic Trade-off: The Price Ireland Pays for Industrial Development." *The Ecologist* 19, no. 4 (July–August), pp. 144–146.

Keown, Arthur J. et al. 1998. *Foundations of Finance*. Upper Saddle River, N.J.: Prentice-Hall.

King, J. B. 1988. "Prisoners' Paradoxes." *Journal of Business Ethics* 7, no. 7, pp. 475–488.

———. "Confronting Chaos." *Journal of Business Ethics* 8, no. 1 (January), pp. 14–19.

Klein, B., and K. B. Leffler. 1981. "The Role of Market Forces in Assuring Contractual Performance." *Journal of Political Economy* 87, pp. 615–641.

Klein, Sherwin. 1988. "Is a Moral Organization Possible?" *Business and Professional Ethics Journal* 7, no. 1 (Spring), pp. 53–58.

———. 1989. "Platonic Virtue Theory and Business Ethics." *Business and Professional Ethics Journal* 8, no. 4.

———. 1988. "Don Quixote and the Problem of Idealism and Realism in Business Ethics." *Business Ethics Quarterly* 8, no. 1 (January), pp. 43–64.

Kreps, D. 1984. "Corporate Culture and Economic Theory." Stanford University working paper.

Kreps, D., P. Milgrom, J. Roberts, and R. Wilson. 1982. "Rational Cooperation in the Finitely Repeated Prisoner's Dilemma." *Journal of Economic Theory* 24 (August), pp. 245–252.

Kreps, D., and R. Wilson. 1982. "Sequential Equilibria." *Econometrica* 7, no. 4, pp. 863–894.

Kuhn, Thomas S. 1970. *The Structure of Scientific Revolutions*. Chicago: University of Chicago Press.

Ladd, John. 1991. "Bhopal: An Essay on Moral Responsibility and Civic Virtue." *Journal of Social Philosophy* 22, no. 1, pp. 19–24.

Lambeth, Edmund B. 1990. "Waiting for a New St. Benedict: Alasdair MacIntyre and the Theory and Practice of Journalism." *Business and Professional Ethics Journal* 9, nos. 1–2, pp. 19–24.

Lasch, Christopher. 1991. *The True and Only Heaven: Progress and Its Critics.* New York: W. W. Norton.

Laughhunn, D., and J. W. Payne. 1991. "The Impact of Sunk Outcomes on Risky Choice Behavior." *Canadian Journal of Operations Research and Information Processing* 4, pp. 106–109.

Leavis, F. R., ed. 1950. *Mill on Bentham and Coleridge.* London: Chatto and Windus.

Leiter, Brian. 1997. "Nietzsche and the Morality Critics." *Ethics* 107 (January), pp. 250–285.

Leland, Hayne E., and David H. Pyle. 1977. "Informational Asymmetries, Financial Structure, and Financial Intermediation." *Journal of Finance* 32, pp. 371–387.

Lukes, Steven. 1977. *Rationality and Relativism.* New York: Columbia University Press.

MacIntyre, Alasdair. 1953. *Marxism: An Interpretation.* London: Routledge.

———. 1966. *A Brief History of Ethics.* New York: Macmillan.

———. 1977. "Utilitarianism and Cost-Benefit Analysis: An Essay on the Relevance of Moral Philosophy to Bureaucratic Theory." In Kenneth Sayre (ed.), *Values in the Electric Power Industry.* Notre Dame, Ind.: University of Notre Dame Press, pp. 217–237.

———. 1984a. *After Virtue,* 2nd ed. Notre Dame, Ind.: University of Notre Dame Press.

———. 1984b. *Against the Self-Image of the Age.* Notre Dame, Ind.: University of Notre Dame Press.

———. 1988. *Whose Justice? Which Rationality?* Notre Dame, Ind.: University of Notre Dame Press.

———. 1990. *Three Rival Versions of Moral Enquiry: Encyclopaedia, Genealogy, and Tradition.* Notre Dame, Ind.: University of Notre Dame Press.

———. 1991. "Incommensurability, Truth, and the Conversation between Confucians and Aristotelians about the Virtues." In Eliot Deutsch, ed., *Culture and Modernity: East-West Philosophical Perspectives.* Honolulu: University of Hawaii Press, pp. 104–122.

———. 1994. "A Partial Response to My Critics." In Charles Taylor, ed., *After MacIntyre.* Oxford: Oxford University Press, pp. 128–140.

"The Man Behind Management." 1998. *Financial Times,* January 30, p. 19.

Marwell, Gerald, and Ruth E. Ames. 1981. "Economists Free Ride, Does Anyone Else?" *Journal of Public Economics* 15, pp. 295–310.

"Master of His Arts." 1988. *Financial Times,* January 27, p. 17.

McGuire, J. T. Schneeweis, and A. Sundgren. 1986. "Corporate Social Responsibility and Firm Financial Performance." *Academy of Management Journal* 31, pp. 845–872.

McMylor, Peter. 1994. *Alasdair MacIntyre: Critic of Modernity.* London: Routledge.

Milgram, S. 1974. *Obedience to Authority.* Cambridge, Mass.: M.I.T. Press.

Milgrom, P., and J. Roberts, 1982. "Predation, Reputation and Entry Deterrence." *Journal of Economic Theory* 27, pp. 280–312.

Mill, John Stuart. 1863. *Utilitarianism.* 1987. Reprint, New York: Prometheus Books.

Miller, Merton H. 1986. "Behavioral Rationality in Finance: The Case of Dividends." *Journal of Business* 59, pp. 451–468.

Miller, Merton H., and Kevin Rock. 1985. "Dividend Policy under Asymmetric Information." *Journal of Finance* 40 (September), pp. 1031–1052.

Miller, R. E. and F. K. Reilly. 1987. "An Examination of Mispricing, Returns, and Uncertainty for Initial Public Offerings." *Financial Management* (Summer), pp. 22–28.

Mishra, B. 1984. "Informational Asymmetry in Finance: Three Related Essays." Ph.D. dissertation, New York University, December.

Modigliani, Franco, and M. H. Miller. 1958. "The Cost of Capital, Corporation Finance, and the Theory of Investment." *American Economic Review* 68 (June), pp. 261–297.

Moore, Jennifer. 1991. "Autonomy and the Legitimacy of the Liberal Arts." In R. Edward Freeman, ed., *Business Ethics: The State of the Art*. New York: Oxford University Press, pp. 14–19.

Moore, Norman H., Stephen W. Pruitt, and K. S. Maurise Tse. 1990. "What Price Morality? South African Divestment Decisions and Shareholder Wealth." Indiana University School of Business working paper, appendix.

Morris, J. 1976. "On Corporate Debt Maturity Strategies." *Journal of Financial Economics* 31 (March), pp. 147–175.

Mulligan, Thomas M. 1990. "Justifying Moral Initiative by Business." *Journal of Business Ethics* 9, pp. 93–104.

Murdoch, Iris. 1971. *The Sovereignty of Good*. Cambridge: Cambridge University Press.

Myers, Stewart C. 1977. "The Determinants of Corporate Borrowing." *Journal of Financial Economics* 5, pp. 147–175.

———. 1984. "Finance Theory and Financial Strategy." *Interfaces* 14, no. 1 (January–February), pp. 126–137.

Myers, S. and N. Majluff. 1984. "Corporate Financing and Investment Decisions When Firms Have Information That Investors Do Not Have." *Journal of Financial Economics* 13, pp. 187–221.

Narayanan M. P. 1987. "Managerial Incentives for Short Term Results: A Reply." *Journal of Finance* 2, no. 4 (September), pp. 1103–1104.

Nash, Laura. 1981. "Ethics without the Sermon." *Harvard Business Review* (November–December), pp. 79–90.

Nietzsche, Friedrich. 1967a. *Beyond Good and Evil*. Ed. Walter Kaufmann, trans. Walter Kauffman and R. J. Hollingdale. New York: Random House.

———. 1967b. *The Will to Power*. Ed. Walter Kaufmann, trans. Walter Kaufmann and R. J. Hollingdale. New York: Random House.

———. 1982. *Daybreak* (Die Morganrote). Trans. R. J. Hollingdale. 1881. Reprint, Cambridge: Cambridge University Press.

Noreen, Eric. 1988. "The Economics of Ethics: A New Perspective on Agency Theory." *Accounting Organizations and Society* 13, pp. 359–369.

North, Douglas C. 1991. "Towards a Theory of Institutional Change." *Quarterly Review of Economics and Business* 31, pp. 3–11.

Nussbaum, Martha C. 1991. "The Chill of Virtue." *The New Republic*, September 16–23, pp. 34–40.

Nystrom, Paul C. 1990. "Differences in Moral Values between Corporations." *Journal of Business Ethics* 9, pp. 971–979.

Okai, Norimichi. 1991. "Financial Scandals and Their Aftermath." University of Michigan working paper.

Pastin, M. 1986. "Managing the Rules of Conflict—International Bribery." In W. M. Hoffman, A. E. Lange, and D. A. Fedo, eds., *Ethics and the Multinational Enterprise: Proceedings of the Sixth International Conference on Business Ethics.* Lanham, Md.: University Press of America, pp. 321–328.

Payne, Dinah, and Cecily A. Raiborn. 1990. "Corporate Codes of Conduct: A Collective Conscience and Continuum." *Journal of Business Ethics* 9, pp. 879–889.

Pearsall, Marilyn. 1986. *Women and Values: Readings in Recent Feminine Philosophy.* Belmont, Calif.: Wadsworth.

Peng, M. K. K. 1990. "The Uruguay Round and the Third World." *The Ecologist* 20 (November–December), pp. 208–213.

Pettit, R. 1972. "Dividend Announcements, Security Performance and Capital Market Efficiency." *Journal of Finance* 27, pp. 993–1007.

Phillips, Derek L. 1993. *Looking Backward: A Critical Appraisal of Communitarian Thought.* Princeton, N.J.: Princeton University Press.

Pilotte, E. 1987. "The Impact on Shareholder Wealth of External Financing by Non-Dividend-Paying Firms: An Empirical Examination." Ph.D. dissertation, Indiana University.

Pirsig, Robert M. 1975. *Zen and the Art of Motorcycle Maintenance.* New York: Bantam.

———. 1991. *Lila: An Inquiry into Morals.* New York: Bantam.

Plott, C. R. 1986. "Rational Choice in Experimental Markets." *Journal of Business* 59, pp. S309–S327.

Polanyi, Michael. 1958. *Personal Knowledge: Toward a Post-Critical Philosophy.* Chicago: University of Chicago Press.

Ponemon, Lawrence A. 1992. "Ethical Reasoning and Selection-Solution in Accounting." *Accounting Organizations and Society* 17, pp. 239–258.

Prior, William. 1991. *Virtue and Knowledge: An Introduction to Ancient Greek Ethics.* New York: Routledge.

Pritchard, Michael S. 1992. "Good Works." *Professional Ethics* 1 (Spring–Summer), pp. 155–178.

Pruitt, Stephen W., and David R. Peterson. 1986. "Security Price Reactions around Product Recall Announcements." *Journal of Financial Research* 9, no. 2, pp. 113–122.

Raghavan, C. 1990. "Recolonization: GATT in Its Historical Context." *The Ecologist* 20 (November–December), pp. 205–207.

Rasmusen, Eric. 1989. *Games and Information: An Introduction to Game Theory.* Oxford: Basil Blackwell.

Rawls, John. 1971. *A Theory of Justice.* Cambridge, Mass.: Harvard University Press.

Reich, Robert B. 1990. "Who Is Us?" *Harvard Business Review* (January–February), pp. 78–80.

Rion, Michael R. 1982. "Training for Ethical Management at Cummins Engine." In Donald G. Jones, ed., *Doing Ethics in Business: New Ventures in Manage-*

ment Development. Cambridge, Mass.: Oelgeschlager, Gunn & Hain, pp. 420–435.

Ritter, J. R. 1984. "The 'Hot Issue' Market in 1980." *Journal of Business* 57, pp. 215–240.

Robbins, E., and J. Schatzberg. 1986. "Callable Bonds: A Risk-Reducing Signalling Mechanism." *Journal of Finance* 41 (September), pp. 935–950.

Rock, K. 1986. "Why New Issues Are Underpriced." *Journal of Financial Economics* 15, pp. 187–212.

Rogaly, Joe. 1997. "Knowledge, Freedom and a Poison Pill." *Financial Times*, March 15–March 16, p. III.

Roll, R. 1986. "The Hubris Hypothesis of Corporate Takeovers." *Journal of Business* 59, pp. 197–216.

Romer, Paul. 1990. "Endogenous Technological Change." *Journal of Political Economy* 98, pp. S71–S102.

Rosenberg, R. 1974. "Adam Smith on Profits-Paradox Lost and Regained." *Journal of Political Economy* 82, no. 6, pp. 14–49.

Ross, Stephen A. 1977. "The Determination of Financial Structure: The Incentive Signalling Approach." *Bell Journal of Economics* 8 (Spring), pp. 23–40.

———. 1988. "Comment on the Modigliani-Miller Propositions." *Journal of Economic Perspectives* 2, no. 4 (Fall), pp. 127–133.

Rostow, W. W. 1960. *Stages of Economic Growth*. London: Routledge.

Ruegger, Durwood, and Ernest King. 1992. "A Study of the Effects of Age and Gender upon Student Business Ethics." *Journal of Business Ethics* 11, pp. 179–186.

Sammons, Jack L. 1992. "Rebellious Ethics and Albert Speer." *Professional Ethics: A Multidisciplinary Journal* 1, nos. 3–4, pp. 77–116.

Schiller, Robert J. 1986. "Comments on Miller and on Kleidon." *Journal of Business* 59, pp. 501–505.

Schmidtz, David. 1994. "Choosing Ends." *Ethics* 194 (January), pp. 226–251.

Schoell, W. F., and J. P. Guiltinan. 1992. *Marketing: Contemporary Concepts and Practices*. Boston: Allyn and Bacon.

Schwartz, Barry. 1990. "King Midas in America." In Clarence C. Walton, ed., *Enhancing Business Ethics*. New York: Plenum Press, pp. 521–529.

Sejersted, Francis. 1996. "Managers and Consultants as Manipulators: Reflections on the Suspension of Ethics." *Business Ethics Quarterly* 6, no. 1 (January), pp. 67–86.

Selten, R. 1975. "Re-examination of the Perfectness Concept for Equilibrium Points in Extensive Games." *International Journal of Game Theory* 4, pp. 25–55.

Sen, Amartya. 1987. *On Ethics and Economics*. New York: Basil Blackwell.

Sherwin, Douglas. 1983. "The Ethical Roots of the Business System." *Harvard Business Review* (November–December), pp. 183–192.

Shiller, R. J. 1986. "Theories of Aggregate Stock Price Movements." *Journal of Portfolio Management* (Winter), pp. 28–37.

Shrybman, Steven. 1990. "International Trade and the Environment: An Environmental Assessment of the General Agreement on Tariffs and Trade." *The Ecologist* 20, no. 1 (January–February), pp. 30–34.

Simmons, Jack L. 1992. "Rebellious Ethics and Albert Speer." *Business and Professional Ethics Journal* 4, no. 2, pp. 42–49.

Simon, H. A. 1986. "Rationality in Psychology and Economics." *Journal of Business* 59, pp. S209–S224.

Slote, Michael. 1992. *From Morality to Virtue.* New York: Oxford University Press.

Smith, Adam. 1937a. *The Theory of Moral Sentiments.* Orig. pub. 1759. New York: Modern Library.

Smith, Adam. 1937b. *An Enquiry into the Nature and Causes of the Wealth of Nations.* Orig. pub. 1776. New York: Modern Library.

Smith, Clifford. 1986. "Investment Banking and the Capital Acquisition Process." *Journal of Financial Economics* 15, pp. 3–29.

———. 1987. "Alternative Methods for Raising Capital." *Journal of Financial Economics* (January–February), pp. 273–307.

———. 1992. "Economics and Ethics: The Case of Salomon Brothers." *Journal of Applied Corporate Finance* 5, pp. 23–28.

Smith, Craig. 1994. "The New Corporate Philanthropy." *Harvard Business Review* 72 (May–June), pp. 105–119.

Smith, Kirk R. 1988. "Air Pollution: Assessing Total Exposure in Developing Countries." *The Ecologist* 30, no. 10 (December), p. 20.

Solomon, Robert C. 1992. "Corporate Roles, Personal Virtues: An Aristotelian Approach to Business Ethics." *Business Ethics Quarterly* 2, pp. 317–339.

———. 1994. *The New World of Business: Ethics and Free Enterprise in the Global 1990's.* Lanham, Md.: Rowman and Littlefield.

———. 1996. *A Brief History of Philosophy.* Oxford: Oxford University Press.

Spatt, C. S. 1983. "Credit Reputation Equilibrium and the Theory of Credit Markets." Carnegie-Mellon University working paper, May.

Spence, A. Michael. 1973. "Job Market Signalling." *Quarterly Journal of Economics* 87, no. 3 (Spring), pp. 355–374.

———. 1977. "Job Market Signalling." *Quarterly Journal of Economics* 8 (Spring), pp. 23–40.

Stanley, Marjorie Thines. 1993. "Multinational Capital Budgeting, Emerging Markets, and Managerial Agency: A Proposal for an Ethically Constrained Capital Budgeting Model." *Business and Professional Ethics Journal* 12, no. 4 (Winter), pp. 87–107.

Stark, Andrew. 1993. "What's the Matter with Business Ethics." *Harvard Business Review* (May–June), pp. 42–49.

Statman, M., and D. Caldwell. 1987. "Applying Behavioral Finance to Capital Budgeting: Project Terminations." *Financial Management* 16, pp. 7–15.

Staune, Jean. 1996. "Science and Management: An Introduction." *CEMS Business Review* 1, pp. 145–150.

Staw, B. M. 1981. "The Escalation of Commitment to a Course of Action." *Academy of Management Review* 6, no. 4, pp. 577–587.

Staw, B. M., and J. Ross. 1986. "Behavior in Escalation Situations: Antecedents, Prototypes, and Solutions." In S. Cummins and B. Staw, eds., *Research in Organizational Behavior.* Greenwich, Conn.: JAI Press, pp. 94–98.

Swanda, John R., Jr. 1990. "Goodwill, Going Concern, Stocks and Flows: A Prescription for Moral Analysis." *Journal of Business Ethics* 9, no. 9, pp. 751–760.

Swanson, Diane L. 1997. "The Problem of Theoretically Reconciling Economic-Focused and Duty-Aligned Research Orientations in the Corporate Social Performance Field" (dissertation abstract). *Business & Society* 36, no. 1 (March), pp. 106–110.

Tavris, Carol. 1992. *The Mismeasure of Women.* New York: Touchstone.

Taylor, Charles. 1995. "A Most Peculiar Institution." In J. E. J. Altham and Ross Harrison, eds., *World, Mind, and Ethics: Essays on the Ethical Philosophy of Bernard Williams.* Cambridge: Cambridge University Press, pp. 4–9.

Taylor, Richard. 1991. *Virtue Ethics: An Introduction.* New York: Linden Books.

Telser, J. 1980. "A Theory of Self-Enforcing Agreements." *Journal of Business* 53, no. 2 (January), pp. 27–44.

Thakor, Anjan V. 1989. "Strategic Issues in Financial Contracting: An Overview." *Financial Management* (Summer), pp. 14–19.

Thaler, Richard H. 1988. "Anomalies: The Ultimatum Game." *Journal of Economic Perspectives* 2, no. 4 (Fall), pp. 195–206.

———. 1992. *The Winner's Curse: Paradoxes and Anomalies of Economic Life.* New York: Free Press.

Thatcher, J. 1985. "The Choice of Call Provision Terms: Evidence of the Existence of Agency Costs of Debt." *Journal of Finance* 40 (June), pp. 549–561.

Thomson, Koy, and Nigel Dudley. 1989. "Transnationals and Oil in Amazonia." *The Ecologist* 19, no. 6 (December), pp. 219–224.

Tinic, S. 1988. "Anatomy of Initial Public Offerings of Common Stock." *Journal of Finance* 43, pp. 789–822.

Titman, S., and B. Trueman. 1986. "Information Quality and the Valuation of New Issues." *Journal of Accounting and Economics* 8, pp. 159–172.

UN Centre on Transnational Corporations. 1985. *Environmental Aspects of the Activities of Transnational Corporations: A Survey.* New York: Author.

Velasquez, Manuel G. 1998. *Business Ethics: Concepts and Cases.* Upper Saddle River, N.J.: Prentice-Hall.

Velasquez, Manuel G., and Neil Brady. 1997. "Catholic Natural Law and Business Ethics." *Business Ethics Quarterly* 7, no. 2 (March), pp. 83–108.

Vitell, Scott J., and Donald L. Davis. 1990. "Ethical Beliefs of MIS Professionals: The Frequency and Opportunity for Unethical Behavior." *Journal of Business Ethics* 9, pp. 63–70.

von Neumann, J. and O. Morgenstern. 1947. *Theory of Games and Economic Behavior,* 2nd ed. Princeton, N.J.: Princeton University Press.

Walking, Ralph A., and Michael S. Long. 1984. "Agency Theory, Managerial Welfare and Takeover Bid Resistance." *Rand Journal of Economics* 1 (Spring), pp. 54–68.

Weber, Max V. 1948. *The Protestant Work Ethic and the Spirit of Capitalism.* New York: Scribner's.

Weizenbaum, Joseph. 1976. *Computer Power and Human Reason.* San Francisco: W. H. Freeman.

White, Thomas. 1992. "Business Ethics and Carol Gilligan's 'Two Voices.' " *Business Ethics Quarterly* 2, no. 1 (January), pp. 51–61.

Wicken, Jeffrey S. 1987. *Evolution, Thermodynamics, and Information—Extending the Darwinian Paradigm.* Oxford: Oxford University Press.

Wicks, Andrew. 1997. "On the Practical Relevance of Feminist Thought to Business." *Business Ethics Quarterly* 6, no. 4, pp. 523–532.

Williamson, O. E. 1964. *The Economics of Discretionary Behavior: Managerial Objectives in a Theory of the Firm.* Englewood Cliffs, N.J.: Prentice-Hall.

———. 1983. "Credible Commitments: Using Hostages to Support Exchange." *American Economic Review* 73 (September), pp. 519–540.

Williams, Oliver E., and Patrick E. Murphy. 1990. "The Ethics of Virtue: A Moral Theory of Marketing." *Journal of Macromarketing* (Spring), pp. 19–29.

Willman, John. 1998. "Large Scoops of Social Values." *Financial Times*, February 9, p. 8.

Wiseman, Jack. 1989. *Cost, Choice, and Political Economy.* Aldershot, England: Edward Elgar.

Wolfe, Art. 1991. "Reflections on Business Ethics . . .". *Business Ethics Quarterly* 1, no. 4 (October), pp. 409–440.

Index

About the Author

JOHN DOBSON is Associate Professor of Finance at California Polytechnic State University in San Luis Obispo. He has published numerous articles on finance and business ethics and is the author of *Finance Ethics: The Rationality of Virtue* (1997).